ROW

Shazad Carbaidwala

ROW

ARPress
ILLUMINATING IDEAS.
EMPOWERING VOICES

ARPress
45 Dan Road Suite 5
Canton MA 02021

Hotline:	1(888) 821-0229
Fax:	1(508) 545-7580

Ordering Information:

Quantity sales. Special discounts are available on quantity purchases by corporations, associations, and others. For details, contact the publisher at the address above.

Printed in the United States of America.

ISBN-13:	Softcover	979-8-89330-281-3
	eBook	979-8-89330-280-6

Library of Congress Control Number: 2024901508

Contents

ACKNOWLEDGEMENTS

Heroes are people that rise above adversity and embody noble qualities. My wife demonstrates those qualities with everything she does. Thanks to my wife for supporting me through the writing process. She is a humanitarian as well as a pediatrician. She inspires and motivates me through her actions to be a better person, always keeping me on the straight and narrow path. She embodies what a role model should be.

She has been my anchor. My protector. The one who keeps me grounded.

I took the road less traveled. It would have eventually been a dead end, but she grabbed me and put me on the proper path.

She accepted my past faults and has made me a better man. The righteous path I follow now is because of her actions. She leads by example, not by words.

She was an instrumental piece for me writing this book. If people read this book and judge me, she will be my guardian. In order to get to me you must go through her. Good luck!

I also want to thank all my family, friends, and adversaries in my life. My family gives me love, my friends give me loyalty, and my adversaries give me courage on how to overcome hurdles they have thrown my way.

Finally, I would like to thank my editorial team, Ron Elbert, Batul Kaj-Carbaidwala, Megan Palos, and Sara Ellenbogen, who spent countless hours editing my book. I would also like to thank my focus group Hozi Raja, Nisreen Al-Qamari, and Husain Koita. Thank you for coming on this journey with me.

TO MY READERS

I am not a writer. This was very hard for me, but after years and years of proofing and editing, it's finally done. This journey began years ago. I threw a Hail Mary back in 2004 when I initially started. *Row* was called *The Life of a Bodybuilder*. I didn't have a lot of depth. Forty pages in, and all my data vanished from my desktop. Something told me it wasn't meant to be at that time.

After a long break, I started writing again. I never realized how difficult it would be writing an entire book. In the latter stages of writing the first draft, I used to carry a notepad and pen with me noting my personal accounts that slipped my mind. This book is fiction with some records of my past life.

In my book I discuss a few of my past experiences and how they changed me. If I didn't change, I would have ended up six feet under or locked in a cell for the rest of my life, probably on death row, which is where this book takes place. This book is a metaphor on how my life used to be before I got my act together. I spend a lot of time on part three titled "Knucklehead Philosophy," because I felt it was important for my readers to understand there were a lot of bad choices made before I finally made a change. Now, I have been sharing my experiences with others through outreach efforts and can hopefully help others with my life story.

The advice I would give to my readers is make your own choices in life. Live by the beat of your own drum. Don't live your life based on others' beliefs. You make your choices, and you live by them. Before I leave this world, I want to make sure I have crossed off everything on my bucket list.

We only live one life; make the most of it.

TO MY MOTHER

Life has its triumphs and defeats. Mom, you have dealt with death, poverty, crime, and betrayal throughout your life, but never let it be the end of your journey.

I want to thank you for giving me the gift of life.

Along my journey, I have faced triumphs and defeats, and I hope I have faced them with the same tenacity you did.

I wrote this book with you in mind. It wasn't easy for me to empty my dirty laundry out to the world, but I want my purpose in life to touch and help as many people as I can.

Dedication

This book is dedicated to my late father Imran Ali Carbaidwala and my beautiful baby daughter Aamena Carbaidwala. She is my angel, my heart, my everything. Aamena, I hope when you get older you read my book and are proud of your daddy for turning his life around.

"The ones who are crazy enough to think that they can change the world are the ones who do."

— Steve Jobs

"He who is not courageous enough to take risks will accomplish nothing in life."

— Mohammed Ali

"Care about what other people think and you will always be their prisoner."

— Lao Tzu

"I am who I am. Your approval isn't needed."

— Jack Nicholson

"Fight for your dreams through actions not words"

"Take pride in everything you do."

— Shazad Carbaidwala

PROLOGUE

All of this started in the middle of the night, when I was woken up by a noise that made me jump out of bed in disbelief.

Stop!

I was still half asleep on my cold steel cot as six baton-wielding goons entered the room. They grabbed me by the collar and started dragging me towards the door like a rag doll. I couldn't believe these cowardly men would attack a helpless man trying to sleep, but I knew these men meant business.

I recognized all of 'em; as these were the same jokers I was conversing with three hours ago, discussing radicalism in the United States. These were crooked correctional officers (CO's) and now they had me by the jugular.

These were tough, take no prisoners type of guys. Guys you don't want to meet in a dark alley on the south sticks of Chicago. These six burly men towered over me. These dudes didn't look like they were selling wolf tickets. I was lone prey in the Serengeti. I was ready to fight these intruders entering my domain. They wanted me, well they could have me, but they better be ready for war. I wasn't going to let anyone come into my home and take my lunch money.

I started hurling punches from all angles trying to keep 'em off me. I was swinging for the fences and was probably connecting on twenty percent of my punches, but at that point it didn't matter because I was severely outnumbered.

It was survival of the fittest now and they were going to have to destroy my will to take my life.

1

My adrenaline had set in and their punches bounced off me like ping pong balls. I fought battles my whole life and was often outmatched. This would be no different. I was ready to become famous and beat six men to death with my bare hands.

I was in the battle of my life, getting thrashed from every direction as blood spouted from my nose like a leaky faucet. I was hurling as many bombs at these men as I could, but fatigue set in. I felt like a major-league baseball pitcher after throwing one hundred pitches as my arms were turning into jelly.

These six brawny men, the hired assassins, were getting the better of me. I couldn't endure any more punishment and realized I would have to succumb to their onslaught. My fury of fists no longer had the same velocity and my vision was blurred from the barrage of blows I took to the head. I landed some light jabs, but I was ultimately rendered powerless. I got down on one knee and curled up defensively. I was throwing in the towel!

They dragged me at least fifty feet from my cell. All my neighbors were banging against their concrete and metal fixtures, watching like this was a Miramax motion picture and I was the star attraction. I knew when this was over I would have the respect of these men, but who cares? I was heading now to my doom.

The onslaught continued while I was being towed to my next destination. I wanted to be alive, to kiss my wife, and hug my loved ones. That's all I cared about now.

I could see my imminent termination and I started to panic. Not only were they going to kill me, but I was going to be in a world of hurt. The thought of torture gave me a tingling feeling streaming through my bones. I felt like a pack of hungry wolverines had devoured my flesh. I could feel my face, and if it wasn't for the adrenaline, I would be screaming for some brake fluid. My life hung by a thread and I knew my demise was coming as soon as a black door was thrust open. My cheeks were bloodied to a pulp and it was difficult to grasp what was behind the door.

PROLOGUE

One of the men opened the door and pulled me in. I could only see a foot in front of me as the men hovered over me, effortlessly restraining me now. They grabbed me and picked me up. I was a rag doll hanging in their arms as they threw me on the chair, which was a tangle of thick leather straps. My eyes rolled and my thoughts were scrambled, I knew this was the start of the execution process. I was now going to meet my maker.

The warden did not grant me my stay of execution, but instead yanked me out of bed weeks ahead of schedule. I was hauled out of my cell while I was sleeping and trampled by new jacks with no conscience. I thought there was some dignity behind all of this. Wasn't I supposed to get a last meal? Wasn't I supposed to have my head shaved? Wasn't I supposed to plan with my family to be witnesses? This wasn't the protocol which was explained to me. I was half unconscious, but I still felt the water slowly dripping from my head. Or was that blood?

At this point, I was immobile. My feet and hands were locked in with a heavy harness. I was moments away from going on the ride of my life.

I was in pure agony, knowing that liquid toxin was going to be released into my body like a freight train. I was dripping beads of sweat as the men in the room stared at the pavement, knowing what was about to transpire. My eyes were wide open, but the room was spinning. I was beaten and battered, yelling for mercy. My clothes were tattered from my body as I lay in a pool of my own gore. I could hear a man whispering, praying beside me. I realized this is where I will be staring at the white light. But I wasn't ready to go. I was a young man with a life to live.

My heart raced and the silence tried to force last-minute thoughts of death. My thoughts spiraled into nonsensical contemplations, as I was moments away from imminent death.

Please don't do this. No, don't pull the lever. Laa ilaaha ill-Allah Mohammadun Rasoolullah.

PROLOGUE

The lever slowly went down and my heart raced. I started to feel liquid coursing through my veins and the burning sensation of toxin, making my body tremble. I was losing. . . .

Suddenly, I jolt from my mattress. The room is black with a shimmer of light penetrating underneath the door. It was all just a horrible nightmare. I was up dazed and aching and start to realize that my days are numbered.

It's time to make peace with God and with death. I am going to be a casualty of the United States judicial system, a product of the enforcement of capital punishment. The blame game and the "why me" is over. I was given due process, and here I am.

"Chow time! Get your convict asses up! It's time to get your daily bread. Eat now or starve."

PART ONE
Con College

DAY 18 JAIL JOURNAL: SOLITUDE

There are many episodes in one's life; some chapters more defined than others, some chapters good natured, some not. Hopefully this book, detailing my chapters, will help add some closure for my family and friends who have supported me, and whom I have hurt.

I am not going to disclose actual events which led me to my captivity. I am conveying my message through this long passage titled, "Row." This extensive document shares the events of my life, weighing on the good and bad of my past doings. In effect, dissecting my life!

American culture has a preconceived notion of what our lives should look like. It gives us an illusion that our lives should be perfect through someone else's lens. Mainstream media uses Facebook, Instagram, WhatsApp, and other social outlets to view different aspects of someone's life. I don't have those channels of communication anymore, so I use whatever outlet I have and that is through this memoir. This book is about the only way I can reach amity. This book is about an individual that has digressed from the conventional norms and is looking to be heard.

Given a choice of life or death, I would have chosen to have never been born because I caused too many important people in my life agony. I was chosen to follow a path and become successful. I had all the outlets to be triumphant but steered away from the yellow paved road of normalcy with children, a wife, and fruitful career to end up doing the things that you will read about.

Some of my writing may not make a lot of sense, as I write when I am allowed under a watchful eye, not having the proper utensils. I am no longer housed with amenities and kept to a bare minimum. Oftentimes I write on walls or on other prison equipment. I sometimes even write on toilet paper. Deemed 5150. Often my thoughts are stale. I started writing this to cope with living in com-

Row

plete isolation from the outside world and maintaining my sanity. I write to block out the noises constantly flooding my head. I strain to interpret my reflections on past and present memories through daily journal entries. Please excuse me if there is some redundancy, as thoughts replay in my mind over and over. I will not have re-entry into society and avenues of rehabilitation. It's too late for that. Back door parole is my sentence.

Sitting down and writing in a confined space is a difficult task for me. I'm not a writer. But this roller coaster called life has landed me in a cage, and as I look beyond the bars at the green pastures and blue pond, I reflect on my thoughts and feelings from my past life, and the words come to me now.

As I developed the basis of my autobiography, I couldn't help getting depressed and then pissed off at what my life has become. I had the world in the palm of my hand, but let it slip through my fingers. I went from a great life, to no life behind bars in a matter of days.

My life has been filled with adversity constantly overcoming some of the poor decisions that landed me in the joint. At one point in time I had it all, determined to be the best, but my inner monsters got the best of me. I was overshadowed by low self-worth and was living a sentence of self-destruction. It was catching up to me like a freight train.

As I started writing this book, I felt a monkey coming off my back, but I knew it would take years to fully understand what really happened that landed me in this place.

I knew writing this book would open the eyes of my loved ones. There are dark secrets that I have kept to myself for a long time and disclosing them may open some deep wounds.

I am hoping this book can reach a wide audience to help aid anyone who has taken a few steps backwards in life, held captive to their own self-mutilation.

I have examined all the different chapters of my life and will replay them until I must make the walk to the executioner's table. I must live the last few weeks recollecting my past because my future is bleak.

I will not spend time discussing my trial. It depresses me. I am hoping this diary gives readers clarity on my life growing up as a youth in Chicago: adored by my family and friends, and ultimately relegated into solitary confinement. But I wanted to shape my life's work before I face my ultimate kismet.

Please forgive me for the sins I have committed. These sins are not what make me who I am today. They are lapses in judgement I made in my life.

❖

They say peer pressure is a bitch, well it wasn't my bitch. I never succumbed to peer pressure throughout my youth and early adulthood. Growing up, I always walked the lonely road. Nobody decided my path. I am the only one at fault for my consequences and my decisions now.

This is not a story of someone who had bad parents or grew up in extreme poverty reverting to criminal endeavors.

God always gives us second chances in life and I had mine repeatedly. I can only do so much now with what I have in my cell.

Life seems to just roll, roll and roll, and I am stuck in a quagmire of steel, rotting. I don't think this was my purpose when I was created, but this is my fate now, so I accept it. I don't live life anymore, I only exist. The only thing I wait for is taking my last breath. The only obstacle I have now is figuring out what moving on means. I don't have the luxury anymore of freedom positioned in my humble asylum.

I have lost touch with civilization and rely on brief exchanges between prison staff regarding news in the world. Society trains us to forget about criminals, to lock the door and throw away the key. I am a figment of everyone's imagination now. A forgotten soul.

I am now waiting to be terminated; like cattle waiting in a slaughterhouse. Each day I write brings me closer to my end. The agony of waiting for my demise is far worse than the actual pain that will course through my body during judgement day. The numbness has already subsided and I can only think about my life from the past.

❖

Have you ever stopped and reflected on your means of happiness? Have you examined the timeline of actual events that have molded you into the person you see in the mirror? Probably not, and my answer would have been the same if I wasn't in here. I would never have thought that I would have completed a book in a small chamber, on the clock. I always wanted to sit down and reflect on my life and analyze each detail, but not caged like an animal.

I believe there are three types of people in this world. The first group of people throw in the towel before life ever begins. They see all the bad things that could happen to them, so they attempt very little. The second group of people try and fail. They get knocked down and stay down. Like the first group they never become who they were meant to be. The third group believe it's never over. They firmly believe the world is their oyster. They allow their failures to bring them new life and overcome any obstacle that is brought their way. I like to think that I was part of the third group before getting locked up.

The thing I feared most in life was being mediocre. To me, being average was just not good enough. Wake up, work a 9 to 5, and then go home, plop down on the couch until passing out in a drunken stupor or a food coma like a dump truck. C'mon, not me. Part of the path I explored consisted of virtue and decency, and the other was self-mutilation and destruction. I just wanted to be revered by humankind. I always envisioned leaping from the top rope like Jimmy "Superfly" Snuka at WrestleMania with a razor-sharp elbow, pinning my opponent and winning the world heavyweight title, or catching the game winning touchdown and jumping into a sea of fans chanting my name.

Why would anyone want to be average? I'd rather do the dutch than be an average Joe. That statement alone gives you an idea about my ideology. I had a zest for new challenges and going to new places. I lived in a vulnerable state, often facing the unknown. Oftentimes my companions would ask me why I was taking on so much at a time. Through the journey of impulsive behavior, I faced many obstacles, most of which I could overcome. I failed and that's what led to my departure from the free world.

God has deployed us on this universe not to be average, but to be great and rise in the face of adversity. We are all great at something and it's our responsibility to first uncover what makes us great and then pursue it with tenacity, conquering it. If Michael Jordan had never picked up a basketball, the world wouldn't have seen his grace on the basketball court. He wouldn't have won six NBA championships, MVP's, Hall of Fame, Best NBA player... the list of accolades goes on and on. To achieve excellence, you must always be ready to pursue different obsessions, even if it is not preferred by the masses. You must be ready to live under personal scrutiny and challenge your yearning for success. I lived my life that way, always chasing prominence. Unfortunately, I haven't achieved my goal yet. I never uncovered the stone to greatness. Maybe greatness will be obtained during the after life.

❖

If I could wake up from this nightmare I would, but I can't, and I never will. My life will always be looking out, wishing, hoping, and praying, that someday I will be able to walk out of my constraints and take a breath of freedom. Remember the saying, "The mind is a terrible thing to waste"? Well that is what I feel every day. I had all the talent in the world and blew it all on a stupid decision. Like Robert De Niro stated in A Bronx Tale,"There is nothing worse than wasted talent."

My days are spent in self-loathing as I re-examine every detail of my life, trying not to sink to the depths of sorrow. I sit and re-piece together all the important aspects of my life, reviewing my feelings and chapters in detail. I don't have long to live so I write as much as I can. I do it to leave behind something of value or purpose. Something to vindicate me.

There have been a lot of twists and turns in my life. When I first started writing this book, writing was effortless. The words were literally going from my brain onto whatever surface I could find until I was finally given a pad and paper. It was painless, until I started delving into my true misfortunes and hardships. Writing about my knucklehead choices was challenging. Some of my confessions in this book were difficult to put on paper for the world to read.

I guess everyone has skeletons in their closet. An individual can do the right things for ninety-nine percent of his life, make one mistake, and have his reputation tarnished for life. Let's look at OJ Simpson's life. He was guilty before even going on trial. Ask yourself, "What if OJ really didn't kill anyone? What if this was all a setup and he was framed?" Since the media presumed him guilty, he was guilty to everyone. Same thing with professional athletes. They never talk about the hours and hours that these amazing people spend in the gym, eating clean foods, sacrificing a social life, and all the sacrifices they make controlling their natural cravings. The media wants to talk about the bad: the domestic violence, performance enhancing drugs, or other criminal activity. Why? Because that is easy and that's what the public wants to hear about.

Life was all about taking chances and I think that I took a few too many. I ate, drank, and injected anything I wanted without concern for consequences. I didn't know another way to live. It was full speed ahead, only to realize down the line whatever I did was wrong. What I was and what I have become made me realize that everybody deserves a second chance. Adversity shaped me into a stronger man, testing my will to transcend. I am a firm believer that things happen for a reason and only the strong survive through misfortune in this world.

❖

I can't remember when I could sleep through the night without waking up looking over my shoulders. Daydreams are the only way I can seclude myself from this nightmarish place.

Every day is a mixed bag of reactions based on my surroundings, derived from the constant noise of the clinging chains, eerie echoes off prison walls, and uproars of inmate rebels. I am trained to become a gladiator because I have no choice, constantly surrounded by turmoil, having to deal with the worst of the worst in the prison system. It's a constant tug of war between the cons and correctional officers.

Inmates think they run the joint, but we don't run nothin'. I am reminded of that every day. I am up when CO's want me to wake up, I eat whatever crap they shove in my bean slot, and I sleep when they scream, "Lights out convicts!" I can't even go drop a deuce in peace. We might outnumber prison staff, but by no means are we in control.

Prisons are large enterprises that have a hierarchy. The warden is the CEO, followed by the deputy warden, and assistant wardens who act as chief officers. Then you have the correctional staff, comprised of prison psychologists, correctional officers, the parole board, and prisoners acting as prison employees. That's the simplified version, but the economy inside correctional institutions could be more closely monitored. Don't let the decor fool you. There is a lot of money changing hands in the joint.

The biggest source of revenue inside the Q, short for San Quentin, are drugs. I am not talking about meds at the ding wing. I am talking about street level dope.

Drugs are prevalent all over the world, regardless of how much societies govern them. Billions and billions of dollars in drugs are crossing over state and country lines every year and a chunk of that makes its way into federal institutions.

Millions of dollars in contraband are being infiltrated every day in prisons all-across the world. Fifty percent of the inmates in US federal prisons are institutionalized for drug related charges, whether those offenses are distributing or using. Inmates need their brake fluid. You got gangbangers slanging crack rock on the streets all over the world. Places like Oakland, Baltimore, and Chicago are just a few, but drugs cross every global boundary. There is very little room for error on the streets and a lot of high-ranking gangbangers with street credit get pinched. What do you think they end up doing in prison? You damn skippy, they end up doing the same damn thing in prison they were doing on the streets. Foot soldiers in every prison are supplying to customers. Gang leaders in prisons make thousands of dollars every day supplying. It's a 24/7 hustle in prison because the profit margins are through the roof.

It's a cat and mouse game between CO's and convicts. Just like in the streets. Bottom line, drugs will never cease. The drug game is too powerful an economic source and too bloody organized to take a back seat to law enforcement. Just like in law enforcement, drug cartels have their chiefs, captains, lieutenants, sergeants, and patrolmen.

❖

Cellblock B always had a long line of consumers waiting for their brake fluid. Just like on the streets, hitters came out holding down their corner with their daily scramble at 5 p.m., while the drug fiends came out from their drug-induced comas like zombies for their daily fix. Same thing happens in prison. Every day, convicts lined up to get their drug of choice, whether it was methadone, Prozac, Xanax, Seroquel, etc.... I saw brawls break out with inmates trying to cut in line tweaking. Apart from the prison infirmary, drugs were also smuggled into prison by visitors. Correctional facilities wouldn't function without drugs.

Correctional staff were constantly striving to shut down the inmate drug trade, but contraband was easier to obtain in prison than on the streets. Ever wonder why? Drugs are penetrating prisons at alarming rates as inmates are smuggling contraband in body orifices, baby diapers, religious scriptures, tennis balls, letters, and even dead pigeons. Cons are coming up with innovative ways of getting drugs into the penal system. You have drug mules stuffing narcotics into dead animals and hurling them over the prison walls. Model inmates obtain jobs cleaning the prison yard picking up trash. They would pick up the dead carcass, remove the drugs, and there you go. Drugs have infiltrated the jails, just like that. That small amount of contraband is worth thousands inside San Quentin.

Day 18: Solitude

Some of the most popular drugs, like Suboxone, are now infiltrating prisons. It's extremely difficult to detect and often smuggled in books. Suboxone is a small orange film the size of a thumbnail. One orange film strip of Suboxone goes for 30-40 dollars on the street, but in prison, each strip can easily go for hundreds of dollars. The demand is much higher than the supply, so drug trade is constantly flourishing. When that type of coin is exchanged, everyone wants a piece of the action, not just the prisoners. If you catch my drift!

Suboxone has hit the prison market, but when Suboxone gets dried up, there will be a new drug that fiends will crave. It's a revolving door. The new drug storming the streets is fentanyl. This stuff is coming from China by the tons and is responsible for thousands of overdoses. Emergency Medical Responders can't respond soon enough to China White overdoses in America. Dealers are cutting fentanyl with heroin to increase potency. The talk in prison is that this new drug combined with heroin can increase its potency by fifty times. Fentanyl will soon make its way into the prisons. Watch and see. I probably won't be alive to see its ramifications.

❖

You are notorious based on your crime and your criminal rank. Nobody cares how bad or how tough you are because there will always be someone tougher. It doesn't matter how many street fights you have won entering the joint. Once you walk into the Q your criminal resume starts.

Most would agree that a maximum-security prison can mold you into a gladiator. You must fight for everything. The guards and inmates are pushing you to the breaking point. Respect is earned. Nice guys don't finish last in prison. Nice guys finish DEAD. Prison code is supreme. You eat when it's your turn to eat. Don't get in line when it's the woods' turn to eat. Don't get in line when it's the blacks' turn to eat. Don't get in line when the Chicanos need to eat. Whites stay with whites, browns stay with browns, and blacks stay with blacks. Period! You hustle when it's your turn to hustle. I have seen what happens to inmates who enter the prison system trying to make a statement because they feel that is the only way to earn their place. Those same men will get boned by a booty bandit before they know what hit 'em.

The things you see and hear about American prisons are not made up. You don't want to go up to the head of the Nazi Lo Riders and break a bottle over his head to prove a point. You keep the peace as much as you can, but prison turns you into a foul human being that wants to destroy people's will and gain the advantage. Why do you think so many people leave prison only to see the same brick walls a few months later?

If someone belittles you, then tighten up and put your shoes on because it's time to take flight. I have witnessed meaningless altercations over whose turn it was to use a five-pound dumbbell in the prison yard. I have seen inmates get hoe checked for making eye contact with a gang affiliate.

Convicts must have street smarts and make judgments that won't keep getting them institutionalized. Once they are paroled and back out on the streets, some cons don't have the resources to survive. They have been institutionalized for too long and will be in and out of prison their whole lives. It's the circle of life for career criminals because gang affiliations, drug abuse, and law-breaking are means to survive.

The US government wants us to believe that prisoners get rehabilitated when they get out of prison. We don't get any treatment and get pushed back out in the streets, expected to play by society's rules. Nobody knows some of the stuff that goes on in prisons. Lifers don't even know fully what's going on in the slammer.

I am finding it tougher to examine how prisons in the United States operate. The United States has over 6,000 correctional institutions ranging from state, federal, juvenile correctional facilities, and local jails. The US has the highest incarceration rate in the world and overpopulated prisons have become the norm. Policies need to change in the judicial system. First, let's end the death penalty. Capital punishments cost millions in taxpayers' money. Most of the world has abolished capital punishment, but the US still has it in place. Second, let's hold our judges and prosecutors responsible for misconduct which lands innocent people in jail. Also, victims who are exonerated should receive compensation for time spent in jail instead of token support from only a handful of states. Third, the US government needs to reduce life sentences for non-violent drug offenses for habitual offenders. Drug abuse is rampant in the US and is a disease. People shouldn't be given life sentences for drug addiction. Aid should be provided to those individuals. I could go on and on, even outlining the misconduct and misrepresentation I suffered in my trial…

The prison system is broken, and citizens' tax money is going to a futile cause.

I became inhumane when I began my journey years ago at this hell hole. Once I arrived through the California Department of Corrections and Rehabilitation (CDCR) it was time to relinquish my rights to the people who would ultimately decimate my existence. I am no longer treated as an individual, but rather as a serial number tracked by the CDCR.

The drive to San Quentin was one of the most frightening moments in my life. I heard stories about violence, but they are only stories until you are on that bus knowing that you are going to be in jail for a long stint; then reality sets in. I realized that the animal house was going to be my residence for the rest of my life. I am going to die here. My buckies are going to be some of the worst criminals that ever walked the planet.

My eyes were glued to the ground and I didn't want to look at anyone's face. This wasn't GABOS, which means, "Game ain't based on sympathy." I interpret this to mean, don't express empathy towards anyone, not the guards, not the warden, and certainly not the inmates, or else that can be interpreted as weakness. There are 3,800 inmates here and I don't want to get to know anybody. The majority are repeat offenders. Here I am with a razor thin rap sheet living in close quarters with some of these guys with rap sheets a mile long. We are talking heavy hitters. That's not to even mention all the crimes they have committed in prison. Murder, rape, extortion, assault, stealing, etc.… These guys are professional con artists molded from Satan himself.

Row

When I arrived, it was a culture shock. I wanted to make sure I had a plan of action. I didn't want to get caught with my pants down, pardon the pun. How was I going to handle myself amongst the violence and corruption?

Everyone in here is trying to survive and the smartest thing for me is to join a gang right away for protection from other inmates. The only problem with joining a gang is there aren't a lot of Asian inmates in the joint. What would we call ourselves; Pakistani Pirates, or Pakistani Pistols? C'mon. When I got incarcerated, I knew I was going to have to fend for myself and at the time I was fine with that until the bus pulled up to the prison. That was a gut check.

Prison is a vile place and life inside the prison walls can end your life in an instant. If I made one false move, I could be looking at a life of pain. I watched hundreds of documentaries and movies about prison life. I even met five murderers outside of prison who each spent time in San Quentin, disclosing their experiences to me. They preached, "San Quentin is not for the faint hearted." When I met them taking a tour of Alcatraz, I told myself, "I am never going to commit a hot one landing me in a place like San Quentin." I was dead wrong.

San Quentin is intimidating, to say the least. It resembles a broken-down insane asylum surrounded by a body of water on the western peninsula. The rumor was San Quentin had great white sharks in the water outside the prison in case any of the prisoners felt lucky. They've never found the bodies of inmates who tried to escape. If you believe the rumors, they were eaten by sharks!

I wasn't in any old prison, but one of the worst maximum-security prisons in the entire world. SQ is one of the oldest institutions in the United States and services seventeen counties in California. The 432-acre California prison overlooks the bay located twelve miles north of the Golden Gate Bridge. It's a majestic place nestled in the mist like an island kingdom, but throughout its history the reality of San Quentin has been harsh. The architecture reminds me of something out of the Old West. San Quentin was the first prison built in California around 1852. During that time, there were 250 inmates, both male and female. The women's unit, referred to as "the hen house" was above the infirmary. Those times were rugged as prison reform wasn't established and inmates were locked away in a brick box called "the stones" with only one bucket of fresh water each day.

It's hard to believe that some of the most hardened criminals in the world are in such proximity to one of the most beautiful cities in the United States. Presently, this reformatory has four large cell blocks, one maximum security cell block, healthcare building, firehouse, and medium security dorm room. All the denounced inmates are housed in San Quentin, awaiting lethal injection.

Nobody cares about prisoners in San Quentin. We are brought here to perish, as most tenants in SQ are on death row, lifers, or on long term prison sentences.

Ruthless killers, rapists, gang members, you name it, San Quentin will house them. San Quentin doesn't discriminate. If you are a career criminal, then you belong in San Quentin. The prisoners here have a PhD in criminality.

I walk the same halls as did notorious inmates like Charles Manson, Charles Ng, and Richard Ramirez. All three serial killers beat and tortured their victims and are some of the most infamous serial killers of the modern era. Richard Ramirez was like a celebrity in San Quentin. This was the same guy that used to kill his victims, ripping their eyeballs from their sockets with his bare hands, and then leaving his mark by putting a pentagram on the wall, praising Satan. Ramirez said he was pushed by Satan himself and the lethal injection chamber was like taking a voyage to Disneyland. While his trial was happening, hundreds of women flocked to his trial just to get a glimpse of him. Before death, he got married to Doreen Lioy, who admired his soul. She stated that he's kind, funny, and charming. I didn't get that type of attention at my trial. I guess I needed a longer rap sheet for women to care.

When I was convicted, the judge informed me I was going to San Quentin. I would have to man up right away. Even though I was going to the worst prison, I was up for the challenge because at that point I did not give a shit about life. My mindset was self-mutilation. All day sentence was meaningless to me. But I didn't get a life sentence. I was going to take the stainless-steel ride.

When you're on the outside it's easy to act tough, but when you get inside San Quentin and the door slams shut with 3,800 of the hardest black mambas ready to spread their venom, you go into survival mode. I was not as tough as I thought I was.

I would not wish this place upon my worst enemy. It is filled with the obscene stench of rotting flesh and zombies crawling around like cockroaches. The vile language can make a truck driver blush. These living conditions are inadequate, which is shocking considering taxpayers pay 39 billion dollars annually to fund these institutions. The average annual cost per prisoner is an outstanding 31 thousand dollars. What is that 31 thousand dollars spent on? It is certainly not on me, considering I have no amenities. I get my three 49-cent trays filled with whatever leftovers the prison issues. J-Cat prisoners deemed to have a mental illness get more comforts than I do.

Most of the inmates in this correctional facility are going to die here, but I will not let this be the last image that goes in my mind before I reach the heavens. You must have mental toughness when you're dealing with all the prison chaos.

When I arrived to San Quentin I was astounded by the actions of some of the other fresh fish coming off the bus. Some were hard wired criminals selling wolf tickets to officers and prisoners in the yard. They were basically putting themselves in harm's way before even entering the institution. I guess they were trying to mark their territory amongst the toughest men on the planet. Those men were truly condemned and going to be rudely awakened by the harsh reality of prison. Those are the same convicts that you will be hearing during blackout, pleading for their lives as they are being gang raped over the cold steel, as their heads are buried in the toilet. They will become a june bug for their remaining term.

First, I had to go through processing. I quickly found out correctional officers were severely outnumbered. To control the inmate population, there were multiple inmates in each cell and each CO was responsible for hundreds of inmates during their shift.

I arrived during the day, when the inmates were out on the recreation yard, which was the worst timing I could have imagined. Our bus pulled in with over fifty convicts with crimes ranging from grand larceny to assault, rape, and murder. One of those criminals included a bug-eyed felon who committed a barbaric crime and was ready to spend the rest of his life in prison, me. I arrived, and all eyes seemed to be on me. I was like a goldfish in a tank with swarming piranhas flashing their razor-sharp teeth. I had to walk from the bus to the prison administrative office to get booked and processed. I walked through the gauntlet as every inmate locked eyes on me, examining each step I took, screaming abrasive profanity, flashing their gang affiliation. The walk was only the length of a football field but felt like miles of treacherous terrain. I was told to keep my eyes forward and did exactly that, but it was challenging with leering eyeballs with malicious intent focusing on me. I tried to envision myself walking through the football stadium tunnel, getting ready for battle. All eyes forward and no distractions. Right away, I familiarized myself with my surroundings and knew this would be home for the rest of my life until my execution. No excuses, I was here for a reason and that reason was my guilt.

My eyes were forward and I didn't say a word. I did exactly what the robocops told me to do. Robocops are the CO's that follow the prison rules to a tee. I was now a prison inmate and lived by the convict oath. I was no longer my own boss and master of my destiny. In San Quentin I was a con.

My life was turned over to the state of California in exchange for my bright orange peel, marked and tattered with past inmate embellishments. I was also given a pair of state issued bobo's and a ladmo bag with stale potato chips, juice box, and moldy bologna sandwich.

If I didn't disrespect anyone or let anyone disrespect me, I would be fine. Respect was everything in prison. You lose respect, you better get transferred to another prison because your life will be compromised every day. The infirmary will become your solitude.

Row

My first day at San Quentin was spent getting booked and obtaining my orientation pamphlet with all the prison guidelines. The booking process for each inmate entering San Quentin can take hours and is extremely painstaking. I was waiting in a holding pattern, so I could get processed. The wait was excruciating because everyone was eyeing each other, ready to start a prison riot at any point. All the new inmates stand in pecking order waiting to get booked, processed, and into the prison system. Many of us felons waiting to be processed were career criminals, no strangers to life on the inside. A lot of them were engaging in personal conversations with the correctional officers. Some of the cons were so familiar with the process they could do it with their eyes closed.

The order began with:

Mugshot
Forfeiting all my personal belongings
Fingerprints
Full body search
Checking for priors and warrants
Health screening

While I transitioned to each order, I waited in a holding cell, anticipating processing like a lamb waiting to be slaughtered. Not knowing where I was going to be placed inside one of the most dangerous prisons in the world was nerve racking. I knew at some point I would be moving to the Special Housing Unit known as the SHU, but I had no idea when. I heard about some of the most notorious villains of our time shackled away in San Quentin's SHU. Am I going to encounter Lawrence Bittaker, Dean Carter, Eric Houston, or Gunner Lindberg? These guys were monsters who kidnapped, tortured, and mutilated other people for days for their own delight. They feasted on others' misery. I didn't belong in prison with those creeps. I'd rather be in a cell with diaper snipers than those cons.

I also received a comprehensive manuscript during my orientation which was designed for new inmates acclimating themselves to prison standards. All it did for me was show me which rules were being broken on a regular basis. For most it provided paper to roll up into a marijuana roach.

As I made my way into the corridor to get fully searched I remember how belittled I felt. It was the closest feeling to getting raped without getting touched.

"Open your nostrils."

"Open your mouth and move your tongue up and down."

"Pull your ears forward and up"

"Run your fingers through your hair..."

"Pull the foreskin back. Pull your sack up."

"Turn around and show me the bottom of your feet, one at a time."

"Bend over and spread your cheeks."

"Squat down three times and cough twice each time."

"Okay, hurry up. Get dressed and get out of here."

You end up feeling resentment towards the correctional staff, harnessing aggression when you see them in the rec yard or chow hall. It's no wonder why some of these punks get shanked.

My first few days at San Quentin, I was in a holding pattern on suicide watch because of how I was perceived by the other inmates and correctional staff. There was a monitoring process used to ensure I wouldn't be a risk. I guess it was precautionary with inmates who are going to be on death row. I never mentioned anything about killing myself, but I learned from my cellmate that my face portrayed a different tale and my lack of interaction suggested dejection.

From my holding cell, I was transported into the general population. I didn't have any friends. I was all alone. If you think you have friends in a place like San Quentin, you got another thing comin. You never see great white sharks in schools like other fish because they are dominant predators. The same goes for San Quentin inmates, constantly on the prowl for fresh fish.

My cellie was a jailhouse OG serving twenty-five years for tax fraud. He was a successful businessman who committed a nonviolent crime. When he found out he would be bunking with me, he requested to be transferred. His claim was that I was a lunatic and couldn't be contained. The guy didn't even know me. When I entered the cell, the first thing I did was make eye contact with him as his pants were around his ankles dropping a load. Yeah, that is another aspect of prison life I needed to get used to and that was no privacy. My business would be displayed every day to everyone. Didn't matter if it was a male or female guard.

My new bucky was wide-eyed and expecting a cold-blooded assassin. I greeted him and thanked him for allowing me to bunk with him. I could tell he was relieved. Pardon the pun.

As days went by, I spent time getting to know my cellie. I didn't expect to build a relationship with anyone in prison. I expected to always have my guard up and temper my expectations regarding associating myself with any- one. I was caught off guard meeting him because he was not what I expected from a San Quentin inmate. He committed a crime, but he wasn't a criminal, and he didn't belong in San Quentin. This place was going to chew him up and spit him out.

Having a cellmate and that companionship all the time made prison time more meaningful. As I stated earlier, my old cellmate was in prison for tax fraud. He was in prison serving twenty-five years for deliberately misrepresenting the true state of his business. He was very honest about his crime and shared in detail. He knew that he had committed the crime and was doing his time honorably. He was not a career criminal and didn't need to be reformed. Our relationship grew as soon as we became cellmates. He was my road dog. I knew I would learn a lot from him over time, but I knew that once my trial was over and I was found guilty I would end up in a different cell, on death row.

Day 18: Solitude

As we formed somewhat of a companionship, he became interested in my story and at some point, I was going to be transitioned to death row. I didn't think he thought of me as someone who was a lawbreaker either, but he didn't know me. I didn't want to share what led me to San Quentin, but, believe it or not, I trusted him, and I wanted him to understand. It was therapeutic for me to be able to discuss my life and it ultimately gave me the idea to start writing.

Prison was never designed for rehabilitation. It was designed for retribution for the crime criminals have committed and keeping dangerous people off the streets. As the saying goes, you do the crime, you will pay the time.

I did the crime and now I have come to SQ to dwell and allow the correctional system of the United States to eradicate me from the free world. I was known as a menace to society and civilization could not tolerate my presence anymore. Instead of paying taxes and being a productive member of society, I am now categorized as a nuisance and a detriment.

I was stuck in one of the worst places on earth, trapped with a bunch of guys that don't give a damn, stone cold gangsters who enjoy the torment of others. They have ice in their veins and don't display any remorse for their actions. True to life boogeymen.

❖

Torture and torment! The correctional officers beating the inmates. The inmates beating other inmates. I have witnessed some of the worst beatings in here. It is said that every single cell in San Quentin has had some sort of slaying.

Prison politics and corruption amongst CO's and gangs occurs all the time. Prison staff don't get involved because of possible repercussions from gang members. Next thing you know prison staff's families are getting threatened on the outside by some of the most notorious shot callers that walked the planet. I mean, we're talking about the Aryan Brotherhood, the Mexican mafia, Crips,

Bloods. Some of the most dangerous thugs on the face of the earth. Men that would decapitate you if you spoke to them sideways.

The Aryan Brotherhood in particular, is a white predatorial gang. Their main interest is extortion, protection of white inmates, narcotics, and violence. They follow a strict code of "blood in, blood out," meaning you kill to get into the gang and get killed if you want out. If you mess with the Aryan Brotherhood you are destined to die, or they will go after your family. This is the same gang that mafia don Jon Gotti begged for protection from, against the blacks inside Marion Maximum Security Prison in Illinois. You think I was going to mess with some of these guys? I wanted to stay clear of them and pray that they wouldn't seek me out.

Being in a prison gang gave inmates an identity as well as protection. These inmates were bound by their gang affiliation over anything else in their life. If a gang member was told to ice another inmate, they better obey their orders, or else they will be dealt with accordingly which often resulted in fatality. It's kill or be killed.

When I first walked into prison I was a ticking time bomb. I didn't care about anything because I felt like I had nothing to live for anymore. My head was full of thoughts of pity. I would do anything to be on the outside. There was no peace and tranquility in the joint. Everyday an inmate is sitting in their cell contemplating doing the dutch. Every day, an inmate is extorting another inmate. Every day, crooked CO's are using extra force on another inmate. This is a Darwinism-based wild kingdom.

Some of the inmates are locked in their cells twenty-three hours a day and maybe once or twice a week, get one hour of rec time outside in a square box with no social encounters. Yes, some of these inmates brought it upon themselves by fighting with guards or inmates, but damn. It's hard not to throw a right cross at a CO barking orders all day long. When you get messed with, you fight back, or you're classified as a hot boy and get lined up for a beating. There aren't many inmates selling wolf tickets in San Quentin. The worst trait to have in prison is to be considered soft. With so many inmates and 600 on death row, being a punk or being soft means, you might as well become someone's bitch.

Entering prison, I was considered fresh fish. Someone new to the prison system is termed "fresh fish" by other inmates. Fresh fish get bus loaded to San Quentin every week. This was heaven for the San Quentin population because it would be a new school to prey upon. These guys didn't care about feelings or winning a popularity contest. They wanted to get their rocks off on antagonizing and making inmates feel inferior to them. They also wanted to obtain whatever goods you had. It's all about goods and services in the joint.

Prison code is simple, but complex to execute. You must walk into prison with a vision of survival and never drop your guard. Even when constantly pressed by other inmates and correctional officers. You must keep your composure and when you do act with malice, you better make your point, or else you will lose respect. You go into San Quentin and expect respect, you will become a target. You will become the gazelle in a savanna full of lions.

With so many hardened criminals inside small quarters, you are walking a tightrope, every day. Every step could be your last, so be careful of what territory you're entering. You step outside your boundary in gang territory without proper consent, you're signing your death seal. There wasn't a Prison 101 class for me to take before I went to prison. I just wanted to lay low and fly under the radar. I didn't wanna beef with nobody.

DAY 17 JAIL JOURNAL: THE CLINK. I AM H67641

I would love for someone to live a day in my shoes, to know that in a few short weeks, I would be processed by the state. Toe tagged and sent out on a stretcher.

When your life is hanging by a thread, I guess you stop caring about being a productive member of the system, stop worrying about hygiene or keeping faith, and start preparing for the afterlife.

My thoughts are empty as my fate lies on the same people that brought me here. I was filthy rich and not a care in the world, but now all that is lost. What I have become falls short of what I wanted to be known for. I have no one to blame but myself. I am going to miss my family and friends. You never realize what you have until it's gone. The decisions I have made may impact my family and friends for the rest of their lives, but I doubt it.

Since I am stuck in my cell most of the day, staring at chipped paint, and surrounded by the stink of urine and metal, I try to write as much as I can. I have a strict daily regimen I try to maintain. When my breakfast is shoveled to me in the morning, I start my process, reflecting on my life. After breakfast, I get in a quick workout, which, ironically, I call a penitentiary workout; a training program I designed in college before I went to bed each night. The workout consists of jumping jacks, pushups, and sit ups. I would do sets of fifties until I couldn't do any more. After I work out, I start writing until I get interrupted, which is normally around lunch time.

I normally spend an hour or two listening to the chatter amongst inmates. I constantly hear the scraping on the concrete of paper transferring from one cell to another. My prison cell is open so I can see past the rusted steel bars. Unfortunately, I don't have any companions on death row to share kites with. I see kites flying by every day with inmates conversing through letters. Gangs use these kites to convey messages through each cell block. These kites are daily reminders that convicts will find a way to communicate regardless of how many CO's are walking the premises. These kites are vital for inmates to convey commands to other prisoners. Kites can be loaded with commands about hits on rival gang members, drug trade, or any illegal activity.

I try to keep busy as much as I can, but the solitude is taking a toll on me. Is solitary confinement torture? Damn straight it is. Yes, I committed a crime, and yes, I should be punished for that crime, but isn't solitary confinement for prisoners who have committed a crime in prison? The judge never said death by lethal injection after solitary confinement. The depression that I have is unbearable.

I wish I was an experienced con and knew how to play the prison game. Corruption and politics rule the prison systems. For some of these guys, life in prison can be better than being on the outside. Living that thug life inside these walls pays off. The perks of being a shot caller means protection from other inmates, as well as getting preferential treatment from the correctional officers and prison staff. An extra ladmo bag or piece of gristle during chow. The guards need the gang leaders to hold order or chaos can break lose. Inmates can outnumber correctional officers 100 to 1 at times. At any time, the inmates can take over the prison, so having a prison hierarchy, establishing order is critical.

Serving time in prison was not supposed to be pleasant, nor was it supposed to include being raped by fellow prisoners or staff, beaten by guards for the slightest provocation, driven mad by long-term solitary confinement, or killed off by medical neglect. These were the fates of thousands of prisoners every year during their stay in prisons all over the world. While there's plenty of blame to go around, it's time that people explore the harsh conditions in which inmates live. I am a firm believer in institutionalism and repenting for my crimes, but valuing humanity is most important. It's almost inhumane, but what can we expect? Monstrous crimes deserve treatment as such.

The purpose of prison was for prisoners to repent and reform, but prison life ultimately consists of passing time on extracurricular activities and maintaining an even keel. I don't know how someone can be rehabilitated with the guidance of prison staff. The constant cruelty by prison staff and lack of empathy doesn't give any of us a chance to be rehabilitated. Our minds are filled with rage and resentment. There isn't enough funding for prisons to fund concrete rehabilitation programs.

The highest incarceration rate in the entire world and there isn't enough money to house 2.3 million US prisoners in 1,719 state prisons. We are the product of our ancestors' decisions, and our ancestry chose that locking someone in a small room, with the bare necessities, was the best form of reformation and punishment.

Not every country operates in this fashion. Why are Norwegian prison systems so successful? Because they firmly believe in prison reform. The statistics don't lie. Norway has the lowest incarceration and recidivism rate in the entire world. Norway's laws are designed to send criminals to prison by adopting a less punitive approach, making sure prisoners don't relapse, which decreases the cost. The intention is to send reformed human beings back out to society to make impactful contributions. Isn't that what prison should be about? Human beings are entitled to make mistakes.

To emulate Norway's prison system, the American Bureau of Prisons would have to tailor each treatment program for each criminal, which is impossible considering that the US prison population alone is a staggering 2.3 million inmates. Out of the 2.3 million inmates, thirty-five percent of those have been paroled, but went back to prison.

The United States spends billions and billions of dollars annually on prison housing and that number is growing. The current state of the prison population is a staggering 500% increase over the past thirty years. Is society getting worse or are officials locking people away on wrongful convictions? I don't know. I can't answer that question. All that I can say is, I committed my crime and now I am doing my time.

US prisons are dangerous places with the worst people in the world all crammed into a petite enclosure being punished for their crimes. We are told to play nice and get along with people who aren't so nice. Looking at the glass half full, US prisons are much safer than international prisons. I almost think that international prisons are secret societies that are set up by inmates rather than the government. I am not sure I could ever survive in an international maximum-security prison. I am fortunate in that regard, I guess.

Rules within SQ are very strict and can't be broken. It is a life and death proposition as prisoners are constantly testing the prison code. There are two codes of conduct, one with the prison officials and the second, an inmate code of conduct. The inmate code of conduct can be life-threatening if broken. For example, if an inmate rats on another inmate, they will face lethal consequences. Cons are told to hold their mud even under the harshest beatings. In some gang affiliations, being a rat is as simple as letting another inmate know where another inmate's cell is located. Lending that type of information can get you a dance on the blacktop.

Prison is not so much about the violence that we endure and see, it's about being confined in such small quarters all the time. We become immune to the violence because we see it so much, but it's being suffocated by space and the dictators that run this place. That is a difficult adjustment.

We are all very resourceful and try everything because we have so much time on our hands. We are stuck in our cells twenty-three hours a day, and sometimes during a lockdown we are stuck in our cells for weeks without even stepping outside our cell. I am sorry, but there are only so many pushups and sit ups I can do. The one-hour session in the rec yard is taken all alone in a small bare concrete exercise yard, walking back and forth like a caged lion.

Imagine you are a low-level convict living in prison with murderers or rapists who have been in and out of the prison system their whole life. They are institutionalized for committing low-level crimes and are left to defend themselves against a gang, 100 deep. White collar criminals are left for dead. Might as well give them a shiv during the booking process.

Let's get something straight, prisons are not made to rehabilitate. They try to, but to rehabilitate over 2 million US prisoners takes billions and billions of US taxpayer money. Who is going to fund that endeavor? Why do you think so many ex-cons leave prison and find their way back? Once institutionalized, you become a hardened criminal. You learn to become a superior con man, acquiring additional felonious qualities and leave prison better equipped to commit another crime. Inmates speak to other inmates all day long. You speak to inmates at your place of employment, then in the rec yard, in the chow hall, and even in the showers. You're in constant communication with other offenders, gabbing about their crime and how they got pinched.

Jail doesn't rehabilitate you to survive in the free world and prosper as a model citizen. Most criminals have been institutionalized for so long that they aren't used to being outside working, paying bills, and making contributions to society.

❖

I immediately sprang up from my bed, half-conscious. Peering outside my 1' x 1' window I can see the wintery white mist set across the prison yard. I walk two paces to the cold metal steel, where I bathe, brush my teeth, and take care of any additional grooming necessities. The monotony of everyday prison life engulfs me. I am a robot operating under strict code. I am told when to eat, sleep, wake up, and am monitored for every action I take.

I live a sheltered presence and feel abandoned and vulnerable. My mind starts playing tricks and I start imagining things that aren't there. I start hallucinating that the walls are closing in, slowly suffocating me.

Boredom consumes me every day. There are occasions when I do come out of my cell and eat with the prison population. I never understood that, but why question it. I crave that human interaction even though it is short-lived. When

Row

I eat with the other inmates, I always get stares and whispers. Everyone knows that my days are numbered. I normally eat alone without any affiliation, but just to hear the inmate chatter is worth it.

If an inmate serving an all-day sentence wants, he could literally live his entire life eating breakfast, lunch, and dinner and that's all. No responsibilities, nothing. No rehabilitation whatsoever.

On the other hand, it could be a beautiful day outside and inmates enjoy the day and suddenly a full-scale riot breaks out and we are all in lockdown for the next three days. You never know what to expect. Prison life is unpredictable. Boredom one day can be followed by anarchy the next. I welcome the animosity because it spices up an otherwise lackluster day. I am already locked away without a trace of existence. I wouldn't even mind an altercation with another inmate just to break up the monotony.

Apart from a few altercations, for me, prison life is not what you see on television. The prison riots, gang warfare, drugs, and BS prison bureaucracy. It's worse! It's like the dream team of criminals all cooped up in one over-crowded concrete structure, constructed from cement, stone, and rubble.

To survive in the general population walking amongst real life gangsters, I became more spiritual and relied on God for protection. I think religion is as strong as one wants to make it. My cellmate was a devout Muslim and he taught me a lot about Islam. He was a spiritual leader and was always willing to share his beliefs. During my early years in San Quentin, I prayed a lot more.

Some of my friends I grew up with are very devout Muslims and follow the religion very closely. I grew up with a strong belief, but it became cloudy throughout the years. I respect the avenue of life my friends have taken, but unfortunately their beliefs and values did not rub off on me during my adolescence and early adulthood. I took the path less traveled and they took the righteous path leading to prosperous, meaningful life. I believe that I am stronger with what I faced, but faith is a strong force and when you have the wisdom of God on your side, you can always overcome adverse situations.

Religion is such a strong force and I see how it has changed my friends for the better. Some of my friends have become great people. A lot of the things I have done in my past probably would have never happened if I had a strong religious background. The thing is, I wasn't a bad person. I have a lot of friends and am loved by my family, but I always felt like something was missing. I always tried to fill the void by adding something in my life. I just never gave religion a real shot and now it's too late.

❖

Vulnerability causes aggression, and inmates in the Special Housing Unit are continuously susceptible. They are prone to violent and confrontational behaviors, whether it's feces thrown on a guard, or constant verbal assault on another prisoner or prison official. When inmates enter the SHU, lifers quickly realize the harsh reality of solitary confinement.

I have been transferred to the SHU for my last few weeks of incarceration before I get put to rest, giving me the time to examine my entire prison sentence.

The SHU is infamous for lodging the worst of the worst in criminality. Its tenants include Al Capone, Tim McVeigh, Ted Bundy, and John Wayne Gacy, to name just a few. These were apex predators with bad reputations for preying on the weak.

I am added to that list of distinguished criminals in American history, because I am in the SHU. It's hard to imagine that I will be following the same road as the worst of the worst.

❖

Maximum security is no laughing matter because of what it represents. Maximum security represents isolation from the free world under the harsh reality of life behind the cold steel bars. I always believed I was one of the mentally toughest guys around, being able to endure pain and anguish without reaching my breaking point. That's what I thought, until I entered maximum security. I knew that when I came to a place like this, my senses would have to improve, and my guard would need to be up immediately.

I reminisce about when I was in the cell block. During the hours of 3 to 5 a.m. you heard an eerie silence in the prison. The cellblock maintained the stink of a mortuary, filled with bodies wasting away like rotting corpses. I was one of those delinquents living a life of broken dreams, eventually sentenced to getting buried six feet deep.

My eyes opened at quarter to 5. Bags over my eyes like I was just in a 12-round title fight. Often, I performed my daily tasks with my eyes closed and oftentimes I had to as there was diminutive light coming from my window during the early hours. On occasion I could hear birds chirping outside my cell, and for a moment I was at peace with myself until I heard the outbreak of prison officials forcefully yelling.

"Chow, convicts!"

That's when I was quickly reminded that I resided in the worst place on earth. Peace and tranquility only lasted a few precious seconds. Soon the entire cellblock was filled with rage and aggression. There was nothing worse than a career convict woken up from his sleep. That was a recipe for disaster.

5:30 a.m. we got ready to start our day walking, chained, to chow hall. Prison nutrition consists of three meals a day. They are vile portions of sustenance, ranging from porridge and cereal for breakfast, a bologna sandwich and a bag of chips for lunch, and dry noodles with bread for dinner. The prison food was awfully close to violating our human rights. The meager portions and lack of variety make it difficult for San Quentin inmates to get their daily nutritional content. Again, that is why commissary was so crucial in prison because it gives inmates some semblance of humanity. I would probably give my right leg for a deep-dish Chicago style pizza.

It took me a long time to acclimate myself to prison cuisine, but we didn't have a choice. It's eat or starve. Inmates during their initial stages aren't allowed visits to the canteen to obtain commissary. It can take months before you have that access. Therefore, you are held under confinement of prison nutrition and allowed three meals a day. I ate every morsel of my grub for every meal, making sure I wasn't losing weight and getting sick. It still didn't make a difference. I needed the energy that every inmate needed to be prepared to battle at any given moment. When I was in the cell block I was always looking over my shoulder.

My body has deteriorated in front of my eyes. I went from a regional and state champion bodybuilder into an emaciated prune in a matter of months. It didn't look like I ever lifted any weight even though I was training every day in the rec yard. I was now a shell of my previous being. I guess it didn't matter since my day of reckoning was approaching.

After breakfast, I made my way to the recreational yard hitting the iron pile. I was granted 1 hour of recreation a day, which was heaven compared to the SHU. For a lot of the non-gang members, recreation consisted of working out, playing basketball, running, trying to maintain some level of activity while being locked away. I would normally weight train for thirty minutes, run for another twenty minutes, and the rest of my time shadow box, or practice my Kenpo karate. That was when other gang members weren't using the weight pile. The non-gang members were always at the mercy of the gang members in the rec yard. If the Mexican Mafia wanted to use the weights and monopolize that area, then I didn't weight train that day. Sharing space and our limited personal belongings is not something a lot of convicts did.

For gang members, rec was a time to keep an eye out on their cartel and make business deals. Everyone was on high alert during rec time as prison riots could explode any time, causing a full out race war. You have gangs scattered strategically around the yard standing guard. The yard was all about gangs carving their own territory. It was a menacing place for me because I was not affiliated with any gangs. The threat of violence was just one part of life on the yard. The yard was also a testing ground for junior associates staking their claim in their gang. If they were told to put a hit on a Chomo or another rival, then it was their duty to complete the task.

Row

After the recreation yard, I took a shower and headed back to my cell with all the other inmates. Time lethargically rolled by after the recreation yard. We were all cramped in the cellblock like sardines in a can, some inmates assigned three to a cell. I was extremely fortunate that I only had one cellie. Some of the cells in my cellblock were half the size of mine.

My cellmate had a lot of talents. He could play the piano, drums, harmonica, and guitar. Because of his behavior in prison and his relationship with the warden he could keep musical instruments in his cell, which he gratuitously let me use. I kept myself busy in my cell learning how to play different musical instruments, and before I got transferred to the SHU, I could read music and play the piano, guitar, harmonica, and drums. I also picked up woodworking and built and designed some gadgets with the tools that he had. I was extremely grateful to my cellmate. Through his generosity, I lived somewhat of an extravagant lifestyle while residing in cellblock B. Inmates in cellblock B did not own musical instruments or woodworking tools.

If you had the juice, then you could live a lavish lifestyle in prison. It was said that OJ Simpson had a big screen television in his cell and hosted Super Bowl parties every year. He was known as the Godfather in prison and was rumored to have countless privileges.

I still remember the day I got transferred to the SHU. I was in my cell waiting to go down to chow hall for lunch when I heard one of the CO's yell, "Transfer cell B-249. Inmate H67641, you're going to the SHU."

There was a sudden uproar of canisters banging against the steel prison bars. I was moved to the death house. I was given three minutes to pack up all my belongings and say goodbye to my cellmate. It was two minutes too much. I looked him dead in the eye, shook his hand, and said, "So long." My stare signified allegiance, solidarity, and appreciation for his candor and kindness. I could honestly say that he became one of my friends. Someone I could confide in within this cold dark place. In an area of crime and corruption, he

38

was a gem. I wished him the best of luck, walked away, and never looked back. I knew once I shook his hand I would never see him again. He knew I was going to be taking the stainless-steel ride very soon.

The CO's knew me at this stage and knew that I wasn't going to harm anyone unless I got antagonized. The ninja turtles gently put the shackles on my ankles and connected them to my hands, and I limped away with my head down. In prison terms this was called a four-piece suit. The SHU was only 100 yards away through the rec yard, up on the fourth floor. The CO's were quiet as we approached the long corridor that introduced the small cages that were now going to be my home for the latter part of my prison sentence.

As I entered the cell, I surveyed my surroundings. I saw a cold metal bed with a very thin, raggedy mattress for my bed, one 1' x 2' pillow to rest my head, an arctic metal sink, toilet, and a small metal table.

I would hear inmates howling and screaming obscenities to prison guards. My cell consisted of very little to keep me occupied. I had my toiletries and a bed with a flimsy razor thin, emaciated cushion, which made sleeping arduous and painful. I was also given a dull pencil and a writing pad. They gave me next to nothing, so I couldn't harm myself, but my cell was still checked twice a day. I was allowed two prison visits per month, but most of my family was across the country and the only visitors I got were journalists who wanted to cover my story before I was executed. No thanks.

The secure housing unit! Those three words give hardened criminals nightmares. It's the idea of losing all your privileges and living under complete isolation that puts the fear of God in convicts. I was petrified knowing that I was going to be alone.

Living in the SHU was going to be a true test of my willpower and resilience.

December 12th was when I was transferred to the SHU. Those privileges I had in cellblock B were now gone. Playing music, gone! Engaging with other cons, forget about it! I went from having a companion, to CO's telling me I got "nothin' comin' anymore." The misery of being in a small, confined space with very limited sunlight and human interaction could make a sane person lose his mind.

Other inmates got to go to breakfast and then went to their jobs to earn money. After their job, they spent time in the recreation yard. It's almost like they were on the outside. Privileged inmates earned their own money by providing services for the prison. Jobs consisted of kitchen duty: scrubbing pots and pans, preparing daily meals, cleaning up the recreation yard, etc…There were hundreds of jobs inmates could have, but with my classification entering prison, I was supposedly a risk to other inmates. I was not eligible for even the easiest positions at San Quentin. I couldn't even get a job cleaning the staff toilets. Back door parole was my moniker.

Cash was king in the joint. Inmates earned money to purchase goods from the commissary. We could purchase food, electronics, books, pretty much everything we needed to keep our sanity. Currency was more important in prison than in the free world. We lived and died by how much money we earned because money could buy safety, drugs, sex, hooch, brake fluid. Currency held a certain prestige and respect and could be used for barter. Having that kind of supremacy in prison could be extremely dangerous, as inmates didn't follow prison protocol and constantly tested their boundaries, seeking favors in exchange for currency.

Currency exchange was critical for a prisoner's well-being because of the lack of amenities. I was stripped of that from day one since I was a high-risk inmate. I was fortunate that I was initially given rec time and a cellie, but I knew that at some point I was going to get transferred to the SHU.

Depression kicked in for me as soon as I realized the reality of spending my remaining life inside the empty white walls. Murder was always the dish that I was served. Every morsel of jail food was laced with my conviction.

Prison life was not only about facing my sentence, but also about facing the emotional burden it was leaving on my soul. I was constantly examining my conviction and how I would repent for my sins. Some inmates examined their trial step by step to someday appeal their case. As much as I tried not to, I was doing the same. I was no different.

Every day was the same agenda repeatedly. I was living in a real-life Groundhog Day.

PART II
Darwinism

DAY 16 JAIL JOURNAL: MADE IN AMERICA

Do you know how difficult it is to write a manuscript with a miniature number 2 pencil with a dull lead and scraps of paper? I have asked prison staff countless times for a notebook and a pen, but I am given the cold shoulder. I am on the pay no mind list. Having something sharp in my cell is not sanctioned. To prison staff that would be like giving Jason Voorhees, the slasher from Friday the 13th, a knife.

I press down on the paper trying to scribe each letter. Exhausting! My forearms are inflamed like I just completed one of my rigid arm workouts. I again requested a sharpened pencil a few days ago, but my request fell on deaf ears. I wish I could see some of these punk CO's on the outside.

Sitting in my cell surrounded by pasty white walls, my imagination is stagnant. It is difficult to reminisce about growing up because it is a lifetime away and my memory is now obstructed with sorrow. I am going to try my hardest to describe my life as a youngster consumed by sports and school. I think this will be a brief passage, as my thoughts from my early childhood are blurry. I want to paint a portrait of triumph because my family overcame a lot of barriers as they began their new life in the United States.

I was under the age of seven growing up in a three-story brick building on the North side of Chicago. Those were great times, but they also came with a lot of adverse situations.

Chicago was a melting pot of different ethnicities. It has a palpable sense of culture and tradition. It's known for its incredible architecture, gritty blue-collar integrity, and its legendary sports figures, like Michael Jordan and Walter Payton. For me it was home and, even though my family didn't immediately thrive, it was only a matter of time before the land of opportunity would open its arms.

Even though the Windy City was vibrant and rich with diversity and one of the most visited cities in the United States, it had a dark side. Growing up on the mean streets of Chicago with my family was tough. My family had financial struggles migrating from Pakistan, and we resided in an area littered with drug dealing and violence. Despite our hardships, we had the most important aspect of life: family. Our family was glued together by love. I was fortunate to be living with so many family members to count on. Even though we were light financially, I was spoiled with love.

We were all united and living in one building, helping each other as much as we could. My family owned a local convenience store, Loyola Food Mart, in a town that was home to a notorious gang in the 80's, The Folk. The Folk nation was a street gang originally colonized in Chicago in 1979. Within the Folk Nation there are multiple gangs spread across the United States such as the Black Disciples, La Raza, Spanish Cobras, and Gangster Disciples to name few. Each one of these sets carried a unique symbol as well as apparel. They were all vicious in nature and murdered at all costs.

During the time we owned Loyola Food Mart, my family was repeatedly attacked. My uncle was beaten with golf clubs during the evening hours one night while trying to close the store. I don't think that the gang members even wanted anything apart from a thrill at someone else's expense. It could even have been a gang initiation. My father and uncle were often threatened with physical abuse trying to protect our family and our only means of revenue.

One wintry night in the Windy City, my cousin was closing the store. Three gang bangers charged the store banging a .44 caliber in the air demanding money. My cousin rendered whatever was in the cash register, but for no rhyme or reason, one of the thugs drew his pistol and opened fire. My cousin was hit multiple times with a .44 slug; once in the shoulder, one missed, and the other a quarter of an inch away from his heart, leaving him helpless. He had the instinct to call 911, though he was bloodied, battered, and barely breathing. Tough as nails! The paramedics arrived and rushed him to the hospital, where he became unconscious due to loss of blood. He was in the intensive care for days as he fought for his life. Fortunately, the doctors saved him, leaving him handicapped for over a month and eating his meals through a straw. Not to mention the trauma of being attacked at gun point for a few meaningless dollars. Meanwhile, the gangbangers walked away scot-free. Why? Because they threatened to kill my family if my cousin ratted. Those thugs robbed my family and almost killed my cousin, and we couldn't do a damn thing.

Those thugs who hid behind the cold steel of a .44 caliber were cowards. They took the easy way out in life by robbing and burglarizing innocent people. Those tough situations my family faced gave all of us tough skin to deal with the pendulum we called "life."

Times were tough, but my family continued to persevere with each other's love and support. Things could have been a lot worse as we could have been living in the Chicago housing unit surrounded by gang banging, pimps, and drugs. Instead, my mother and father scraped up every penny they had and bought a building keeping our entire family living together.

My immediate family lived in a dingy three-bedroom apartment on the first level, while other family members were on the second and third level. I loved the fact that my family was in the same building.

Growing up in Chicago was an adventure for my family. My family would do everything in their power to triumph and beat all odds. We were all hustling for our place on US soil. Violence and poverty were just stumbling blocks on the path to success.

I was young a boy just getting a taste for life. I didn't realize then how much my parents fought to get us out from the shadows of poverty and into better living conditions. I still don't know, but I appreciate everything they did. They are real heroes in my book.

❖

I started playing sports competitively at five years old and participated competitively till the age of thirty.

As a teen, I wanted to be recognized. I wanted to walk in a room and have people adore me. Why? I aspired to become something in the public eye, envisioning a line of people requesting my autograph. I feared not being somebody, not being in the limelight where everyone knew me. Mission accomplished. Everyone now knows me as a hardened criminal. My mother didn't raise me like this; I only have a handful of days left on this earth and making choices or changes now doesn't mean anything. I need to make peace with myself and turn the page to the new chapter of my life, which will be titled, "The Afterlife."

During my youth, I thought becoming an athlete was the way. I wanted to be admired in whatever sport I chose to compete in. The head honcho, the don, the main attraction. Pictures in the newspaper, interviews, magazine articles, whatever social media channels there were at the time. Becoming a distinguished athlete consumed me and molded my mind. Everything I participated in had to be sports related. That competitive drive fueled me every day. I was rigid and wanted to win at all costs, even if that restricted me from having a social life. I would outwork my opponents as well as my teammates and coaches. I couldn't stand going home at the same time as my teammates, not having done anything extra.

After football practice, beaten and battered, I would stumble into the gymnasium to run a few extra sprints or push a few extra repetitions on the bench press. I punished my body to the limit, so I could excel on the field. My coaches would catch me training after hours, and, fearful of me burning out before games, grounded me from the weight room. I always snuck in somehow through the back door. My high school football coach got so fed up with me sneaking into the weight room that he made me my own key and told me to lock up. He told me I was the hardest working player he ever coached. I always thought I was invincible and indestructible because of my preparation. Nothing could hurt me as I was strong in spirit and powerful, performing like a well-oiled machine.

I was an overachiever, but never got the satisfaction of relishing the moment. It was like winning the gold medal and being on the pedestal feeling that I did something wrong. Thinking I hadn't perfected my craft. No matter what I did, I wasn't satisfied. First place was never good enough. It's a trait that some people have, but I think that in me, it was extreme.

When I was a bodybuilder, I was always looking at a skinny kid in the mirror, thinking I was never big enough, or lean enough. I would do push-ups and sit ups watching television. I hated compliments because they made me complacent. When I was in the corporate world, I was never satisfied with my accomplishments. It's supposedly a characteristic of psychopaths to never feel gratified in their current state. Some people overestimate what they can do in their lifetime and try to achieve the impossible. Most people underachieve and fall short of their hopes and dreams. I wouldn't say that I'm a psychopath, but I think I have characteristics that resemble some modern-day serial murderers. I'm an overachiever and if someone told me I couldn't do something, I always had to prove them wrong. I needed that negativity.

During my adolescence, I was always getting into something. I was always out of the house hanging out with friends, playing sports. Childhood in the 80s and 90s for me was much different from the childhood of youths today. There weren't a ton of gaming systems and computers to pollute our youths' minds. When I was a youth, if I wasn't in a competitive sport, which was rare, I came home from school, threw my book bag to the floor, and vanished for a few hours. I was playing whatever sport was on the docket that afternoon. It was wholesome fun without any restrictions. Everything was much less complicated back when I was growing up. We went to school, hung out with friends, played sports, and did our homework -- sometimes. None of this social media crap rotting our brains. We weren't consumed with posting on Instagram, tweeting about some nonsense, or posting what we ate for breakfast to the masses. It was as simple as that. None of this emotional outlandish behavior raging out against the world. Times have changed and it's scary to think that our youth are going to be running the world. The children of today will soon be the future of tomorrow. I sound like a fortune cookie.

At an early age, I knew that school was not my cup of tea. I hated going to school because I wasn't a gifted scholar. I wasn't grasping the subjects in my early years. When I was in first and second grade, I was often removed from class to assist with my reading, writing, and arithmetic. School didn't come easy to me and I had a learning disability coupled with a hot temper, oftentimes chin checking one of my classmates. Growing up, I always had beef with someone. I was a lone hooligan. I won some and I lost some, but I thought the most important aspect of fighting is earning the respect of your adversary.

During my second-grade spelling bee, I was eliminated because I couldn't spell "cat." CAT! There are two-year old's that can spell cat. Tasks were not easy for me and I always had a short fuse, displaying my frustration. I wasn't a terrible kid, but I wasn't an angel either. I ended up in the principal's office talking my way out of problems quite a bit.

I defied authority, often rebelling against school officials. On one occasion I provoked the school principal by calling him by his first name to his face. "Hey Al."

Row

My aggressive nature in school was probably why I excelled on the gridiron. I had so much aggression that if I didn't play football and release some of that, I would have ended up in a youth detention center. I wasn't concerned with consequences back then because I didn't care about penalties. My actions were decided based on the now and not the future.

I didn't take my education seriously. It was never a priority. I always wanted to be outside creating havoc. Whether it was throwing M-80's in people's yards, egging one of my enemies' front porch, or TP-ing someone's house. It was extremely difficult for my parents to put me in a box. I wasn't interested in spending time in the house during daylight hours. I would rather be outside.

When my family and I lived in Chicago, I went to Saint Ignatius grammar school. It was a decent school in the North Side of Chicago and both of my older siblings went there, so I felt somewhat protected. Well, that was what I thought, at first.

Saint Ignatius thickened my skin at an early age, as it was the first time I ever got bullied. Christopher Teagan was his name and he was my arch nemesis. He was the Joker to my Batman, the Detroit Pistons to my Chicago Bulls, and the Green Bay Packers to my Chicago Bears. He made first grade hell for me and took advantage of me every chance he had. He was a street punk and, at the time, I didn't know how to deal with someone who could out-power me mentally and physically. I fought back, but was never a match.

Teachers never seemed to care about his antics and constant barrage of abuse. He was an eight-year old trapped in a fifteen-year old's body, preying on me every day like a ferocious crocodile devouring a helpless mouse. He sought me out in the hall, at lunch, gym, recess, and after school with his older brothers who were just as menacing. He kept me in his back pocket as his daily ego boost. I was his Red Bull and he seemed to get a rush from pinning me against the locker or punching me every chance he got.

I recall one instance which scarred me for a long time. We were in detention after school, sitting right next to each other. Chris was hurling whatever he could find in his backpack at me, all while the teacher was completely clueless. He then proceeded to get off his chair and tackled me to the floor like a linebacker and started endlessly dropping bombs on me. He was stronger and knew how to wrestle. I was outmatched. The teacher was completely oblivious while I was being pummeled. I don't know how someone could be so undisturbed while one of her students was getting beaten by another. The torture ended once my adversary was exhausted and decided my face had taken enough of a beating. I peeled myself from the ground and wobbled back to my desk, tattered clothes and all.

Without Chris and his bullying ways, I don't think I would have grown up with such tough skin. I had to develop a certain level of mental toughness and discipline trying to deal with constant abuse. It isn't easy going to school when you know you're going to get beat up black and blue without the teachers getting involved. He ruined my learning experience in 1st grade because every day I went to school, I walked the halls in fear. I was like a scared little kid who was living in a dream with Freddy Krueger trying to decapitate me. I remember being nervous every day before going to school, anticipating a beating. Kids my age were ultra-excited about going to school, but that feeling was taken away from me. It made learning difficult.

What I would do to meet good ole Chris now. I dreamt of him walking into my cell on the first day of his sentence. Coming into my cell trying to be buddy-buddy, not having a clue how much pain he inflicted and how much pain he was about to endure. I would welcome him with open shanks. Anyone that leaves that type of mark, you remember.

Even though that prick caused me a lot of pain, I still would not wish San Quentin upon him. I can't wish harm or harbor ill will towards anyone. We were just kids. I am not the judge or jury of his actions and I have made a ton of mistakes in my life. Who the hell am I to judge anyone?

The bullying went on from one school to another. I wasn't exactly getting bullied anymore as I was the aggressor, to a certain extent. My family moved from the city of Chicago to the Northwest suburbs in 1987. Suburban schools were much different from city schools. Children in city schools were tougher and more rugged because of their environment. City students had to watch their backs.

People from city schools weren't scared to take flight on anyone. I came from that environment. I also came from being assaulted by my bully every day. Entering Thomas Jefferson in Hoffman Estates, I had a chip on my shoulder. I was entering that school as a menace to society, sporting Metallica Ride the Lightning attire, rocking out to hairbands like Skid Row, Pantera, Guns and Roses, and

Black Sabbath. I was also watching WWE matches idolizing some of my favorites like Macho Man Randy Savage, Ultimate Warrior, Demolition, and Legion of Doom. I couldn't get enough of watching guys beating each other to a bloody pulp for my sheer enjoyment. I enjoyed the battle between two brutes so much that my brother and I would reenact our own WrestleMania matches, often beating each other until submission.

Instead of being the sheep, I became the lion, exerting my dominance. I didn't want to get punk'd anymore, so whenever anyone said anything derogatory, like calling me "dot head" or "dirty Indian," I molly whopped 'em pretty quick.

Experiencing violent behavior early toughened me and gave me an edge when my family moved to the suburbs. It was like moving to a different world, like going from chaos to complete serenity. The problem was that I never conformed to the structure of suburban living until I got much older. I was still living in the jungle instead of becoming domesticated. I walked into Thomas Jefferson Elementary School on a mission not to meet another Christopher Teagan and if I did, I would check his chin before he checked mine.

One channel of aggression opened the door to another and that is when I started watching football. Once I started, it was hook, line, and sinker and I wanted to start playing. Moving to the Northwest Suburbs gave me the opportunity to join Hoffman Estates Athletic Association. The association was only a few minutes from the house, making it easy for my mom to take me to practice every day.

I wanted to make sure that I was never going to be a victim again.

Moving to the suburbs was like living in Disneyland. We had a beautiful five-bedroom house, a huge backyard, and friendly neighbors. Everything my family ever wanted and dreamed of was now a reality. I had my own room, which I decorated with posters of my favorite WWE wrestlers, NFL stars, and rock bands. Our backyard was used for baseball, football, soccer, cricket, and volleyball games. You could always catch my brother and me playing some sport with our friends in the backyard. We were living the American dream.

My dad owned a video store, Select Video. It was the only video store within a 5-mile radius and was just a few blocks from the house. My brother and I would walk there every chance we got. Back then there was no streaming, downloading, YouTube, or Netflix. None of that crap. VHS, all day. My father monopolized the territory with his video rental store. The business was flourishing in a magnificent location across the street from the pond.

Residents of Hoffman Estates were content. Residents lived a life of luxury with large houses, big back yards, and a successful outlook on life. We were in middle class suburbia, and, for us, that was a major upgrade. No more looking over my shoulder. This life was homage to my mother and father's moxie, standing together and overcoming the odds to get their children out of the slums.

Life was great and my family was on the right track financially. I now had all the privacy I wanted living in a peaceful environment. It was everything I ever wanted and I was grateful to my parents for working hard and removing me from the streets of Chicago.

❖

My second-grade year at Thomas Jefferson was a blur. I was never in class and I was getting into a ton of scuffles. Someone would say something to me and they would get a knuckle sandwich. I didn't like structure, and the suburban schools had a lot of that. Wait in line for lunch, wait in line for recess, hold hands when walking down the halls. C'mon. I also had a learning disability the first few years of school and my attention was always somewhere else. I was fortunate that my parents were such positive influences. When I entered second grade, I felt like I was in a whole new world. I didn't have many friends at my old grammar school, so I wasn't missing friendship, but living in a new environment gave my siblings and me a new territory to explore.

I knew, entering the schools in Hoffman Estates, that my experience would be much different from what it would have been in the city schools. There would be Christopher Teagans not only in school, but for the rest of my life. Experiencing that abuse gave me the vigor to push through hostile situations. As much as I hated being bullied, that experience made me resilient when I made it to high school and college.

Row

High school was a breeze and I was finally starting to realize the importance of education and accepting that it didn't matter if I excelled at athletics. Universities look for scholars first and athletes second, unless you're in the top five percent in the nation for your sport. That wasn't me.

There were a lot fewer distractions and I could concentrate on my studies. I had friends, I was playing sports, and my family was on the right path financially. I went from growing up around poverty to white middle-class suburbia, littered with golden retrievers surrounded by white picket fences. My best friends were a football, baseball glove, and basketball. I didn't have to worry about a thug encroaching upon my enjoyment. I was also on a schedule that allowed me to focus on my schoolwork instead of vampires trying to loot me. Life in Hoffman Estates was fantastic and I was getting an education superior to what I was receiving in the city. Playing sports undeniably inspired me and grounded me, keeping me on the right path to succeed which eventually resulted in a scholarship and the chance to continue playing football. It seemed like I was turning the page. Well...

My first few semesters in college, I didn't take my academics as seriously as I should have. I was gazing in the bright lights and screaming fans. Playing college ball was all I cared about during my freshman and sophomore years. I hadn't decided on a major, and I was living an independent life without any adult supervision.

During the beginning of my college career, going to classes was never a priority. The priority was maintaining my eligibility, training, and running down the field busting wedges. Mix that in with a few college bashes.

My early college life was a life of debauchery and time wasted with my teammates in our football dorm room, Solberg Hall. A lot of shuckin' and jivin'. I was a student athlete and was working at the same time, but it was the time of my life, and I wouldn't trade it for the world.

Playing sports gave me a social advantage. I didn't have to rely on mingling with people and making new friends, as I already had 100 teammates to socialize with on a regular basis. There was also a lot of support from the professors and student body following our football team. I loved the attention that I was getting for all the hard work I was putting into college athletics.

Day 16: Made in America

My normal daily routine would consist of attending class, then proceeding to the film room to study the weekly opponent, attending mid-day football meetings, practicing, and hitting the weight pile. After that, I'd work for a few hours for the grounds crew, recruiting coordinator, or weight room attendant, before heading back to the dorm room to crack open the books. Okay, probably not homework. More like hittin' the PlayStation joystick.

I like to think of my experience at North Park as a learning experience. I made a lot of poor choices which lead to my dismissal from the University in 2001. I wasn't ready to live on my own, and my inner inadequacies manifested during my residence at the institution. I was a young punk sporting gold plated hoops around my ears, blonde highlights, and tattoos. I was trying to be someone I wasn't. I was a wannabe tough guy. I was a knucklehead.

A few of my teammates and I decided to reside on campus heading into our junior year. We all lived in different vicinities in the Chicagoland area, prohibiting us from training together during the long, backbreaking summer training sessions. We planned to work during the day and then train as a team in the evening hours. There were five of us that trained every day and then a handful of teammates joined periodically. We had a solid rapport and hit the weights hard. Our summer training sessions were grueling and we pushed each other to the limits.

During one of our training sessions the dean of student affairs walked into the weight room. The dean of students at NPU was a colossal booster of the football program and frequently visited us training. He would often ask us how our training was going and about our prospects for the upcoming season. Rain, snow, sleet, or shine, he attended every game. He was a true fan of North Park athletics and wanted the football program to excel. He was also a professor, teaching a course in critical thinking skills. The class curriculum consisted of watching movies and writing about their significance in modern society. This class was held at the dean's house across the street from the football stadium, and it was normally filled with football players who needed mentorship.

My teammates and I put in a lot of work during that summer and the dean recognized our commitment to make North Park a contender in the College Conference of Illinois and Wisconsin. He rewarded our hard work at the end of the summer by offering us residence at the North Park president's summer home during the school year. When he propositioned this to a few of us, he requested our allegiance to maintain pristine occupancy.

Row

Well, we did not live up to our promise and throughout the course of the year we held Motley Crue type gatherings, disassembling the apartment. We left thousands and thousands of dollars' worth of damage requiring complete destruction of the property. Doors were missing, kitchen appliances were removed, glass windows were shattered, stains were left all over the carpet, enormous holes were left in multiple locations, messy scripture graffiti was displayed on walls, tobacco cups piled with spit were exhibited everywhere collecting bugs, and filth was present everywhere. The place looked like a tornado hit after we were done with it. The sheer debauchery and lack of maturity we showed that year was flat out disrespectful to the whole North Park community. My roommates and I were all disgusted with our actions, but those were the choices we made. We had to go to the college board and discuss the destruction we caused. We destroyed property that wasn't ours and, thus, it was time for me to leave campus and start attending another university.

North Park University treated us with the utmost respect and gave us multiple opportunities to become role models for the institution and set an example by providing us a beautiful apartment. We were the big men on campus. Instead, we decided to destroy the apartment. I was very remorseful because I let down the dean of students, who was a close friend. I had also wanted to finish out my college education and college football career at North Park University.

I think everything happens for a reason and we learn from our trials and tribulations. I missed North Park and the camaraderie I shared with my teammates, but it was time to move on or else I would have never graduated. I ended up transferring to Benedictine University, in a town outside of Chicago.

When I transferred to Benedictine University, I was determined to graduate and completely focused on my studies. I went from spending endless time in the gym to splitting my time between the gym and library. My class schedule was booked Monday – Friday, with seven courses. I was also working at General Nutrition Centers as a sales associate and continuing my training. It was time to man up and start taking my studies seriously or else I would be a seven-year student. You know, like a doctor, except I was a business major.

I was all set to graduate with a BA in Business Management and Organization Behavior, taking twenty-one credit hours my last semester. After approximately fifteen years of schooling, my college career was finally ending, and I could start working and supporting myself. I was excited about closing the chapter and moving onto greener pastures. There was still one stone unturned.

I wanted to obtain my master of business administration degree. This was always a goal of mine, especially because of the academic troubles I had in grammar school. I wanted to prove to myself that I could further my education and obtain my MBA. I believed that obtaining my graduate degree would also carry me in my corporate career, give me business knowledge, and fulfill a lifelong goal.

I was also working at the time and speaking with graduate students; a lot of them stated I couldn't hold a full-time job and be a full-time student. I knew that if I didn't jump right in, I would never go back to school. This was probably my one and only chance to get into graduate school, or else too much time would have elapsed, so I decided to obtain my MBA. I accomplished this while working a full-time job and getting ready for my first bodybuilding show. I was committed to my office, my gym, and the library. That time frame sucked, but, looking back it was well worth it as I graduated Cum Laude.

I wonder what any of these cons would say if I told them I had a graduate degree. College degrees don't mean a damn thing in prison.

DAY 15 JAIL JOURNAL: CHUMBAWAMBA

Count! Don't these fools realize I ain't going anywhere? Nobody leaves this dump.

How do you expect an individual to live in a cement box? Not allowed to have contact with the outside world or partake in any rehabilitation opportunities, or even go outside and enjoy the fresh air, and then expect them to be rehabilitated when they enter the outside world?

This happens repeatedly in the United States jail system. Inmates come into prison as convicted criminals, and then leave prison with stronger ties to the criminal world. The number of prisons that leverage rehabilitation tools is far from promising. So, where is that money going? It's going into the pockets of the fat cats in the courtroom. It's not going to prison staff because they are constantly complaining about their salary.

I will never walk outside these walls again. I know that. I don't care how tough you are, when you are living in isolation it hurts like hell. I feel like I am buried alive in a cell, while everyone is walking on top of me. I feel forgotten and nobody cares. Like Tom Hanks in Castaway. People did mourn my death sentence, but after a while everyone forgets and starts living their life. I become a distant memory rotting away.

If you listen closely, you can hear the rage that builds amongst the other inmates. Little things will make you go crazy in here; if you don't get mail a certain time, if you feel you're not getting enough food on your tray, or if one of the CO's uses excessive force when they cuff you. These meaningless vices can burn a violent notion in an inmate's mind and will eventually make them act out.

Row

The only sounds I hear now are inmates scratching at the walls seeking another refuge, knowing damn well there is nothing outside their cell except a bullet to the head.

There is a lot going on in my mind leading up to my execution and my days on death row are numbered. I could easily go insane thinking about my last few weeks and wondering if my soul will ever find rest.

I think about the past condemned who took the stainless steel ride like; Leanderess Riley, a former San Quentin death row inmate who assassinated an innocent bystander in a Sacramento robbery. Riley fought tooth and nail with the officers, gripping the handrail, pleading for mercy. Even when the gas was distributed, Riley put up his hands to cover his face. Eventually, he too succumbed.

I am not going to be executed in this manner. I want to die with dignity, with my eyes exposed to my audience so they could see my disposition. I didn't want the chamber to dishonor my last few moments.

Before I get put down, I request to examine the lethal injection chamber. I am denied by the warden, as he thought that would elevate my anxiety. The San Quentin chamber is called the Chamber of Horrors and has slayed over 500 men.

I lie down and stare at my empty jail cell, staring at white-walls. I get lost in my own thoughts. Meditation is the key to my survival. Constantly asking myself, will I do the time, or will I let the time do me?

It doesn't look like my end is going to get any easier. My fate is now controlled by God. I don't know what each day is going to bring. My disposition that day is going to dictate the way I write. I am not going to apologize if I offend anyone. If you don't like what I write, don't read it. I am not trying to become a bestselling author or make money. The feeling I have now is surreal. In a few weeks, I am going to relive my life in a flash.

When you are alone, you reflect on your thoughts. You analyze everything and those reflections can cause deep-rooted depression. Ask yourself, "Can you live in a bathroom for 10 years?" Anyone who says, "I would love to live a life alone," hasn't truly been alone.

Every time I leave my cell, I must strip, get shackled from my hands to ankles, and have multiple rifles pointed at me, as if to say, "Make one false move, asshole, and I will blow your head clean off." I get it. I am a criminal, but I am also a human being.

When I got incarcerated, I was left with memories. Everything in my past was a distant memory. All the adversity I faced in my life is nothing compared to what I am about to face.

❖

During my life on the outside, sports were always my first choice. Competition is where I thrived. It was where I learned to be a man. The playing field is where I learned to deal with injury and diversity. I put my body through the grind day in and day out. I used and abused my body like a prizefighter that fought one too many fights. Injuries were a way of life for me. I just bandaged and put some Flex-All on whatever injury I had and kept going. If I was in pain, I took a cortisone shot. If my head was pounding from a big collision on the football field, I took smelling salts to wake up and play the next series.

I always tried to live life to the fullest, but with that, I caused a lot of harm to my body. Competition was an important aspect of my life because it made me stronger having to fight through the adversity. Apart from all the injuries I endured playing sports, I managed to do a lot of stupid things to my body. There was a time my friends and I would play chicken. We would take bats and get it close to our skin until somebody stopped and quit. Well, back then, quitting at something like that was a cowardly act and who wants to be perceived as a coward in front of fifty testosterone-induced football players? I don't recall how many times I burned a bat on my hand. I don't know what I was thinking. Knucklehead philosophy.

I was still young, but I was a train wreck with all the broken bones, head trauma, strains, pulls, and tears. To tell you the truth, I wouldn't have it any other way. A pristine physique hasn't been physically tested. I am not talking about competition in the backyard with your homeboys tossing the pigskin. I am talking about competition with athletes who wanted to rip my head off. If you have gone through life without feeling the pain of a break or tear, then you are lucky. I pulled my hamstrings, quads, calves, hip, triceps, groin, tore my bicep, my MCL, ACL, my abductor, broke my fingers, my arm, chipped a bone in my hand, and suffered multiple concussions, sprains, and multiple surgeries. The list goes on and on.

I was a mini Evel Knievel with all my injuries and battle scars over the years of wear and tear. I was always getting into something when I was an adolescent, whether it was fighting with older kids, or playing football, bodybuilding, weight training, self-medicating, torturing my body for kicks, or working labor intensive jobs. I put mileage on my body going from one injury to the next, never letting my body go through the repairing process. I could play through some of the agony, sometimes succumbing to the severity of the injury.

It seemed like everything I did, I ended up getting wounded. I was always in some sort of cast or bandage. Back then ACE bandages were my best friend. My mom wanted to put me in a bubble, securing me from the outside world. She endured all these injuries with me. Every time I would come home, I could see the sad expression on my mom's face. I knew that it would affect her, but what could she do? She couldn't keep me caged in the house forever. Sports were my life. I was just too aggressive as a young boy and needed to get my aggression out on something. That is why my mom got me playing sports at such a young age.

I enjoyed the competition and learning how to play different sports, pushing myself to try as many as possible. I can't tell you the number of times I was on the brink of passing out, or shaking from extreme muscle fatigue from a triple drop set, or running that extra sprint. I tried different fascinations in life and pushed the envelope, or else I found myself in a rut. I didn't want to be the one to look back on my life and ask myself, "What did I accomplish?" or "I wish I would have completed a goal on my bucket list." Everyone on this earth has a stopwatch ticking away until we pass. I wanted to try everything on my bucket list. Shoot, I wanted to try everything, period! I didn't want to keep any stones unturned.

I lived my life by trial and error and to do that, I had to humble myself. When I tried different interests, I stepped outside of my comfort zone because it required putting my trust in someone else's expertise. I put my faith in a coach to always provide the precise path to succeed, and heeding your teacher is challenging because we all have that defiant nature. When a mentor provides guidance, it is human nature to defy and question their tactics; you have to let go of your ego.

That becomes difficult as we get older. We tend to act self-righteous. We think we know everything, but what have we truly accomplished. What goals and obstacles have we overcome? How have we defied the odds?

Apart from football and bodybuilding, I tried a lot of different sports; Olympic lifting, wrestling, boxing, track and field, baseball, soccer, swimming, and mixed martial arts. I had competition in my blood starting at the ripe age of six and endured the punishment on my body with all the injuries I racked up throughout the years.

The first sport I participated in was soccer while we were hustling in the windy city. My mother wanted me to participate in a sport at an early age to learn discipline and how to work in a team atmosphere. I loved playing soccer because I could run around and be a kid. No stress, no pressure, and soccer was the only sport that I don't remember whether I won or lost. Every other sport I played, I remembered what our record was. As I got older, winning became imperative. I was a great winner, but a horrible loser. I didn't prepare and work endless hours to lose.

The sport that I loved to play was baseball. It was another sport that I played in middle school and those spring days were great. There is nothing like playing baseball in the spring. No pressure, no stress, just enjoying America's oldest pastime. I played for the sheer enjoyment.

I guess when you start making it up the ranks, a lot of politics interfere with your love for the game. I only played for three years and at a low level, but loved every second of it.

When I made it to high school, that is when the real competition started. The stakes got much higher and wins and losses counted now. Second place ribbons didn't matter anymore. Second sucked!

Apart from bodybuilding and football, wrestling was probably the hardest sport in which I competed. I wrestled for three years. The training was rigorous and having to maintain my weight was difficult. I was already very small and starving my body to make weight was not the smartest thing to do. This was especially true because my other goal was to gain size, so I could play high school football. Wrestling toughened me up, though. I had to endure the weight cuts at an early age and then go out on the mat and compete. I also learned about body control and out-leveraging my opponent. Wrestling was short lived because it was very counterproductive to getting bigger for football. I also sustained multiple injuries. I only wrestled for three years after breaking my arm in a wrestling meet my freshman year. It was a blessing in disguise because I enjoyed wrestling, but I couldn't prevent my body from growing anymore. I had to decide to ditch wrestling and spend the winter season conditioning for the upcoming football season. I didn't learn about nutrition until college, but not having to starve my body anymore and having a full season to train for the gridiron was exactly what I needed.

Boxing was another sport I pursued in high school. I wanted to box to work on my footwork and quickness for senior year in football. I heard some of the best NFL running backs boxed in the off-season to work on their agility. I wasn't a running back anymore, but then again, football is all about quickness and agility. I took a beating in boxing, constantly sparring with opponents much bigger than me. For hours, I sparred, shadow boxed, performed agility drills, conditioned, and weight trained.

I was constantly sparring with as many dudes as possible to hone my skills and develop coordination and footwork. My hand eye coordination improved dramatically as well as my muscle endurance from sparring with heavy gloves. Sparring was tough; your gloves go from being 16 oz. to feeling you have two bowling bowls hanging from your arms. The sparring, ropes, shadowboxing, and learning proper technique are only a small part of what I had to do to become an effective boxer. It came easy to me because of all the other sports I played, as well as the scuffles with classmates. I only boxed for a year, but that was all I needed. I sparred toe to toe with fighters who competed in the golden gloves, the most prestigious amateur title. I attribute a lot of my success on the gridiron my senior year to my boxing coach and sparring partners.

In middle school, I was known for my speed. I could always rely on my speed in whatever athletic activity I participated in because it came naturally to me. I didn't have to work hard to be fast. I started to run competitively in middle school and continued through my sophomore year in high school. Even though I could run, I knew I wasn't going to make it far in track and field. I had speed, but I didn't have that freakish speed, nor did I have the stride to compete against the fastest in the state. Some of those sprinters were thoroughbreds. No matter how hard I worked on my stride, form, and speed, I was always outmatched by the sheer genetic speed of some of the all-state sprinters. My stride wasn't nearly long enough and I would have to turn over much quicker than the taller sprinters. When I initially started competing in track, it was easy. When I tried out for the track team, I was already inserted into four events. At the conference and area level, I would place in the top 3 because I was flat out faster than my opponents. My form sucked and my stride was short, but I was just faster.

I loved track and field because of the events, but the training involved was demanding, especially in high school. A typical day consisted of a mile warm up before we started our workout.

The toughest workout I ever endured was thirty-six 200-yard sprints that all had to be under thirty seconds. I have thrown up, almost passed out, bled, torn and pulled muscles during workouts, but after this workout I thought I was literally going to die. This was a Navy SEAL workout designed to weed out the weak. Out of the thirty athletes that attempted this feat, there were eight of us left. I will always remember this workout and our track coach informed us that it would be a notch on our life belts if we could make it through the entire workout. I did make it through the workout, but it was painful and I ended pulling my hamstring in the last 200 meters.

By the end of the workout from hell, if I had to go to the bathroom there would be nothing stopping me because I couldn't control my body anymore. My legs were shaking and I quickly jumped into an ice bucket.

That was pretty much the end of my track and field days. I hung up my running shoes my sophomore year.

❖

The last sport I competed in before I was incarcerated was mixed martial arts. I always talked about competing in mixed martial arts and combat sports. I wanted to take part in a discipline that didn't require as much brawn, but technique and strategy. I started to take part in Ed Parker's Kenpo Karate, learning different self-defense techniques. I didn't realize how challenging it would be to learn the different techniques and the amount of discipline I would need to excel. Kenpo karate requires flexibility and technique to perfect the kicks and punches.

When I joined Kenpo karate, I met the owner of the academy, who was in his late sixties. He was a 10th-degree black belt. Yes, you heard it correctly, a 10th-degree black belt. There are only a few 10th-degree black belts in any discipline and he was one of them. This guy trained in Kenpo for over forty years and could kill someone with a finger. A trained assassin. He could dismantle a group of people with his bare hands. His academy taught self-discipline and dedication while teaching each Kenpo technique and learning the true art of it. He didn't hand out promotions very easily and moving up belts was very difficult. You earned a higher degree belt after months, even years of dedicated work. When it was finally time for my promotion, he brought me in and made me do a cardiovascular workout, recite the Kenpo creed, perform the kata, exercise each technique flawlessly, and then absorb a front leg kick in the ribs from the sensei.

I would have continued to train in Kenpo if I wasn't incarcerated. I took Kenpo when I needed to because you better be ready for war in prison, and defending yourself is crucial to earning respect and, ultimately, your safety.

The days of competition taught me a lot about self-discipline and dedication.

DAY 14 JAIL JOURNAL: IRON WILL

I wake up every day and endure the stares and the whispers of "dead man walking." I stare ahead and look through to my adversaries, as if to say that death does not haunt me, but inside I am succumbing to the harsh reality that my time is coming near and I don't know through which door I will be walking. The pain that I endure daily inside solitary confinement is not living life, but I guess if you're conscious with a heartbeat, you have a life to live. The unknown petrifies me.

I always thought the ultimate sin was doing the dutch, prison slang for committing suicide followed by a murder rap. I committed the second worst sin, so I must anticipate my fall walking through hellfire and brimstone, staring the devil in the face, and atoning for my crime. My expressions and demeanor probably give the impression that I am ready for the seat at the chamber, as many death row inmates have faced. I know at some point my day of reckoning will come, but as the day comes closer and closer, I can't stand the anxiety. Every day, I dread the words "lights out" because all becomes quiet and the prison becomes like the middle of the ocean where predators are lurking. You are left with your thoughts as the darkness engulfs you. I am contemplating the pain of the execution. I get the feeling of chills running down my body and then come the overwhelming panic attacks, which paralyze me down to the core.

I am a murderer, and, in prison, inmates respect that and correctional staff fear those inmates. The inmates that commit the penniless crimes get treated differently by the staff as non-violent offenders. It is hard to explain, but you see it. Fear and intimidation is a resource that cons use to get what they want and the inmates that walk into prison with a reputation of taking whatever they want by whatever means necessary normally become the alpha males in prison. Those inmates become the CEOs of prison and are called shot callers. They roam the prison yard like sharks ready to feast on anyone weak, often showing their blood-stained teeth as an act of intimidation.

I recall getting ready to battle with the opposition, putting on my armor. There is an eerie silence in the locker room as you hear the loud breathing and cleats hitting the concrete. Players pacing back and forth by their lockers like ravaged lions seeking prey. The bathroom stalls are filled with players spewing their breakfast, while others are staring out into nothing, ready to annihilate their opponent. The boom box is shrieking "Welcome to the Jungle" by Guns N' Roses. Coaches in their office are silently reviewing their schemes, going over last-minute checks, and making sure their game plans are all in order.

Before we headed to the stadium, we congregated before the school chaplain. We bowed our heads and prayed. After prayers, we chanted the Viking school song piercingly so the rival in the locker room next to ours would hear our battle cry.

Everyone got ready for confrontation differently, but we all had the same goal, and that was complete annihilation of our opposition. There weren't any mercy rules and order wasn't settled until all four quarters were concluded. When the other team was down, that was when you slowly stepped on their throat and watched them choke as they were gasping for their last breath.

My adrenaline was at its pinnacle when standing shoulder to shoulder with my teammates. Like soldiers, we were standing in a straight line, full salute, guided by our coach. Cleats hitting the pavement, the stadium at full capacity with fans roaring, the speakers blasting AC/DC "Thunderstruck," and the band marching to the beat.

During pre-game, there was a lull when you could hear the constant thud of pads colliding. That thud sound would be amplified 10 decibels when we collided with our adversary. There weren't any other stressors apart from school, football, and putting it all on the line in front of thousands of people.

There were games when we were in enemy territory, getting barraged with vulgarity and heckling from opposing fans. That was when I didn't hear anything apart from the cleats hitting the pavement. Everything else was silent. Click, clack, click, clack from eighty players in a straight line, all focused on complete domination. It was music to my ears, especially when we were moving into enemy territory. Our focus was on the green pastures that lay ahead of us.

Two decades removed, and I still remember how a family acquaintance approached me when I broke my arm during sophomore football practice and uttered, "This game is not for our type of people." Talk about kicking someone when they're down. Well, earning multiple awards, captainship, and all-conference honors, proves this game is for people like us.

I spend a lot of time reminiscing about the gridiron in here. Reflecting on my playing days and all the great players who graced the battlefield, Dick Butkus, Walter Payton, Jerry Rice, Jim Brown, Gayle Sayers, just to name a few. It gets me through the day. In my childhood those were the players that I looked up to because of the passion they played the game with.

Guys like Jerry Rice who was arguably the best wide receiver during his tenure in the NFL. He has surpassed 20,000 yards receiving and scored over 150 receiving touchdowns during his Hall of Fame career. He was the epitome of tenacity and always outworked his teammates. He would endure grueling workouts in the summer, so he could outplay his counterparts on the field. He is still known for his workouts, and he would invite anyone to join him during his run up the two-and-a-half-mile treacherous incline known as the Hill. There were stories told where world class athletes would join him during his workouts and make it through a quarter of his grind before collapsing in sheer agony. The man was a true superstar and worked harder than anyone in his time.

Imagine being the very best at a trade, being told that you are exceptional and truly world class on a regular basis, given every compliment, and held up on a pedestal. You have become the pinnacle of success in the field you have chosen. Now imagine someone coming along and blowing right past you, then coming back and asking if you need assistance. Jerry Rice was exactly that. He was all world, but even more so, he was world class, constantly teaching and educating the best athletes. He even taught the athletes who wanted to take his position. He made everyone around him not only better in his sport, but better in life. To this day, he is an inspiration and holds over 18 division one college football records and 14 NFL records in his illustrious 20-year NFL career. If the National Football League were to hold a distinction higher than the Hall of Fame, then Mr. Rice would be first ballot.

Row

That is who I wanted to emulate with my preparation not only for football, but in life.

Growing up as a young athlete I wanted to climb the ranks of football glory and someday strut Hallas Hall playing for the Monsters of the Midway. I didn't look at how much money NFL stars were making, or the business side of the game. I looked at NFL players as supernatural beings that were larger than life. I wanted to mimic the NFL stars and someday make my mom and dad proud by playing on Sundays. I had a dream just like everybody else.

When I was young I looked at the purity of the game. I had tunnel vision and limited myself to the righteous part of the game, the part of the game that has thrilled Americans for a century.

When I started competing on the gridiron, I questioned why there were forty seconds between plays and why we had to spend the amount of time we did watching films, meetings, and preparing. I just wanted to hit people. From an outsider's lens, it seemed like a lot of unnecessary procrastination, but I quickly learned the magnitude of the approach for each play. The casual fan who has never played just watches a bunch of barbarians hitting each other for entertainment value, but the individuals who have stepped on the gridiron understand the preparation that goes into each game.

Each play had hours and hours of strategic planning by the coaches. My college playbook was over 200 pages designed to put me in the best possible position to make plays. Every single position on the field had an assignment which interlinked with the other positions to make one cohesive unit. It's all based on the other team's strengths and weaknesses.

Football is the ultimate team game which involves all three phases: offense, defense, and special teams. Players have to understand opponents' tendencies, weaknesses, and strengths, and they need to react within a fraction of a second. Every play only lasts a few seconds, so being in the right place was critical. That type of anticipation took hours and hours of preparation on the field and in the classroom.

I loved football for the camaraderie and teamwork it took to play. You must be prepared for the highs and lows and how to properly deal with setbacks during a game. The team that will prevail will be the team that limits their mistakes and counters the other team's blunders. During a week, we watched films on our opponent, attended meetings, practiced for hours, and then we finally got to play.

Day 14: Iron Will

After a week of preparation, we knew our opposition inside and out. We knew their tendencies, strengths, weaknesses, plays, key players, etc.

Go full speed, play hard, and play with intellect. Think and react. Fast twitch muscles. That was football's motto. Don't complicate the game. When you play at a high level, politics can take a major role. You got boosters telling coaches how to coach, players taking bribes, media making up stories. All that political BS takes away from the game. When you watch the greats like Brett Favre, Tom Brady, and Ray Lewis, you can tell they truly enjoyed playing. You would see them smiling, playing with confidence and complete focus. They played the game the way it was meant to be played, with honor and dignity. Football is hard enough with all the distractions. Every player has their own set of distractions dealing with school, work, religion, and adversity that comes with life.

Sacrifice!

During my high school and college playing days, I wanted to make a career out of the game. I wanted to play professionally, but I knew I was fighting a major obstacle, and that was breaking my genetic barrier. My playing weight was only 5'6, 200 pounds at my heaviest, running a 4.69 40-yard dash. Those numbers won't get you a paycheck. That is when I found out that my football career would probably end in college.

Football always set me apart from my family and friends because I was the only one playing in college. You don't see a lot of Pakistani football players sprinting down the field, busting heads. Playing a position called madman. My career was all about playing above my athletic ability, outworking my opposition, and seizing whatever opportunity I was given. My hard work always got me on the field. I realized I wasn't going to step on the football field and become the silver back gorilla, taking over the game. In college, I would have to earn my playing time, initially playing special teams, making plays like blocking punts and making tackles downfield. Then I would earn my playing time on defense, practicing hard and spending time in the film room studying my opponents. Not to mention hitting the weight pile every chance I had. I had great strength coaches and mentors guiding my training. I was measured on my performance, but football is truly a team sport. Playing with thousands of fans cheering after months and months of preparation lit a fire in my belly to go out and perform. I was doing the small things to prepare for each game. If I had a thirty-minute break between classes, I went to the film room. If I had fifteen minutes before a meeting, I went to the gym and knocked out some pushups and pullups. Before bed every night, I would do pushups, sit ups, and dips. I did whatever I could to gain a competitive edge.

The game was pioneered over 100 years ago, when Rutgers played Princeton. Now it has grown to millions of athletes and is televised all over the world. You can go to smaller US towns and hear a pin drop from local businesses as young men take the field, battling for bragging rights. Stadiums filled to the brim and Friday Night football across America is taking precedent.

Football is America's favorite sport and Friday nights was where it all took place. There was nothing like playing high school ball under the bright lights. Screaming fans, school colors draped across the field, band marching in precise order, the smell of fresh cut grass. It's hard to explain, but you could ask any former or present football player and they would say their high school playing days were the best. College was great and the experience was memorable, but nothing trumps the sheer surge of energy I experienced playing under the Friday night lights.

When I lay my head down, I start thinking about some of the best moments of my life. I think about all the great memories playing football… The backyard games I had with my friends and all the great memories with my teammates. Playing games with my brother's friends, and then going home battered and bruised, turning on the television to watch the Monsters of the Midway playing at Soldier Field. Those were the simple times, when I didn't have punk ass guards to worry about. Going to school, then to practice, preparing for battle under the bright lights of Hildenbrandt Stadium, playing in front of the entire student body. Sporting my neatly pressed green and white uniform in school during game day, fielding all the high fives and good lucks. Going in the middle of the auditorium as team captain during the homecoming pep rally, stating a few words of encouragement as fans chanted the school song.

Those were my glory years playing ball on Fridays and Saturdays.

I feel like Al Bundy from the 1980's comedy show *Married with Children*, always dramatizing his glory days playing high school football for Polk High School.

Day 14: Iron Will

❖

Tracing back to my roots, I developed a love for the game because of my mother. My brother and I were not terrible kids, but we weren't angels either. After begging and pleading, my mom finally signed us up for Pop Warner football. At the ripe age of nine years old, I started my football journey in Pop Warner football and stuck with it all the way to 23 when I hung up my cleats. Football was the way of life for my family during that time.

That is where I met Coach Trow. This guy was a bulldog of a coach. Former marine, who kicked ass and took names. He would make us run until we couldn't run anymore. "I wanna see one of you maggots puke." We screwed up a play, take a lap. We were offsides, take a lap. We were late to practice, take a lap. After my first year, coach Trow had me eating lightening and crapping thunder.

My brother and I were excited to finally play because our friends were already participating in youth athletics. I was finally going to put on pads and hit someone, replicating my favorite NFL players like Mike Singletary, Chuck Cecil, Mark Carrier, Brad Muster and so many of my favorites from that era.

That was the whole idea behind Pop Warner football for me. I put on pads and hit people in a controlled manner, taking out my aggression, so that when I went to school, I would behave. From that point on, I knew that I wanted to play football. As soon as I put the pads on, I felt right at home. I was never scared to hit anybody and was never timid about approaching someone who was larger than I was. I couldn't be, or else I would never have played. When you're five foot nothing, everyone is bigger than you. Football was a game of warriors and gladiators. You must have a certain swagger to play this game in the land of goliaths.

In grammar school, football was a big part of who I was. I always carried a pigskin in my hand, tossing the ball around with my older brother. My older brother was instrumental in my football career during my adolescence. I always played pick-up games with his crew who were much bigger and older than I was. I was required to use my agility and speed to elude them. It gave me the foundation I needed to play against stiffer competition.

Because of my size, I was always at a disadvantage. Football is a game of giants and only the toughest athletes are qualified to endure the grueling season. What got me by was my ability to out-leverage my opponents. I became a student of the game and studied each position.

The game changed my life and gave me an avenue to express myself. Kept me off the streets. I loved the controlled violence and team camaraderie. All for one and one for all. It was the closest thing to being a soldier apart from going to war.

What I learned as a football player was something I will take to the grave. I had no idea how much of an impact playing this game with a little pigskin would make on my life. The adversity I faced playing football taught me about life and how to overcome the obstacles; rigorous training in miserable weather, playing with breaks and pulls, doing homework after a grueling 3-hour practice, cardio sessions in the blistering heat with thirty-five pounds of equipment, just to name a few. It forced me to become dedicated to something.

The beauty of football is that it is a true testament to someone's will. You must play through pain, injury, fatigue, blood, and sweat. Starting in early August, I woke up at 6:30 a.m. and made my way to the practice field knowing that each day would be a test of my will and dedication. I was strapped with thirty-five pounds of equipment ready to battle with my teammates. Soaked with sweat already as coaches have us lined up to do 100-yard suicides. 16 hundred-yard sprints under 16 seconds. Can't do it, then hit the bricks, and hand in your playbook.

It's one of the only sports, apart from hand to hand combat, where you can feel your opponent's breaking point. Seeing a receiver racing across the middle of field anticipating an easy catch, de-cleating him, watching him hit the floor in agony, limping back to the field...

To this day, that feeling gives me goosebumps!

It is a faded memory since I walked the halls of Fremd High School as a scrawny youth, sporting my crew cut, flannel button downs, and torn up jeans.

I was probably classified as a high school jock always playing a sport or training. High school athletics brought me great joy because of the mentors that guided me. My head coach was the mentor who was always by my side. He built me up when I did well and always let me know when I did wrong. I still take the principles my head football coach has taught me in everything that I do. For him, it

Day 14: Iron Will

wasn't all about winning on the football field; I think it was more about winning in life. He instilled in me the skills to succeed in life by not leaving anything on the field and always dotting the i's and crossing the t's. Success was not always granted, but the odds are much higher when you put in the grind.

High school football was pure. There weren't financial gains from playing in high school. I played for the true love of the game. I often reminisce about those nights during the fall, a field of freshly trimmed blades of grass, the fall foliage, the marching band playing the school song, the bleachers painted in green and gold, and our school mascot parading the field, spreading school spirit.

The game seems barbaric in nature, but takes intellect to play and a brilliant mind to coach. I need to spend some time writing about my high school coach and what he meant to me throughout my life.

Iron will!

It was the motto that he instilled in his players. "Iron will" meant having the determination, dedication, work ethic, and moxie to win at all costs. It meant putting in the time and hard work to win not only on the gridiron, but in life. That characteristic was branded on me at an early age by my high school football coach.

He was my Vincent Lombardi, the Hall of Fame football coach of the Green Bay Packers. He made me a better football player and better person, which carried over for the rest of my life.

The principles that he taught me at an early age were that life is not stress-free and you have to strive for what you want. Put in the hours in the training room, film room, and practice field, and success will follow. Preparation was the key to success. He probably doesn't realize the impact he has made on my life.

He touched so many lives during his tenure as the head football coach at Fremd High School that when he retired, over a hundred former players came to watch his last game and celebrate his illustrious career.

He treated me with love and respect and gave me 100%, just like I gave him. Before games he would approach me and always whisper words of encouragement. Before one game he told me that he had a dream about me and the success that would be forthcoming at the college level. He guided me as a player and as a young man.

Row

When I was competing at the college level, he used to keep a picture of me in the high school weight room. There were NFL players and other professional athletes that walked the halls of Fremd High school, but my coach recognized the commitment I made to the team and tried to instill that into the rest of the underclassmen. That is what made my coach remarkable. He rewarded effort and playing above your capabilities rather than rewarding genetic superiority. He recognized iron will.

He was committed to making men out of his players. Not only did he teach his players to play with great will, but he made his players respect our teachers in school and our parents. I feel like there are only a few people you will come across who will truly make an impact on your life, and my high school head coach was one of them. He never let me take a play off or develop bad habits on the field. He held me accountable to perform in the classroom and on the field. He was tough on me, often screaming and yelling at the top of his lungs, but that was because of the love he had for me.

Iron will!

Before games, Coach would spend hours with his players around a campfire discussing life. We would discuss the impact of religion, family, education, work, and life. His impact on my life has been tremendous and it is no surprise that his players go on to become natural born leaders and successful people. What he would say if he saw me now...

He led his team to 13 state playoff appearances and broke the conference winning total. The will to succeed in leading a team to the state playoffs every year and breaking the coaching career win mark was unprecedented. I am sure if you asked Coach what his biggest achievement was, he would say molding hundreds of youths into well rounded men. He didn't care about rewards and accolades. On the outside, I operate under the same principles that he taught me and that was to have discipline and the drive to succeed, to not let anything stop you from achieving your goals. Since I graduated in 1998, I have gone on and achieved great things, but I have also made poor choices along the way. A lot of 'em.

It was a true honor and privilege to have played for Coach. He pushed himself to the limit for his players and demanded excellence from himself and, in turn, wanted the very best out of his players, which is a trademark of a Hall of Fame high school coach. I remember when he fainted during one of his practices, due to physical exhaustion from constantly over-exerting himself for his players. He needed to be helped off the field, probably needing weeks to recover. Not Coach, he was out there the next day, shouting out plays.

Coach, thank you for everything you have done for me, from your teachings on the football field to your mentoring in life.

❖

The National Collegiate Athletic Association was formed in 1906 and is the general legislative and administrative authority for men and women's intercollegiate sports. Basically, the NCAA is the gateway into the professional sports arena. If you aspire to play professionally in your respective sport, you better not piss off the NCAA.

NCAA athletics is a business, recognizing billions of dollars in revenue annually with over 450,000 representatives. NCAA is filled with top-notch blue chip talent and coaches taking whatever measures necessary to land the next big recruit. There are college stadiums across the US seating over a hundred thousand screaming fans. Teams are battling each other every week trying to move closer to receiving a bid to an honorary bowl game, where a college can receive up to $10 million in revenue.

There weren't many schools that were offering me a chance to play at the next level. Out of the schools that I could have gone to play college ball, I chose North Park University. North Park University was a Swedish covenant school in the heart of a bustling Chicago suburb. Chi town was an impressive city filled with great skyscrapers and bold architecture. The campus was on the outskirts of the city, highlighting both a suburban and city feel. The biggest appeal of going to North Park wasn't the facilities or the coaching staff, it was being close to my family. Being less than an hour from home was ideal. It would also mean my parents coming to my games on Saturdays and watching me play.

I only took one recruiting visit to North Park University before I fell in love with the university. It wasn't a difficult decision, as I wanted to attend a school that had a football pedigree that was on the rise and a prodigious business program. North Park University provided me a scholarship and grants to attend and compete in NCAA athletics. That's all I wanted.

Row

August 11, 1999 will be noted as one of the most significant dates in my life. That was the date I entered manhood. It was the first day of college training camp. That was the day that my parents unleashed me on the world. They dropped me off at college, closing the chapter of dependability and releasing me into the world of adulthood.

When I started college, I was extremely tense. I was going from a small student body in high school where everyone knew me to the new kid on the block. There would be less attention from the teachers and a lot more pressure to excel in the classroom. I had to excel both on the football field as well as in the classroom to maintain eligibility and preserve my scholarship.

College football was a whole different level from high school. You must live and breathe football at the college level and you're in it all the way or else don't let the door hit you on the way out. It was that simple. It was a full-time commitment, oftentimes I would spend more time studying my playbook than my text books. It was a game of attrition. There was no participation award for riding the bench. Yes, you got the luxury of telling people you play college football and might get some notoriety for that, but you must look at yourself in the mirror every day and pretend.

Playing college ball, I enjoyed traveling to different institutions, staying in hotels with the team, and competing in enemy territory. It took some time, but I had my feet firmly stationed on the ground now, scoring good grades and excelling on the gridiron. I had a world of opportunities at my feet and it was my responsibility to take advantage. Being a college football player, I was given certain benefits. If anyone states collegiate athletes don't get preferential treatment, they're lying to you. The commitment it took to excel in intercollegiate sports while going to class was extremely taxing. Other students felt that preferential treatment is unfair, but when do you get thousands of fans filling up a stadium to watch a science fair? Some sports and athletes were given preferential treatment because they brought in the most exposure and revenue to the institution. They deserved it!

I still remember my freshman year summer when I was getting ready for training camp. The day of camp orientation, all the freshman met in the auditorium for a short congregation with the head coach. This was an initial introduction and welcoming by the head football coach. Shortly after, we would be meeting the upper classman.

I stepped into the auditorium and met some of the incoming freshmen. I was 5'6" 150 pounds, soaking wet. My jaw dropped meeting some of these dudes. These physical specimens were fully grown men sculpted out of granite. It's like they were born eating raw eggs and flipping tires. I felt like retreating and prematurely terminating my football career. Imagining some of these guys in pads and then thinking about how much bigger the upperclassmen were going to be made my head spin. For the first time in my life, I was apprehensive about playing football. I was always the epitome of hard work in high school. Now, thinking about starting all over again and trying to earn their respect was going to be a hard pill to swallow, especially being outsized by a foot and eighty pounds by some of these behemoths.

During our freshman introduction, the first freshman I met was an all-conference, all area, tight end who played at Leo High School who was built like Hall of Famer, Shannon Sharpe. In fact, he was a bigger version of Sharpe and he was only eighteen years old. This guy was 6'5" and 240 pounds, built like a professional bodybuilder. When he shook my hand, he enveloped my hand and peered down at me. He probably thought I was the equipment manager or something. This guy was a mammoth. Talk about genetics. Seeing the other freshmen was a shock. As much as I was intimidated, I was also excited to get out on the field and see how talented our team was.

After freshman orientation, the rest of the upperclassmen entered the auditorium. I was officially integrated with the entire roster and was classified as fresh fish. Go figure. I could tell right away who the starters were compared to the second and third stringers. It was obvious just by the coaches' reaction when they greeted the players after summer break.

As I walked into the auditorium, I got a nod and a handshake from the coaches. I always played college with a chip on my shoulder because I was never the biggest, fastest, or strongest. Coaches look for those blue-chip athletes who could light up the scoreboard or stop a bus from crossing the goal line. I was never given special attention, nor did I need it, and that was my fuel. That was all I needed every year, to hit people with everything that I had and watch them limp back to the huddle in misery. Snot bubbles! I always loved when a player would tell me after a game that they have never been hit so hard by another player. That was the fuel that burned inside me. I trained and trained and trained some more for that reaction.

We had about 120 players try out for the team, so getting repetitions as a freshman was difficult. We had a mixed bag of players. We had highly touted recruits from out of state, walk-ons, inner city players, suburbs, transfers from other colleges, even a few players from overseas. We were so diverse we even had some players that were active gang members. Yep, you heard it. That's okay, though, because on Saturdays we all bled blue and gold.

I liked the players from the inner city. They were tough, blue collar, no non-sense hit-you-in-the-mouth type of guys. Skirmishes were daily occurrences on the practice field and they were usually in the middle of it, but that was okay. It made for interesting and intense practices. That was the difference between high school and college. Not only were the players more talented, bigger, faster; they also had attitude.

I would give some of the inner-city guys a ride home on the weekends. That was an experience! I remember being told during car rides to turn off my headlights approaching a rival gang's territory, or seeing a dead body decomposing in a car.

I remember driving one of my teammates home. He insisted on me coming into his home and meeting his family. So, I obliged, not knowing the trouble around me. We parked about a block away from his house in the dead of night. As soon as we walked ten paces I heard, "What's up nigga? What set you from, Blood?" They were strutting and slanging gang signs right at me. When they got close, they noticed my teammate who was from the same hood. Thugs don't normally go to college, so when they knew my teammate from the same set playing ball, all hell broke loose. The compliments rained down on us. They shook my hand gang style and we went on our way. If that gang didn't know my teammate, I probably would have been shot and tossed in a dumpster for trespassing. I was sporting my blue and gold team colors. Big mistake in Blood territory. I dodged a bullet.

With so many players, I relied on mental repetitions and busting my tail on special teams because that was the only way I was going to see the field as a true freshman. It was rare for a true freshman to play on game day. Most of the freshmen end up playing on scout team, getting the first and second team ready for games and then redshirt to maintain four more years of eligibility. I didn't want to be a player that only practiced and didn't dress on game day. I might not have been faster, stronger, or talented than a lot of the players, but I knew I could out-work these guys in the gym and in the film room. You can't pit genetic framework against work ethic.

Training camp every year was grueling and could be extremely dangerous. On average, twelve football players nationally at every level died each year due to dehydration, heat exhaustion, heat stroke, and other complications. Picture putting on thirty pounds of padding on the hottest days of summer, and practicing twice a day, for three hours each practice. That was no exaggeration and three weeks of these practices, filled with conditioning, hitting, and training, were truly an act of valor. Getting through training camp injury free was an accomplishment. During the intense heat, there were a ton of pulled muscles and muscle cramps sidelining players.

Training camp was always backbreaking, but you walked away from each training camp a dedicated player with true appreciation for the game. I am sure if you read this and have never gone through a training camp, it's easy to discount the magnitude, but I can tell you firsthand that camp was one of the hardest experiences I've ever had to endure.

During training camp, I would count the days until school started because we wouldn't have to practice twice a day anymore. And I hated school with a passion!

Our bodies constantly fought pulled muscles, dehydration, and nagging injuries. You don't play NCAA college football without years and years of prior training and a collection of injuries. You have honed your skills for years before you hit the college scene.

Camp was a demanding three weeks battling with my teammates trying to gain a roster spot. Every college football team in the United States goes through this process because coaches must weed out the weak.

We had 120 players try out for the team and by the end of training camp we had around 70-80 players left.

Row

Stepping on the college practice field was an eye-opening experience for me. I would need to fight for every repetition. The college atmosphere compared to high school was a lot more intense. Players were always trying to make the next big play to catch the coach's eye moving up the depth chart. Everyone wanted that coveted starting spot.

By the end of training camp, we had about fifty guys sitting on the sideline with some sort of injury, and some flat out quit. I couldn't imagine quitting, no matter how difficult practice got. My freshman year, I had two pulled hamstrings and a pulled calf. Struggling to sleep, I had to lie on my stomach with three ice bags on my legs. Pain and anguish were part of the recipe at training camp for every player, but it was a necessity for coaches to judge the talent and prepare for the season. Every day after practice, I immersed myself in a tub of ice to assist with recovery. That ten minutes sitting in a tub of ice was torture. Maybe even worse than solitary. Nah.

I firmly believed that our program was on the rise. Unfortunately, we had too many players who thought they were better than they truly were. They didn't think they needed to work and hone their skills in the weight room and on the practice field. A lot of us were the best on our high school teams, received accolades, captainship, recognition by teammates, and newspaper article features. Superstar treatment was expected at the next level and it just doesn't work that way. We had too many prima donna players that didn't play for the love of the game.

My college had a weak football tradition. The fans were aching for a winning product. We had extremely loyal fans that would come out every fall sporting their blue and gold, chanting our school's fight song, giving our opposition a fearful visitor experience, but most often the outcome was bleak. It was frustrating putting in hours in the film room, practice field, meetings studying the scouting report, and then not being able to cash our paycheck. It was like working without receiving any pay.

We had our first scrimmage against Xavier University. Finally, we were able to hit someone else for a change. I realized quickly that this wasn't high school anymore. During the third quarter, our starting quarterback was picked off in the corner of the end zone. The defender sprinted fifty yards, slamming the ball to the turf and parading down the sidelines. I was amazed by his athleticism and how he intercepted the ball with one hand, having the speed to outrun our offense down the sideline.

Day 14: Iron Will

First few weeks of the regular season I was like a deer in headlights. I always tried to keep eyes in the back of my head. I was playing cornerback. I wasn't nearly fast enough to play corner back at the college level. I only ran a 4.7 forty-yard dash and that speed was like comparing a Corolla to a Lamborghini. There were guys on my team that could run a 4.4 forty-yard dash, which was moving at the speed of light. When you are handicapped in a speed game playing with thoroughbreds, you must make it up somewhere else. I did that from a strategy standpoint. I studied the game like Peyton Manning, understanding teams' weaknesses and tendencies. I wanted to be a field general. I always knew where I was on the field and I knew where my teammates needed to be. That kept me out of harm's way, giving me the ability to make plays.

By the end of my freshman year, I had blocked three punts and made countless tackles on special teams. At the end of the year, I received special teams' player of the year honors, awarded by the coaching staff.

My freshman year came and went. I put a huge effort into conditioning my body to compete at the college level. By the time we were leaving for summer break, I was twenty-five pounds heavier. I was putting in hours and hours pumping iron at the gym, not only working on putting on muscle but becoming more explosive. Bigger, faster, stronger was the key to success and I didn't want to sit on the bench my freshman, sophomore, and junior years before getting my shot to start as a senior. That was loser talk.

My sophomore year was a tough year because the coaches decided to change my position from cornerback to strong safety, which they called a mad man. The position was designed to follow the ball and hit everything that moved. It was the best football decision they could have made for me because I wasn't fast enough to play cornerback. I was designed to play mad man. When I came into camp, I was hungry to play and knew that I could make an impact at strong safety. I wasn't required to play a lot of man coverage. Instead I could roam around the field like a lion searching for prey and then attack. It didn't take a lot of time for the coaches to observe that they had made the right assessment. The position was designed to act as a fourth linebacker, while still being able to cover different zones on the field.

Row

The season was a success apart from my injury. I partially tore my ACL, fully tore my MCL, and tore my meniscus the last game of the year in the third quarter. It was devastating because I knew it was going to keep me from participating in winter conditioning and spring practice. Since I got injured the last game of the year, the coaches pondered whether I would be ready to compete during spring ball and the upcoming season. The last thing I needed was to be sidelined while others were coming up.

I still have vivid memories of that day. Last game of the year. I was never excited for the season to be over. I was one game, one year, one day closer to hanging up the cleats and never playing again. It is a nightmare for any athlete to give up their love, and football was my love.

Our last game of the season was against Illinois Wesleyan University at Tucci Stadium on an arctic December evening. We didn't have any hopes of making the playoffs, but bragging rights were in order.

Illinois Wesleyan was a powerhouse in our division and they normally pounded the ball down our throats, leaving our team battered. It was a war when we took the field against them and this game was no different, especially since it was the last game of the year. At that point, nobody on the field was playing one hundred percent healthy; all were nursing some sort of injury.

I took the field on kickoff return as a blocker. I was not too fond of that position because I was blocking for our kick returner as the opposition stormed down the field like semi-trucks, bulldozing anything that comes in their way. The kickoff team had people that were called wedge busters and their goal was not to tackle the ball carrier, but run full speed into the blockers and knock them over, creating complete chaos. Not a fun job for me, but what the hell I needed the experience.

It was the third quarter, and IWU kicked the ball to us. The kick returner fielded the ball clean on the 5-yard line, burst to the 15-yard line, and dodged several would-be tacklers.

I normally set up my block around the twenty-five-yard line, giving the kick returning enough real estate to operate. I never wanted to crowd the ball carrier because they were normally the fastest players on the field and needed running room. I made a great block, overpowering the IWU player charging down the field. I got the better of him, but as I turned to the side, I saw that our kick returner was getting tackled. I kept my block, while the ball carrier got pushed down right behind me.

The tackler made a great play, eluding several blockers and running down the ball carrier. As the ball carrier was getting taken down, he rolled on the back of my knee, immediately dropping me to the turf.

I could only see white while lying on the turf, staring at the sky. I was in excruciating pain, trying to get a grip on what had happened. My teammates were screaming for the trainers, sensing my agony. The pain was out of this world but, I had made an oath to myself that I would never get carried off the field. No matter how much pain I was in, I would walk, crawl, limp off the field under my own power. As I saw the trainers running towards me, I knew I might be carted off, but I could do nothing but scream in pain. My world was turned upside down and I sensed a career-ending injury. Ten seconds ago, I was upright, trying to help my team win, and now I was on the ground in sheer pain, trying to make it up to my feet to preserve my dignity.

With all my might, I stood on my feet as the trainers tried to carry me, and slowly hobbled off to the sideline on my own. Once I got to the sideline, I took a seat as the trainers gathered around, examining my knee. They knew that I had torn a ligament based on a few preliminary tests. Their facial expressions told me and the coaches all we needed to know; it wasn't looking good.

Last game of the year and I was realizing my offseason was going to entail a strict rehabilitation program. One partially torn ACL, MCL full tear, and meniscus scope to take care of and I was good as new.

After my sophomore year, I was in line to start at strong safety. The safety in front of me graduated and went on to play professional football for the Sioux City Bandits in the Indoor Football League.

My injury was healing and mobility was slowly coming back. I was busting my hump rehabbing. I wanted to play spring ball. Entering spring football my sophomore year, I was hit with a reality check. I knew right then and there, this wasn't high school football anymore. This was a business and we were the ones that kept the coaches' jobs intact. I was too much of a liability. I had a broken wheel.

When my team came back from winter break, we all met in the auditorium for winter conditioning and spring practice. Entering spring ball deliberation, I noticed a few unfamiliar faces. These unfamiliar faces were built like NFL defensive backs and were well over 6 feet tall. As I entered the auditorium, they were eyeballing me with some familiarity. I was sensing that both guys were brought in to add additional depth to our defensive unit.

The coaches addressed the team and welcomed all of us to spring ball. He then announced and welcomed the unfamiliar faces. "My name is Blank, strong safety from Iowa University. My name is Blank, strong safety from Wichita State University." That was the last log that was needed to feed my internal flame. Both guys were recruited to replace my spot in the upcoming year. Both guys were much bigger than I was and played D1 ball. Big deal!

I was down to third string on the depth chart. That year I kept my mouth shut, head down, and trained furiously. I was pissed! I kept hearing North Park praised, kept hearing how glad people were that North Park had acquired two Division 1 players and they were going to be the staples of our defensive unit. I came into camp with one goal in mind and that was to outwork everyone. I dwelled in the weight room, constantly preparing for the upcoming season.

I took every measure to make sure that I maximized my training. I even spent the entire summer on campus in a dingy, hot dorm room so I was walking distance from our training facility.

I spent so much time in the weight room that our strength and conditioning coach introduced me to his protégé, Mark Levell. Mark was an Olympic lifter who qualified for the 1980 Olympics before they were boycotted due to the Soviets invading Afghanistan. The boycott was a travesty because Mark was one of the top Olympic lifters in the world, clean and jerking a whopping 392 pounds, under 150 pounds of body weight. He was projected to medal during the Olympic games, ousting the Bulgarians, whose training regimen was ahead of their time. Mark's life during his Olympic campaign was devoted to winning at all costs, and he won multiple national titles in Olympic lifting. When the Olympics were boycotted, Mark decided to dedicate his life to helping athletes. Mark was the Mr. Miagi of Olympic lifting and only worked with a select few. He was a no-nonsense wise guy Italian!

Right away, Mark took an interest in my ability. He taught me how to properly perform Olympic lifts, including snatch, cleans, clean and jerk, and power press. The goal was to help me get bigger, faster, and stronger. He showed me the proper technique and shared some of his lifting accounts while he was training for the Olympic trials.

Mark's daily schedule was to wake up in the morning, have breakfast and head to the gym. He would come home, have lunch, and then return to the gym for another session. Then he went back home for dinner before going back to the gym for his third session. He trained three times a day. That type of dedication and mentorship fueled me.

When I met Mark, he was retired from Olympic training. Back then, he could easily press 400 pounds. Now he was only a shell of what he used to be. Not being able to represent his country was devastating, but it inspired Mark to help me. He was willing to share his insights into the world of Olympic lifting. He was an inspiration and mentored me during my sophomore year. I adopted his principles, training hard at all costs. He fought multiple injuries throughout his training career, which inspired me to overcome challenges in my own career.

I met Mark on Saturday mornings. This was apart from the conditioning program my strength and conditioning coach at North Park designed for me. That Saturday morning workout with Mark was the hardest workout I endured in my entire life. Balls to the wall training with no break. Talk about pushing the envelope. It was harder than the conditioning sessions in the August torment, playing with a broken arm, the thirty plus 200-yard dashes during track and field, the sparring sessions while I was boxing, carb depleted training sessions wearing a sauna suit...I pushed myself to the brink of exhaustion, typically leaving my shins a bloody mess from the bar constantly scraping with each rep... If you are into Olympic lifting, you know what I mean regarding the bloody shins.

I thought I endured pain. I didn't know what pain was until I met Mark. He made me a better lifter as I enhanced my pain threshold and truly discovered the meaning of training hard while facing exhaustion. I parlayed everything I learned from Mark to the football field and eventually on the competitive bodybuilding stage. I used his training theories and adopted those principles in bodybuilding. He was a true ambassador for Olympic lifting and loved to teach. I was fortunate to have a mentor of his caliber.

One of my fondest memories of my training days with Mark was the time he requested a training session at the Brickyard instead of our normal spot in the dungeon at Lake View High School. The Brickyard was the chamber of horrors, with memories of past lifters who trained under harsh conditions. The Brickyard was the hub for elite Olympic and Power lifters located in the south side of Chicago. The Brickyard was filled with white chalk hovering over the clean and jerk platforms and squat racks. It was designed to break your spirit. The gym, if you want to call it that, was not for the faint of heart. The faint smell of vomit and dried blood tainted the atmosphere. There was no air conditioning or heating, just dead air. Many gladiators have walked through the Brickyard never leaving the same. This place left vivid memories for the rest of my life.

I was reluctant to go because of the crime wave and influx of gang affiliation in that area, which was rampant with the Bloods and Crips. I was concerned about my safety as the Brickyard was not a place for the timid, filled with world-class athletes and world-class gangbangers. Police officers were even reluctant to drive to the South Side, widely recognized as the homicide capital of the world. Gun violence and murders were widespread throughout the area and I was heading there as a lone sheep. These were the days before GPS so if I got lost I was in a world of hurt.

As I parked my car, I kept my eyes wandering through the streets. The wintery mist was settling on my sweatshirt. There wasn't a soul in sight in the morning hours. The houses were boarded up and graffiti was rampant. The deprivation of inhabitants in the South Side was shocking. I didn't realize what I was walking into until I set foot in the Brickyard.

As I arrived, I was greeted and welcomed by Mark. "Ready to train with the best?"

I walked into the Mecca of Olympic lifting, meeting national Olympic and world champion power lifters. These guys were the best of the best and I was training amongst them. During my lone water break, Mark introduced me to an eighty-five-year-old ex-Marine and national snatch champion. He snatched 150 pounds right in front of me, for a double. I could only wish to be eighty-five years old and still walking, let alone snatching even close to that weight. Mark wanted me to see the tenacity and work ethic a champion exhibited. He wanted me to witness and examine their approach to each repetition. I walked away that morning with more wisdom and insight on how to train with a champion's drive and concentration.

This was the methodology I adopted in my training going forward. My training became more efficient and laser focused on every repetition.

DAY 14: IRON WILL

I started my Junior campaign as the third string strong safety. I was behind both our Division 1 safeties who were specifically brought in to replace the previous starter. I guess the endless hours of preparation in the gym and film room didn't matter to the coaches. Well, hard work and perseverance does and will always overcome perception. The perception was that these two D-1 athletes were prototype safeties, billed as tackling mercenaries, and brought into the Chicago heartland to save the North Park Vikings and bring home a conference championship.

The season arrived and the blue chipper from Big Ten Iowa University couldn't make it through training camp due to dehydration. He ended up catching the chain out the door. Mr. Wichita State from the Missouri Valley Conference couldn't play a lick of strong safety and was transitioned to outside linebacker, rotating in on defense and playing special teams. Ali started at strong safety during that campaign and led the defensive backs in tackles. Work ethic would prevail over raw talent and they may have been D-1 caliber, but they didn't have the daily grind.

I was happy with my personal accomplishments, but our team finished a miserable 3-7. My junior campaign ended and our entire coaching staff was fired. A new regime was marching in, which I wasn't going to be a part of due to my early departure from the university.

My college career was ending and the reality of life without football was full steam ahead.

After my 2001 season, I did make one last-ditch effort to get invited to try out for a professional arena football team in Sioux City. I was shocked getting the phone call after my senior year season, which was plagued with injuries. The Sioux City Bandits were part of the National Indoor Football League playing in the Central Conference in Iowa. A number of former North Park alums played for the Bandits.

When I arrived at the Sioux City Municipal Auditorium, I was ready to compete. I was looked over, poked, and prodded. The team's medical staff also measured my hands, neck, and arm length. I felt like I was getting measured for a suit. Unfortunately, my measurements didn't leave the Bandits' coaching staff in awe. I sprinted the forty-yard dash, ran multiple shuttle runs as they assessed my quickness, high jump, broad jump, multiple safety drills, and bench pressed 225 for repetitions. I also took an aptitude test. I impressed the coaches, bench pressing 225 twenty-six times and performing well in the quickness drills. When I left the facility, I was exhausted. I had performed those drills hundreds of times for scouts and coaches, but never under the watchful eyes of potential employers.

I fulfilled a dream trying out for a professional team. Unfortunately, I didn't get a contract to continue my football career. After twelve years playing for the love of the game, I couldn't fulfill my lifelong goal. It was a tough pill to swallow, but I knew that my competitive fire was still burning, and I needed something else to fuel it.

I would have loved to be a world-class football player, but I didn't have the God-given talent. What helps me sleep at night is that my goal was to play football professionally and I did everything to accomplish that goal.

I was gratified by my accomplishments on the gridiron, and looking back on my career, I didn't shy away from anyone.

I loved the comradery that we all shared. We all went through the struggles together. Practicing twice a day in the blazing heat in August, watching films, and participating in all the other activities: meetings, training sessions, media events, team meals, interviews, travel, hotel stays, and individual discussions with our coaches. We all made that sacrifice together.

Every team I played for was my second family. I have lasting memories I could replay in my head. When you spend so much time with the same group of people, you build a bond that cannot be cracked. If any one of my teammates in high school and college needed my help while I was on the outside, I would be there in a crack of a whip. We had a small fraternity and shared that field together as one. We won together, we lost together, and we bled together. We did it together! One heartbeat.

Day 14: Iron Will

The twelve years that I played, I sustained multiple injuries. Three broken arms, broken fingers, torn MCL, partially torn ACL, torn meniscus, pulled muscles, multiple concussions, and countless sprains. Not to mention all the nicks, cuts, and scrapes I endured during a long taxing season. Why would someone endure this type of torture? Why did I play football? These were the questions that I asked myself during those scorching 110-degree practices with thirty pounds of equipment while my friends were enjoying their summer. I would do it all over again.

When I think about my years playing football, constantly talking and analyzing the game, I was satisfied hanging up my cleats. I enjoyed the game and I knew football was going to be a part of my life forever. I was going to use some of the life-long lessons I learned on the gridiron and employ them in the real world.

Sitting in my cell thinking about playing ball makes me smile. It makes me reflect on the simpler times when all that mattered was between the lines.

Tick tock, tick tock. When you're in solitary confinement, you're living your life on the brink of insanity. The noise never stops. I'm trapped inside an empty concrete box while the walls seem to be closing in. I don't have a clock in my cell, so I never know what time it is.

Stuff I try to think about. Stuff I try not to think about. Suicidal thoughts are always spinning in my head. Imagining how I would pull the feat. What tools would I use? How could I turn the metal contraptions in my cell into a lethal device? I am surviving on borrowed time. Why is the California State Correctional Institution hell bent on executing me? I could be cleared of my crime, walk the streets, and be a productive member of society, but I am condemned.

When I had my freedom, I was living the life of solitude every day. I am alone in my own seclusion, feeling imprisoned from the outside world.

As I reminisce, I remember waiting backstage at the 2005 Midwest Iron Man Championships ready to compete. This feels like a lifetime ago, but it was an important aspect of my life because of the work that I put into the sport of bodybuilding. It was my first bodybuilding competition and I was prepared to get my name out there in the world of diet and exercise. I was young with tunnel vision, not knowing there was another world outside the cold steel dumbbells. I had worked so hard for over ten years weight training, doing cardio, calculating what nutrients went in my body, posing in front of the mirror each night, driving hours to the south side of Chicago every week to meet my nutritionist, and all the other little intricacies it took to get ready for competition. On top of that, I was a full-time student getting my MBA, and working a full-time job. I was determined to succeed at every aspect of my life, never looking back or feeling sorry for myself.

This was only my first bodybuilding competition, but I already wanted to compete in the Super Bowl of bodybuilding. I wanted to be a contender on the pinnacle of exercise and nutrition. Entering the USA contest and competing against the best in the world was my main goal. Becoming a professional athlete dominated my thinking in early adulthood. It was an addiction.

My life from the ages of thirteen to thirty-one was consumed by the world of exercise. Buying Flex, Muscular Development, and Muscle and Fitness magazines from every newsstand, striving for the competitive edge. My physique was my temple and I wanted to train all the time, trying to become a champion. A champion in something, but God didn't show me the light yet. Little did I know that with that entitlement there was a lot of commitment. I could not imagine my life without bodybuilding, as it was my means of solace. I would find myself getting lost in deep concentration during training sessions, able to escape into my own contemplations. It took me away from the rigors of life and into my own world. Often, I would be training and have 100 people around me working out, but I always felt isolated. I was in my own refuge.

The long sleeves, wrist straps, elbow braces, knee brace, and partially tattered track pants accompanied by my headphones blaring Disturbed, Godsmack, and all my favorite 80's rock compositions. The stench of Flex All permeated the room. The metal 100-pound dumb bells with white mist spattered in the air from chalk as I stared in the mirror, scrutinizing the musculature on my body, disgusted with my physique, and desiring perfection.

Not a lot of people understood the sport of bodybuilding. Most thought it was all alpha male egos, steroids, and sheer vanity.

Bodybuilding is a sport for a few, revered by many, and criticized by the naïve. It is easy to look at the competitors and knock the athletes for taking drugs because most can't attain that muscle maturity, symmetry, and density. The amount of dedication and iron will it took me to step up on stage was huge; years and years of sacrifice, years and years of Friday and Saturday nights in the gym alone, years and years of missing trips with friends because I didn't want to miss a leg workout. You train endless hours to enter a competition and win a small trophy. There was no gratuity in bodybuilding. There was no paycheck waiting for me if I won.

DAY 13: GENERATION IRON

The awards that I won can never be measured with a monetary distinction. Those awards were eighteen years of hard work, blood, and sweat.

The weight room was my battlefield. I was on a collision course, challenging myself constantly. I pushed myself into submission. I invited my clients to come train with me and the poor souls that did left with pain and anguish, but their level of respect for bodybuilders was raised to epic proportions. The transformation your body undergoes in such a short amount of time was what drew people to the sport. People like to see freaks in any walk of life. When you go to the zoo you don't want to see the goats and sheep. You want to see the lions and tigers. You want to see the biggest and most ripped guys on stage. Who cares if they took steroids, if they looked good?

What is it like to be so big? How much do you bench? How big are your arms? Can I feel your muscles? I would never want to be that big. Juice head! That is disgusting.

I was the blonde girl with double D breasts for a very long time, committed to my craft, but hating the attention, often sporting sweatshirts and track pants concealing my body from the world. Towards the latter part of my bodybuilding career I often trained in my own refuge when nobody was around, in scorching, unventilated garages, warehouses, and basements, hidden away from outsiders. To most, I was the circus animal people wanted to pick and probe.

I despised the attention. People came up to me and constantly asked me stupid questions while groping me, staring at me like I was a circus animal, like I was a freak, constantly under a microscope. Everywhere I traveled, I attracted immediate attention. The glares from people as they pointed, whispering in each other's ears, the constant whispers I would hear when I entered a room, and the constant barrage of questions regarding sports enhancing supplements. Sometimes it was too much and I wanted to crawl away into a cave.

In football I had my teammates who were getting a lot of the same attention. It didn't bother me. I wasn't treated like an oddity. In bodybuilding I was all alone. That is when I realized that I didn't want any of that crap around me. The more I won the more attention I got. Whether, it was positive or negative I didn't want it. Erase my muscles; would people really give a damn about Fayaz. Hell no! People will question all the good things they hear about you but believe all the bad without a second thought.

Row

Some "friends" were interested more in my physique as a status symbol than in who I was as a person. They wanted to tell others, "Yeah, I know Fayaz. He trains at the same gym, or he is a good friend of mine. See? I have his number on my cell phone." I realized having muscles demanded attention and respect not only from people in the fitness industry, but everywhere. I gained notoriety and a false sense of kinship from people. People wanted what I had, but didn't want to put in the hard work training when injured or when others are at social gatherings, like I did. People liked unique individuals who stood out. I was treated like a celebrity and everybody loves a winner. When you fall from grace is when you find out who is truly your companion.

I was 230 pounds with under fifteen percent body fat in the offseason. I was never content with being a regional champion, Illinois state, Iowa state, and Wisconsin state champion. That didn't matter because I was always chasing a goal, trying to fulfill my own prophecy. I wore XXL shirts, arms erupting from the sleeves, shoulders popping like bowling balls. I was never gratified and that was why I exercised with reckless abandonment. I wanted more.

When I finally retired from bodybuilding, I was happy with my accomplishments of being in magazines, signing with a reputable sponsor, winning multiple state titles, and making a name for myself. I parlayed that into a nutritional consulting and a personal training business, but something was always missing and I never figured it out. I was never satisfied and was always wanting more, which was good because I had the fire burning inside me to pursue something else.

I guess I was used to solitude before I even came to prison, equipped to handle confinement from my bodybuilding career. I was often traveling to competitions alone, sleeping in hotels, and traveling across state lines, chasing state titles. The life of a bodybuilder was desolate and consumed with fear of failure. The monotony of the constant pounding, pushing 140-pound dumbbells, pressing 420 pounds, and squatting 500 while every muscle fiber was screaming for submission. When people asked me what I enjoyed, that was my answer. I loved training and seeing how far I could push myself.

Loved the process and loved the result, but hated the principles in the sport of bodybuilding. It's probably one of the most misunderstood sports in the world, filled with the greatest physiques in the world and the emptiest pockets. Of all the sports in which I participated, bodybuilding required the most discipline. There were no cheat days or out-of-office replies.

Champions are made when nobody is watching.

Michael Jordan didn't become great with millions of fans watching him. He became great in the gym perfecting his craft, taking 1000 jump shots every day. He was never satisfied.

I was never content in bodybuilding. When you're content and start drinking your own Kool-Aid, that's when someone comes by and steals your thunder.

There was no such thing as God-given talent in bodybuilding. You train harder than anybody else to become a champion. There were no shortcuts, no cutting corners, no cheating, period. That was the process I enjoyed about bodybuilding. I knew if I trained harder and more efficiently than anybody, I would have success. I didn't have to gaze at an opponent across from me, 6'5" 220 pounds, while I was genetically inferior.

My goal was never to step on stage and flex my muscles, but to the uneducated, that's what was portrayed without examining the process. My goal was always to go through the rigors of dieting 16 weeks, training twice a day, food preparation, sizing and weighing each morsel of nutrition fueling my body, practicing my posing, executing my cardio, tanning, and analyzing my physique with my team. Then comes the self-promoting, sponsorship obligations, etc, all the while carrying out all my other responsibilities in life. My aspiration was to be steadfast in carrying out all of my duties and still maintain a bodybuilding lifestyle. That was the challenge.

Where was the cost benefit in all of this? The rigors of everyday life added to the constant struggles, making sure I was eating every two to three hours, consuming over 5000 calories daily, pounding protein shakes, guzzling raw egg whites like Rocky, and making sure I trained twice a day was what made the outcome that much sweeter. I didn't need a paycheck or a pat on the back. Money from the sport would come later.

Bodybuilding was my getaway from the real world and my haven to learn about myself. How could working out define someone as a human being? Well, during my early adulthood, weightlifting made me develop traits that I would never acquire elsewhere. I never wanted the limelight that the sport had to offer. I never wanted to be acknowledged as a body builder. When you train as much as I did, you learn about fortitude and discipline as well as breaking barriers. In the gym, I learned lifelong lessons, forcing myself to attempt weight I never imagined I would be able to lift. Squatting 500 pounds, bench pressing 420 pounds, military pressing 315 pounds…. That level of physical stress I put on my body embodied mind over matter. Lifting that much took years and years of grinding and pushing myself through those pain barriers, continuously battling through injuries.

Fine, I was strong, but what life lessons could I learn lifting weights? When you're training and pushing yourself to the breaking point of blacking out, then a lot of adversity you face later in life won't seem as demanding. I can't tell you how many times I would be racing to the bathroom after a heavy set of squats, throwing up, and returning to the same squat rack to perform another set. Set after set, I performed the same exercises, determined to squeeze every muscle fiber, eyes bulging out of my eye sockets, and veins pulsating. Bodybuilding for me was a metaphor for life and enduring the everyday struggles.

Breaking the pain threshold was one of the toughest aspects of bodybuilding. What separated bodybuilders from guys that trained every day was that bodybuilders performed those extra repetitions even when their bodies were giving out.

The truth about being a bodybuilder was unfathomable even for the recreational lifter. Championship bodybuilding meant not only lifting the heaviest weights, but also eating clean and taking the right supplements ALL the time. You couldn't succumb to that little square piece of chocolate, even if your body was screaming for sugar. It had to be your whole and only way of life to succeed.

From the 60s to the 90s, fans started getting fascinated with the world of bodybuilding. You would see the freakish physiques walking around the gym and you wouldn't know how they got so tanked. There were a lot of unknowns about the sport back then, and that enticed fans to start watching, building the fan base for bodybuilding.

Bodybuilding, in the early 70s was becoming very popular and was now getting televised recognition. Fans were becoming intimate with the competitors and getting to know their larger than life personalities to go along with their larger than life muscles. Bodybuilders like Arnold Schwarzenegger, Franco Columbu, Lee Haney, Lou Ferrigno, Sergio Oliva, and Samir Bannout. These guys had the classic physique with broad shoulders, small waist, and flaring lat muscles also known as the v-taper. They not only looked aesthetically appealing, they also had personality, which brought a lot of attention not only to them, but to the sport that needed exposure at that time.

Don't get me wrong, bodybuilding was never in the same conversation as America's great pastimes like football, baseball, and basketball, but fans were now flocking to theaters and auditoriums to catch their favorite bodybuilders.

Bodybuilders back then were not as enhanced as the athletes today. The modern-day International Federation of Bodybuilding and Fitness pro bodybuilder makes the previous bodybuilders look like miniature replicas. They walk around the offseason close to 370 pounds and on stage at 270 with five percent body fat.

In the late 90's and early 2000's, the bodybuilding physique was changing. The "mass monster" was the fan favorite; 300 plus pound goliaths like Ronnie Coleman, Markus Ruhl, and Dorian Yates. Those guys made the old greats look tiny. The sport started to become less about aesthetic appeal and personality, and more about how freakishly big some guys could get. Fans wanted to see the mass monsters on stage, and the aesthetically pleasing physiques of Frank Zane and Arnold were still appealing, but not nearly as appealing as the monsters. I believe that is when bodybuilding started getting a bad name. Fans couldn't relate to the athletes anymore.

As years went on, the bodybuilders started getting more and more size, and everyone was looking for that cutting edge formula to take their physique over the top. Instead of having a few guys to compete against, bodybuilding was now attracting the masses.

Bodybuilding was starting to gain a lot of momentum, and then *Pumping Iron* hit center stage. *Pumping Iron* was a documentary about the world of bodybuilding, mainly focusing on the athletes getting ready for the Super Bowl of bodybuilding, the Mr. Olympia competition. The Mr. Olympia competition showcased the preeminent physiques in the world. The winner walked away with the coveted Sandow trophy, a briefcase full of money, multiple endorsements, and the designation as the best bodybuilder in the entire world. The best IFBB pro bodybuilders were showcased at this competition. *Pumping Iron* focused on the poster children of bodybuilding during the 70s, Arnold Schwarzenegger and Lou Ferrigno, as they battled for the coveted title of Mr. Olympia.

Pumping Iron brought to life these characters and how they lived their daily lives in and out of the gym. The sport was now on the map and these larger than life mythical figures were worshipped. Fans all over the world were flooding the gyms in Venice Beach, California, the mecca of bodybuilding, to catch a glimpse of these athletes training. Fans were not only keeping track of their favorites; they were also trying to gain notoriety on the amateur stage. The sport was becoming popular and did not have an off season like the mainstream sports. No rest for the weary. Bodybuilding was an all-year sport, showcasing these guys all the time.

Unlike in the mainstream sports, fans were able to engage with their favorite bodybuilder. Guys like Arnold and Franco were at your local gym in Venice, accessible to their adoring fans. They were walking amongst us all. You never see professional athletes in everyday places anymore. When was the last time you were in a coffee house and Peyton Manning strolled in? You knew the pros because their muscles couldn't be hidden away by even the largest garments. They demanded attention.

You see competitors on stage flexing their muscles in a posing suit, performing various poses. Easy enough, right? In-order to get competition ready, I became an expert on nutrition and exercise. I understood what I was putting in my body and how much energy I was exerting. I became a scientist and my body was my experiment.

I became very critical and extremely selfish. Sacrifice and simplicity was the name of the game. Bodybuilders aren't married, don't have any kids, don't travel unless it's at a competition, and avoid hardship that would take them away from training. Life revolves around their physique.

The drawback that I had in my bodybuilding career was the sacrifice that I had to make in order to have success and find that balance. The time I spent in the gym and in preparation for competition took away from the time I spent with family and friends. I knew with great sacrifice came great reward, but sometimes the sacrifice was greater than the reward. I couldn't answer that question because I didn't enjoy bodybuilding competitions. What made it worthwhile was the body transformation in a short amount of time and the process of making that change.

It was truly amazing how you could transform your physique with proper diet, nutrition, and grit. I marveled in that theory and wanted to prove I could obtain a bodybuilder's physique. Why not? I spent hours and hours in the gym pumping iron, so why not try to obtain what ninety-nine percent of the common gym goers couldn't?

As I peeled the onion and examined the sacrifices needed to be successful, I began to appreciate the sport. I didn't get a chance to examine my bodybuilding career until I walked away from the sport. Some would say that its ending was premature, but, believe me, it was my time to say good-bye. I accomplished everything I wanted to. I knew it was my time because I never looked back. It was my identity for a very long time and that was what people associated me with. When I was introduced to people, I was always introduced as the bodybuilder. I gained a lot of notoriety and respect from the sport of bodybuilding, but it was more the sheer fact that I was an anomaly. I was doing something that most didn't want to do or couldn't. If I had a penny for every person who told me they wanted to body build, but couldn't handle the diet...

When I started my bodybuilding journey, I didn't realize all the great athletes had a team whom they were working with. Bodybuilding was not an individual sport.

Growing up, I played individual and team sports, so making the transition into bodybuilding was effortless. The best thing about bodybuilding is that there are a lot more aspects to it than just pushing metal. Nobody can push you to go into the gym every day, take the proper supplements, eat the right foods, drink enough water, and then do it all over again day in and day out, not knowing how your body will respond until the last few weeks of your diet, before you step up on stage. I prepared to eat, sleep, drink, and think about my physique every minute of the day. I didn't take days off and enjoy a cheat meal, or else I eliminated success. There was no room for error.

It didn't matter how I felt on the inside. The only thing that mattered was what I looked like on the outside. What mattered was how muscular I was, how symmetrical I was, how vascular I was, how I posed, how I appealed to the crowd, and how comfortable I was on stage. It was easy to see who was prepared to compete and who wasn't. I was always prepared to compete because I knew I did my homework. I trained twice a day for years, so I knew I outworked everyone in my class. I worked on my posing for hours on end so when I was on stage I wouldn't suffer and my muscles wouldn't shake. I even started tanning weeks before the competition, so I was darker than my competition. I didn't take any shortcuts with my diet. If I was told to eat six ounces of chicken and three ounces of vegetables, I would weigh each nutrient to make sure I was exact. I probably wouldn't have been competitive if I didn't aim for perfection.

Success in bodybuilding did not come overnight. I had a small bone structure, working with a 5'6" frame so I needed to make sure that my workouts were calculated exactly based on my needs and that I was accurately performing each exercise. I couldn't afford to take shortcuts in my training. Playing sports through college gave me the necessary insight into my body composition and how to train with the right intensity to succeed at bodybuilding.

Results from training came slowly for me and winning took years and years of rigorous training. I trained for over ten years before I stepped up on the competitive stage. Bodybuilding was a marathon and it took me years to obtain a champion's physique.

In a sport for giants like football and bodybuilding, I was roaming the playing fields. I wanted to be successful in a sport that was comprised of genetic monsters. I didn't have a level playing field, but I couldn't be successful in life making excuses. I put my head down and fought for what was mine. I never took bodybuilding as a 9-5 job. I took it as a 24-7 job and lived my life in a silo. I had to, or else my physique would never maintain its shape and I would fall short every time. It was all or nothing. I put my social life on the back burner, pursuing this chapter of my life. I lived a sheltered existence for a period. I didn't see my friends or my family, often training in seclusion. My thoughts were always on the prize.

Everything I did was to improve my physique. I ate, trained, and slept on a strict regimen. I have an addictive personality and when I love something, I do everything in my power to obtain my goal. In this instance, I was trying to obtain the perfect body.

During my journey in bodybuilding and my life as a gym rat, I met a lot of different people. Former gang members, professional athletes, celebrities, musicians, drug dealers, ex-cons. You name it, I met them. At one point I even befriended a former biker gang member who was convicted of attempted murder! He had some very interesting stories. I was always approached by people requesting advice. I had a target on my back for people to approach me. I was stopped in the middle of the street by people asking me how I got so big. Approached in restaurants, airports, shopping malls, grocery stores. I ended up dreading that attention.

When I first started competing, I didn't realize how much of an impact it would have on my life. The journey of dieting, competition, and transforming one's figure was incredible, a roller coaster. During the last few weeks of preparing for my first show, I would stand in front of the mirror in awe of my transformation. I was never one to admire my physique. I always wanted more, but I guess everyone was like that to a certain extent. My body looked leaner and more vascular each day. At that point, I went from doing one show, to competing for years, becoming addicted to the process.

When I committed to competing in my first show, I didn't realize the dedication and time commitment. It was a full-time job getting contest-ready. When I started dieting, the only aspect I was familiar with was to eat a lot of protein and stay away from carbohydrates and sugars. Piece of cake, right? Wrong! The misconception of stripping carbs and fats while dieting was not true. I was wet behind the ears trying a new endeavor about which I had very little knowledge. It was a learning opportunity and my goal was to get on stage and do it for myself. I wanted to see if I could push myself to the edge.

During the early part of my diet for the 2005 Midwest Ironman competition, I was buying whole chickens from the grocery store each day. I had no clue how to diet and did not have a mentor. The national level guys who convinced me to do my first show were now training at another gym. I was alone.

I started training with a friend a few weeks later who was committed to training hard and getting in shape. Not exactly the bodybuilding mentor I had in mind, but I didn't have a choice. He was a blessing in disguise, helping me through the entire process. He was with me every step of the way and I couldn't have done it without him. We developed a strict training regimen consisting of high intensity workouts, exercising each body part to physical exhaustion. Each workout was an hour to an hour and a half, training two body parts each workout. He made sure I was on point with my workouts and taking in the right nutrition. We were tag team partners.

Row

Even though I had a reliable training partner, I was still missing direction from a veteran competitor. I needed someone who had been through the trials and tribulations of getting stage ready for a competition. I needed to know what it was like backstage at a competition and what it is was like the night of the event. I wondered what it was like, how I would know if my body wasn't adapting to the diet. I also needed guidance on posing, proper nutrition, supplementation, and everything else bodybuilding entailed. Even though I had been training for years, bodybuilding was different.

My training partner and I were both doing a lot of experimenting with our nutrition, when I received a phone call from a friend who knew I aspired to compete. He was surprised, probably thinking my aspirations to compete were simply a pipe dream, but he gave me the 411 of the only IFBB professional bodybuilder in Illinois at the time. He also owned one of the only hardcore gyms in the state, focusing on kicking ass and taking names. He was one of the few great gym owners who helped competitors get ready for bodybuilding shows by supporting them with posing, supplementation, tanning, nutrition, and personal training. He was the whole package. I couldn't pass up that opportunity to learn from him.

There was a lot of uncertainty when I drove to his gym an hour south of my house: USA Gym in Bridgeview, Illinois, located in the middle of nowhere, the drive filled with back roads and pot holes. I felt like I was walking into the Mecca of bodybuilding with championship trophies showcased and the walls covered with past champions. I heard stories of the best bodybuilders on the planet working out at USA Gym, Olympic Champions like Jay Cutler, Ronnie Coleman, and Phil Heath, just to name a few. I was going to meet with a legend in the bodybuilding community, someone who trained champions and was also a champion in his own right.

I had no idea how he would critique my physique. Would he laugh when I stripped down and kick me to the curb? He was the first professional bodybuilder I ever talked to and he was very accomplished not only as a bodybuilder, destroying some of the best pros like Dexter Jackson, winning over twenty competitions, but also as a businessman, owning his own gym, and working as a fireman, saving lives every day. This guy was the real McCoy. I did not want to come across as naïve or disrespectful, but I needed him to take me seriously. I didn't train for years to have someone look at me for ten seconds and make a snap judgment. We spoke for about thirty minutes. Initially, I thought he was not going to work with me and tell me to hit the bricks. This dude had a posing studio with wall-to-wall mirrors, able to critique each mandatory pose. By the end, he was impressed with my muscle density and overall physique and he gave me the green light to start dieting. Having his blessing gave me the realization that this was not outside the realm of possibility. He was a great mentor and working with someone of his caliber was extremely helpful for my morale in my first show.

We arranged to meet every week, so he could train me, make sure I was on the right track, and show me the intricacies of getting ready for a competition.

Bodybuilding can be mentally exhausting because I was my own worst critic, constantly thinking I looked worse than I did. I needed someone that had been through the rigors of dieting and experienced the mental anxiety that a bodybuilder experiences. I didn't understand how some of the top pros got nutritional advice from people that have never competed before. I heard a lot of pros going to different dieticians that didn't know what it's like to get up on stage, depleted and dehydrated. It surprised me that some of the top pros in this industry took this route, but who am I to say? These guys were at the pinnacle of the sport.

To me, bodybuilding was the culmination of all the sports I played from Pop Warner through college. My calling finally came in the sport of bodybuilding because it was all on me to prepare for each competition. I did the hard work and I received the rewards. The pictures and lights didn't lie. If you cheated during your diet it would be captured in the competition under the bright lights, in front of thousands. Nobody could sell wolf tickets in this sport. Competitors would be holding extra fat and water in certain places and, believe me, it sticks out. You won't get away with it, and I knew I would never take that approach. I was all-hands-on deck, pouring my heart into this sport.

The hardest part of bodybuilding was not the training, but everything that came with it and around it. Ninety-nine percent of bodybuilders aren't making money in the sport. I was the one percent, but I wasn't making enough to live off the sport, so I had another hustle. I had a normal nine-to-five gig along with my bodybuilding career. I was a grinder going to gym twice a day, not taking days off, and overcoming the monotony of doing the same thing. Apart from having a bodybuilding career, I was managing my families' properties, operating a nutritional business and a personal training studio, and maintaining a sponsorship with Pride Nutrition. There was no time for friendship or relationships. It was all or nothing.

Row

My daily regimen consisted of two training sessions, daily food preparation, supplementation, and eating. It was not easy always being on the run, but I wouldn't change it for the world because it made me feel alive. It gave me purpose and motivation. I had daily responsibilities and prioritized my day around my workouts. It wasn't easy managing all my responsibilities and then dragging myself to the gym, lifting 100 plus pound dumbbells, but that was my release. I knew that no matter how frustrating my day was I could take it out on the weight pile and release my tension.

When I became a bodybuilder, there was a certain aura that I carried around with me. There was a certain sense of confidence that I had from competition. Sometimes when I walked into the gym, I felt like a superstar because that was my domain. There were only a handful of bodybuilders in each gym and everyone knew who they were. I was the CEO of my gym, always getting VIP treatment. When I needed a machine, the person using it stepped aside. When it was time for me to eat, I sat in the general manager's office and ate. My face was plastered on the gym Wall of Fame, as if to say I was at the peak of physical perfection. I was the only member on that Wall of Fame. It was all a false sense of security. I wasn't really making a difference in anyone's life but mine.

When I was training, I stuck out in gyms like a white guy at a rap concert. I would get my daily questions, like how much I benched or how big are my arms. I would get the monkey mouth people asking me how much I cycled, or the name of my source. People I didn't even know would walk right up to me and ask me questions about a specific exercise or body parts as though I had some welcome sign on my T-shirt, or some secret that nobody else knew. No introduction or greeting. My answer was always the same: hard work and dedication. There was no weight room etiquette when I was a bodybuilder. Everyone always wanted the cutting-edge information, whether it was a supplement or training style.

Bodybuilding was my getaway; I could crawl into the trench and get seclusion. I put on those headphones, blasting 80's rock and got lost in a trance. No more tenants disturbing me with maintenance complaints. No more employers calling me to answer a question that could wait till tomorrow. Diet and exercise questions from clients; forget about it. It was hard to believe that picking up a bunch of heavy metal rocking to Def Leppard would bring me such euphoria, but it did. I lived and breathed bodybuilding for over ten years. It brought me a lot of happiness and success.

Day 13: Generation Iron

When I told family and friends that I was going to compete, I didn't get the warmest response. "Aren't those the guys who put on baby oil and strut on stage in their Speedos?" Kinda true, but...After my friends and family saw me compete for a number of years, their dispositions changed. Yes, they would come to shows and see men and women flexing their muscles, but they also understood and appreciated the hard work it took to get them on stage. They witnessed the sacrifice I made and my dedication to the sport. I didn't just train for one or two years to become a bodybuilder. It took years and years of rigorous training. I also dieted 16 weeks and isolated myself to become stage-ready.

Being on stage didn't entice me to become a bodybuilder. What fascinated me about the sport was the process. Unlike other sports where you can take plays off, in bodybuilding if I had one cheat meal I would have never made it on stage. Bodybuilding separates the pretenders from the contenders. If I had a dollar for everyone who came up to me pleading to compete or promising to compete at the next show, I would be rich. The fact of the matter was people made fun of what they didn't know or couldn't do. It's easy going to the gym and pump up when you are not dieting and devouring all the calories. Try to train with the same intensity when your carbs and water intake are low. That is the difference between bodybuilders and the rest. Competition only comes after years and years of proper diet and exercise. Hard work is the true catalyst of success.

December 3rd, 2005. What a day in my life! That was the day that I stepped up on the bodybuilding stage for the first time. Normally when you do something for the first time, you are a deer in headlights, but I was composed and prepared to win. I spent hours and hours perfecting each pose. I kept my diet clean and had the best training partner and personal trainer. I didn't care who my competition was because I outworked everyone on that stage. Nobody was putting in ten to twelve workouts a week and nobody was posing one to two hours every day. Hell, nobody was even tanning as much as I was, which gave competitors that dark enriched look that bodybuilders desired under the blistering lights. I did everything I needed to be at one hundred percent when I took the stage. From August–December, I lived a Spartan lifestyle, adhering to a strict regimen. I trained, ate, and slept. There was no such thing as a social life for me. The goal was to make a statement and possibly have a career. I never knew how I would fare because I didn't have the genetic makeup to compete in a land of oddities.

Row

When I started my in-season competition phase, I had no idea how my body would develop. I started my diet at 231 pounds, the heaviest I had ever been. I was walking around at about fifteen percent body fat. I built a foundation over the years so muscle development and muscle maturity was not the issue. I made sure I didn't suffer any significant injuries when I got close to the competition. You can easily tear or pull a muscle because you're holding very little water and fat.

I felt great training for my first competition. I had no injuries and my body was adapting well to my diet. The last few days before the competition, my team successfully implemented the major changes, like carb loading and water depleting. This is when your physique changes the most and it's the hardest part of the diet for a bodybuilder. It was tough choking down chicken breasts without any water, oftentimes spending over thirty minutes at the dining room table trying to stomach the last few bites without choking. The last few days are miserable and could make or break your physique and your spirit. One wrong move could leave your muscle bellies flat and make you look completely emaciated after all the hard work. I learnt that the hard way in my second competition.

The last few days of training were full body cross training workouts. The main objective was squeezing every repetition and getting as much blood volume into my muscles. During this time, carb loading while also slowly depleting water from my diet was critical. This was the method I implemented when my physique was on point. Other times, drastic measures needed to be taken if my body was not responding well to the carbs. I wish the last week before a show never existed because the last week was brutal.

The diet was going per plan and all the calculations my team and I made were working. The night before the competition, I introduced simple sugars and eliminated water slowly. For most, the night before the competition, you're up introducing carbs and depleting water. This helps increase vascularity and rounder muscle bellies. Every thirty minutes I was introducing new carbs like rice cakes with grape jelly and handfuls of Skittles washing that down with a swig of honey. It couldn't have gone any better as my vascularity in my arms and legs were piercing out of my skin. Vascularity was a benchmark in the judge's eyes. The more vascularity, the tighter the skin around the muscle bellies, meaning less fat. It demonstrated someone who was ripped to the bone.

I had my last meal of the day before bed and took a water pill to make sure that I was getting rid of any excess water. Taking diuretics is always a risky proposition as too much can be dangerous and risk dehydration, or possibly even cardiac arrest. It can also cause severe muscle cramps and eliminate vascularity. But, what the hell, I wanted to win at all costs. By any means necessary.

I woke up the next morning feeling better than ever. I was ready to compete. I officially went through a full diet without any real setbacks apart from a minor pulled hamstring, but that only kept me from training legs for a week. I was ready to win and stake my place in the bodybuilding world.

I arrived in the morning to pre-judging at the Gateway Theatre home to all the major Illinois bodybuilding competitions. Gateway Theatre housed some of the baddest bodybuilders of all time. Olympians like Jay Cutler, Sergio Oliva, and Phil Heath; I was about to walk up on the same stage.

Pre-judging was when I would find out who was going to win. It's the first time I would meet my competition. I would be judged side by side next to everyone in my class, executing each pose. The trick in posing was performing each pose while illustrating your best features. When you're asked to flex your biceps in a front double bicep pose, the judges want to see how you are holding your abs tight making sure your quads are still separated. They are reviewing the whole package, not just the featured pose. Having symmetrical muscle balance and muscle density was the winning formula.

Even though it was my first show, I was ready. I knew how to pose, had enough Pro Tan, pumped up properly off stage, took in the right foods minutes before stepping on stage, and properly carb loaded. I dotted every *i* and crossed every *t* during the last week of dieting. I hit every pose on stage flawlessly. There was no hesitation and each pose was in smooth transition.

I ended up winning my class and caught the eye of a lot of sponsors that night. Well, that's what I was told. In bodybuilding, just like any other sport, you can be great one day and then old news the next.

After the show, I took a month off from the gym to give my body a break from the constant pounding of heavy lifting and stringent dieting. When I returned to the gym, I was treated like some kind of war hero. Come on! I was given a false sense of accomplishment from my gym peers. The staff at the gym asked me to autograph the Flex magazine where I was pictured. Gym rats were approaching me shaking my hand, congratulating me on winning. I hated that attention. I didn't want it. I started to train at odd times to get away from it. I knew I was getting that attention because I won. People wanted to circle themselves around winners.

I was excited about possibly having a career in bodybuilding, but I knew I had a long way to go. I obtained a sponsorship opportunity, which was a rarity in bodybuilding. I had that fire burning inside me to continue progressing. Bodybuilding wasn't my dream. I enjoyed training and the challenge of transforming my physique, but it was never in my life itinerary to step on stage. I guess God had other plans.

Now that I started becoming a name in the sport I had to start marketing myself, which for me was difficult. The other side of bodybuilding that many of the competitors neglect is the self-marketing. You must get your name out there by being your own biggest advocate. It's also important to establish a solid network to obtain additional opportunities and get your name and pictures in magazines. I knew if I continued to compete, that would all come later. There were a ton of guys that compete one time and never compete again. I didn't want to become a one hit wonder.

My first and second competition were a year apart. The judges wanted to see me on stage sooner, but I wanted to put on more size before stepping on stage again. For my first show, I went from 231 pounds to less than 150. I compromised too much muscle and didn't have the roundness in my muscles. I worked extremely hard to put a better package on stage the second time around. That didn't go according to plan.

My second competition was difficult. I made some reckless decisions. Two weeks before the show I tore my left bicep. I was in too deep and decided to continue to train.

I went to the gym ready to train biceps, triceps, and calves that day. Nothing unusual, just a typical day in paradise. I was well-hydrated and felt remarkable for being close to competition. I was performing machine preacher curls going at about eighty percent. I was controlling each repetition and trying to prevent an injury during the final stages before the competition. Any injuries in the latter stages of a pre-contest diet can be devastating.

DAY 13: GENERATION IRON

Unfortunately, I didn't have lady luck on my side when I was performing my third set of ten repetitions and I felt a twinge in my left bicep. This didn't feel like a big deal; I always got those twinges, so I proceeded to perform the sixth repetition and that was when I felt a pop. It felt like a gunshot exploded into my left bicep. Something was terribly wrong; I dropped the weight, unable to complete the full set. I was wearing a sweater, so I could not see my arm. I knew something was off because my left arm felt numb and I was having difficulties removing my hoodie.

When I finally pried my sweatshirt off, my left bicep looked like a rainbow which was a telling sign that I tore the muscle. About one minute after, I started to feel nauseous, like someone punched me in the gut. I darted to the bathroom spewing everything I ate that day.

I drove home, ready to make a doctor's appointment. I heard bodybuilders continue to train after a major injury. I didn't know how because I was in excruciating pain and thinking about training with a torn bicep, let alone performing my daily tasks, was going to be pure hell. I knew my bicep was never going to look the same and having an augmented muscle in bodybuilding was not exactly a judge's delight. I was determined to forge ahead and try to make it through the next two weeks. I was in too deep to stop. Every workout was now a challenge; every rep, every set. Everything I did, I was in pain. Before each workout, I would wrap my bicep with an ACE bandage, hoping the wrap would keep my bicep protected and not cause more injury. I don't know how I trained with a torn bicep as those two weeks were the most painful of my life. I look at my mutilated arm now and see the battle scar plastered on my left bicep.

The night before my second competition I felt and looked much bigger than I did the year before. My muscle bellies were much fuller and rounder. I went through all my mandatory poses with no cramping and my back didn't overpower my entire physique this time around. I did my homework. My bicep was still in bad shape, but I dealt with it. I felt good before I went to bed and decided to take more diuretics than advised. I was holding a little bit more water in my upper hamstrings and lower abs, so I took a little more of the water pill, not realizing the dangers. I completely ignored the advice I was given. I made the judgement call for myself thinking it would help me get that extra water out of my system before pre-judging. That was the biggest mistake I ever made in my bodybuilding career. I ended up staying up all night, urinating over 150 oz. of water. As I was urinating, my muscles were deteriorating right in front of my eyes. The separations and vascularity in my muscles were disappearing little by little. It was tragic watching my hopes flushed down the drain minute by minute because I took a little white pill.

The anxiety was making my body go into a catabolic state. With no sleep, I ended up going to pre-judging weighing eight pounds less than the night before. I could not hold a pose without severe cramps. There I was, with a torn bicep and sick from the diuretic the night before. Every pose I hit, I cramped. This was the perfect storm and my chance of winning was gone.

I tried pumping up forty-five minutes before I stepped on stage, but I couldn't even lift a five-pound dumbbell before cramping. Panic set in and I ended up taking a few potassium pills, which didn't help. I was fifteen minutes from going on stage straining to hit a pose. My physique was not responding to the carbs. My muscle bellies were not peaking anymore and I had lost all my vascularity. I made a monumental mistake by taking more diuretics than prescribed. I put in a year of training, eating, and sacrificing for this moment and one pill the size of a Tic Tac cost me the competition. There was nothing I could do at this point except to man up and compete. I stepped on stage flat and did whatever I could, but my adversaries were prepared. I hit every pose as best I could while cramping. The pain was relentless from a tear and cramps on top of that. I felt as if my muscles were tearing away from the bone as I had to keep composed on stage. I did the best I could, but I knew it wasn't good enough.

After the show, I was demoralized. I gained a tremendous respect for bodybuilding that night because a simple error can sacrifice the entire competition. Just like football, bodybuilding was a game of inches.

I didn't want to compete again, but there were goals I promised myself and quitting because of a stupid pill was a cop out. I made a mistake and had to man up to it.

❖

The more I competed, the better I wanted to look and took drastic measures to come in tighter, bigger, leaner, more vascular, whatever it was going to take to win. Anyone who tells you they are competing just to go on stage and try their best is giving you the business. If they are a true bodybuilder, then they are not competing to win a consolation trophy. They want to step on stage and have everyone's jaw drop, crushing the competition. They want to leave with a hottie on one arm and a first-place trophy on the other.

After my second show, I ended up taking two years off from competitions, making sure I was healed. It was a calculated two years because I needed time to grow and be honest with myself. I wanted to be a contender, not a pretender. If I wanted to get featured or even mentioned in magazines, I needed to put on more size. The mass monster era was in effect and I needed to buy into the times. I would never tip the scales at 250 pounds, but the bigger the better.

I hit the stage in 2009 and instead of doing one show, I decided to compete in three consecutive shows. I did some crazy shit that year. At one point I was walking around with a bowl of salt. I was chugging down salt every few minutes. The idea was to add salt into my diet to retain water and then suddenly eliminate the salt and introduce a diuretic. Crazy! I would diet for twenty straight weeks, which was an entire month longer than my previous competition diets. I planned carefully, but damn, eating clean for that long! I could easily over-diet and watch my physique crumble, like what happened to me during my second competition.

I wanted my 2009 campaign to be memorable. My goal was to step up on stage ten lbs. heavier than previous competitions. Adding ten pounds is not difficult as you add more calories to your diet, but adding ten pounds of rock-hard muscle is completely different. Adding ten pounds of quality muscle is next to impossible without the perfect regimen. I surrounded myself with a team of diet and exercise nerds.

When I competed in 2009, my muscles were much rounder and I was a lot thicker. I did compromise how lean I was previously, but I didn't want to overdo it and drop too much weight. I ended up competing in all three shows and won two out of the three. In the show that I didn't win, I came in second, which was not acceptable in my eyes, but the judges made the call. I looked better and felt better than I did in my previous competitions.

After the competitions, I started marketing myself a lot more. I competed in five shows and it was time to get more connections through media outlets. I competed in Wisconsin, Iowa, and Illinois in 2009. It was important to me that I present myself well in my own backyard first, before I even tried to start to network in other areas, outside of the Midwest. If you looked good, you looked good, but there are a lot of dudes that do extremely well in competitions and all they get is a trophy.

Bodybuilding ain't cheap, and without any sponsorships or endorsements, I had a very expensive hobby. Bodybuilding was not a hobby for me. I needed to win competitions and parlay that into sponsorships and business prospects. Winning meant possible sponsorships, endorsements, magazine articles, etc. I wanted to strike while the iron was hot, so the first thing I did was create a website revealing as much information about my nutritional business and bodybuilding career as I could. This was before the age of social media where everyone knows everything about you. Back then, the way to get media attention was to create a website and there were only a handful of personal bodybuilding websites out there. It baffled me that most of the top pros in the world didn't have websites. There were very few channels for fans to engage with their favorite bodybuilders.

When I created my website, I drew some buzz from local media agencies. My alma-maters, Benedictine and North Park University, both did a piece on my bodybuilding career and that was the start. Those stories grew into bigger stories from major bodybuilding companies. Both *Flex* magazine, *No Nonsense* magazine, and Bodybuilding.com did a piece. The more interest I drew, the more magazines and papers I was in. Things were starting to happen.

I was sponsored by Pride Nutrition as well. Getting connected with a supplement company was the lifeline for a successful bodybuilder. Pride Nutrition was a local Chicagoland supplement company. In order to be sponsored, I pushed their product, went with them to different competitions, worked their booths, wore their thread, and took their supplements. In turn, they promoted me on their website and provided me with supplements. Sponsorships are rare and it was one of my goals in my bodybuilding journey.

I knew my competing stint was going to be short lived. I loved the process of dieting and training for a competition, but sustainability was always going to be an issue while adhering to all the stressors in life. I wanted to have a family someday and that would not have been possible if I continued to compete. Those life goals were important to me and were on the back burner while I explored the opportunities that bodybuilding provided.

DAY 13: GENERATION IRON

When I competed at the Wisconsin State, little did I know it would be the last time I stepped on a bodybuilding stage. It was by choice, as I accomplished everything I wanted to, and it was now time to experience other challenges. I knew once I stepped away from competition I was going to step away from bodybuilding for good. I wouldn't attend anymore shows or help anyone get ready for competitions. I was going to close that chapter in my life.

I knew I couldn't compete forever and I put a lot of miles on my body when I was at the pinnacle of the sport. Bodybuilding was a full-time job. I didn't have time for anything else, and I was at a time in my life when I wanted to travel and start to settle down.

When I look back at the years of competition and what it meant to me, I know that I walked away satisfied and content. There was a lot of good that came from my sacrifices and dedication. The days of waking up in the morning and pouring half dozen raw egg whites in a shaker cup filled with orange juice are now over. The days of pounding protein shake after protein shake are now over. The days of weighing my food and counting my calories are now over. No more trips to the toilet after a heavy superset. God wants you to do things on his watch. My time was up and it was time to put the weights back on the rack.

Thank you to everyone that helped me and supported me through that journey. My family and friends who came to my competitions not knowing what to expect. My team who helped me through the entire lifecycle of a rigorous diet. Lastly, all the people that told me bodybuilding was just a pipe dream.

PART III
Knucklehead Philosophy

DAY 12 JAIL JOURNAL: THE KEY TO MY CELL

Condemned in the bowels of prison to pay the ultimate price. Death. Bleak isolated private interiors of San Quentin. Criminals committing the worst crimes are doomed to wither away.

Iron maiden, quartering, hanging, buried alive, burning at the stake, electric chair, gas chamber. These early and violent execution tactics haunt my imagination. My horror will be different. My execution will stake claim in history books adding one more to the list of departed by the hands of the justice system.

Capital punishment was suspended from 1972 to 1976 in the United States by the Supreme Court. Since then, 1,264 inmates have been executed in America, with the needle pointing up. The most death penalty slayings in America occurred in the 21st century. Why the hell did we restore capital punishment when it was suspended? Who made that bonehead decision? Why am I being used as an example? I am a decent human being who can do great things in this world, but some jury filled with incompetent people decided that the death penalty was appropriate. Just because I committed a crime, that doesn't mean my family should be punished. It doesn't mean that my mother should get a phone call letting her know that her son was strapped to a chair and executed.

There are no more good days in this hell hole! This place just sucks the life out of me.

Who knows if any of my writing is going to get into the right hands? I might just be writing with false pretense. I am so sick and tired dealing with these people and the corruption. Every move I make, I am being watched. I sit here and rot like I am terminally ill and told by a physician that I am on borrowed time.

Before I get executed I want everyone to know that I never gave up on anything and whatever I committed to I made sure I followed through. I paved my own way in life, whether it was a path to the pearly gates or a path to hell.

❖

I guess during our adolescence we make some bonehead mistakes. I made some when I was a freshman at North Park University. I was a young buck trying to be somebody, entering new worlds of NCAA athletics and adulthood without my parents. I was fulfilling a lifelong dream of playing college football, while hearing whispers, "You're not big enough", "You're not good enough." Only six percent of high school senior football players will play college ball, and on my high school team, we only had four. My mindset entering my freshman year was football, football, football. Nothing else mattered except for proving the naysayers wrong. I would do anything to see the green pastures on Saturday in stadiums filled with cheering fans.

My first day was surreal as my parents helped me pack all my belongings in a tiny jail cell dorm room with all the other football players. Sohlberg Hall looked more like a penitentiary than a college dorm room. All it had was two bed frames with no mattresses, no T.V, two drawers for my teammate and me, no air conditioning, and a tiny closet. I was waiting for a correctional officer to hand me my moldy bologna sandwich and juice box. This was what the NPU coach was referring to when he said you better be ready to come to camp and work. He told me that there are no distractions and once I kiss my loved one's goodbye and closed the dorm room door, I belonged to him. For the next month, I was going to be his soldier. I wasn't even allowed to make a phone call unless I was in dire need. I guess that is why they called it "hell camp."

The dorm looked like something out of a horror movie, with small shoebox rooms and a killer stalking each room, lurking for its prey. I would call the movie "The Sohlberg Asylum."

Day 12: The Key to my Cell

There were times when doubt was crawling in my head; as I tried to figure out why I made this choice to abandon my comfort zone. All my friends were going on trips and broadening their horizons, and I was entering hell camp. I could have easily gone to Harper College, which was 2 miles away from my house, and then transferred to a four-year university, but my decision was to take one more step towards my dream and to continue my football career. Just those two words combined still bring me goosebumps. Nobody can ever take that away from me. I can be called a convict, a stone-cold killer, a bully, whatever, but nobody can ever tell me that I wasn't good enough to play college ball. Out of my high school graduating class I was the only one who played all four years at the college level. To me it was a big deal.

During my first year playing at the collegiate level, I ended up putting on 20 pounds through the offseason conditioning program. We had great strength and conditioning coaches who concentrated on specific exercises for me, getting the right nutrition to help me put on more size. It was the first time I figured out how important nutrition was for growth. I was constantly eating. I was like a fat kid at a doughnut shop.

Every player wanted the competitive edge. We all wanted to accomplish team goals, obtaining a conference championship, and putting that diamond ring on our finger. We all had individual goals of becoming captain, all-conference, and obtaining other distinctions.

We lived by the creed, "Whatever means necessary." Sports-enhancing supplements were around me all the time. Teammates had jugs of protein, creatine, amino acids, or whatever the fad was at that time stacked in their locker rooms. Around that time, Androstenedione was hitting the market and was the new supplement craze. Hey, if Mark McGwire had it in his locker room smashing record-ing-breaking homeruns, so did I. We all wanted to achieve greatness and see our names in lights. The question was, what would I do to achieve greatness?

Spectators that are not involved in sports have no idea. Competing at the college level took preparation, commitment, dedication, a whole lotta luck, and slew of other intangibles. The sacrifice we all made for the sheer love of the game was never enough for me.

Row

During the offseason training program at North Park, a few of the upper-classmen I looked up to were training. These guys were the captains of the team and head honchos on campus. When they trained, spectators always watched. Our starting outside linebacker who had tryouts with a few pro teams made a video, of him deadlifting a car and dragging a bus. At the time, these guys were the strongest people I ever met pushing some serious weight. We had one guy that could bench press 550 pounds and another that squatted 700. I knew some of my teammates were on something, but I did not want to ask. It was their business. They worked their asses off in the gym. As time passed we got to know each other a little better because I lived in the North Park athletic center. I was starting to gain their respect with a simple head bob or acknowledgment when I would pass. Nobody spent more time in that joint watching film and training than me. As much as I didn't like the interaction, being an introvert, I knew everyone that walked through that door.

I was training one Saturday afternoon. The gym was empty as I was blaring the Rocky 4 sound track, "No Easy Way Out." Our starting defensive tackle and highly recruited teammate walked into the gym and walked straight up to me. It was the first time we spoke. He was a man amongst boys, sporting a crew cut and tank top showing his twenty-inch pythons to the world. He commanded respect and being a scrawny freshman runt, I craved that physique.

We were both training by ourselves and since both of us didn't have a spot, we decided to lift together. He was someone I looked up to because he was the strongest guy on the team and a true leader of our defense. He was a motivator, constantly picking up our teammates. He mentored the new guys like me on how to work out with the right intensity. In my early years of weight lifting he was a true inspiration. He was positive and looked out for the up and coming freshman players. He was a true ambassador for the North Park football team. We spent that training session sharing a few words. He told me how impressed he was with me and told me that I was the hardest worker he ever met. That meant a lot coming from him, but didn't get me a starting position on our defensive unit. Hard work only got you so far.

Playing college ball at my weight was like being a cub in a lion's cage, filled with full-grown lions. Seeing the older players without pads, I thought they were gigantic and then they put on the pads, which made them look even larger.

DAY 12: THE KEY TO MY CELL

As my off-season progressed, I was putting on some serious weight, but I still wasn't as strong as I wanted to be. I needed to crawl before I walked, but some of my teammates were already sprinting.

In high school I trained with the offensive linemen. My senior year in high school, I was one of the strongest guys on our team playing outside linebacker. I was undersized for that position, but was strong enough. I went from being one of the strongest on my high school team to being in the lower percentile in college during my freshman year. I wanted to get bigger by any means necessary. Why spend all that time in the gym to sit on the bench? I didn't want to be a number on a team of many. I wanted to start.

At the time, I was reading a book by the great Motley Crue musician, Nikki Sixx. He kept a journal tracking his drug addiction. In the book, *Heroin Diaries*, Nikki talks about drugs he was taking while writing his memoirs. He was hallucinating on crack cocaine and heroin. He thought wise guys were heading to his house to gun him down. He would spend weeks in his closet with drugs and a shotgun.

His vices were crack, heroin, pills, alcohol, and probably any potent cocktail he could get his hands on when he was a multimillion-dollar rock star. He spent years abusing drugs, spending countless days in the most unimaginable places. He talked about being on tour with Motley Crue and the wild side of sex, drugs, and rock and roll. You want to talk about a guy living his life on the edge of a cliff. Nikki took so much heroin on one-night partying, he blacked out, waking up in a dumpster. He was told that he overdosed and was declared dead. Nobody wanted to take him to the hospital, so they threw him in the dumpster like a piece of trash. What a way to go!

Nikki Sixx wrote a lot of Motley Crue's songs during his addiction period. He would write for days in his closet, wasted. He lived his life balls to the wall playing hard rock, partying after shows, and living life on the edge. Reading his book made me realize I had to go balls to the wall. Not taking drugs, like he did, but having that attitude in my life. I didn't cater to anyone's views about how I should live my life. I lived my life the way I wanted to live. If I wanted to try something, I did it. Life was too short to constantly be worrying about what others felt about me.

Row

During Nikki's period of addiction, he was high more than he was sober. He would perform in front of thousands high as a kite, but he was always prepared. Preparation for a concert was his sobriety. I wanted my drug to be training. His life on the edge was my metaphor. I wanted to take whatever necessary steps to get bigger, faster, and stronger. WHATEVER MEANS NECESSARY! Second string was not an option.

My training philosophy changed after reading that book, from training once a day, to training twice a day. Whenever I had free time I would do push-ups, sit-ups, and jumping jacks. I tried to lift whatever I could. I would walk around on campus with a tennis ball, constantly clutching the ball and squeezing the life out of it until my forearms exploded.

At this point, I established myself as a no-nonsense guy that wanted to be left alone while I was training. I put my headphones in and was locked and loaded.

❖

One afternoon I was training alone. Those same teammates that trained with the same tenacity approached me and asked if I was interested in taking a trip. I looked up with an acute look of irritation and politely asked them not to disturb me while I was training. I didn't appreciate them disturbing me, but was intrigued by the invitation. After my workout, I met up with them and that was when the plan was formed. This trip would change my life forever.

I didn't realize that it would be one of the biggest mistakes of my life.

They wanted to take a trip across the border to Mexico, visit the pharmacies, bring back as many anabolic steroids as we could. This endeavor was a lot easier said than done, but we did it by whatever means necessary. Little did we know that this would be a monumental lapse in judgment.

Some words of advice for anyone traveling to Texas and thinking of smuggling drugs across the border: Listen to their slogan. Do not mess with Texas!

I remember that day frame by frame. We were planning on taking my beat-up Ford Escort with over 100,000 miles to Mexico from Chicago, Illinois.

I was only eighteen at the time and living with my parents. I was wet behind the ears and had no idea what I was getting into. All I knew was my summer training program was starting and I wanted to start my cycle as soon as possible, walking into the football season bigger. I needed to build on my freshman year performance and fight for a starting position on our defensive unit. That's all I cared about.

All I saw was the result, which was starting strong safety on the North Park University defensive unit. I was naïve, not fathoming getting into trouble and I had no idea about the stiff penalties of drug trafficking, in Mexico. I was a selfish fool. Bottom line was that I wanted to be a great college football player and didn't want my size to handicap my career.

I would be leaving for Mexico with people I barely knew. Granted, they were teammates, but what did that mean? We didn't share the same blood. This did not go well with my parents; they were adamant that I stay home. Parents always know what's best for their kids, and in hindsight I should have listened. Damn, I should have really listened. I was a knucklehead at that age, thinking I knew everything. I didn't have a damn clue, leaving the house around 9 p.m. with no driver's license and just my North Park University student ID. I left for Mexico with no official government issued ID!

There were three of us bozos heading down to Mexico around 11 p.m. Remember, this was before the times of GPS and smart phones. We were held to using a paper map to track our journey across the border.

We all had the same mindset: to get what we needed and get the hell out of Dodge. At the time, I did not realize how long it took to get to Mexico from Illinois. I took the car to the mechanic the day before and told him I was going to drive cross-country. Dude took one look at my ride and advised that there was no way in hell my old banged up Ford Escort was going to make it to Mexico. The mechanic advised that there were issues with the car needing immediate attention. He insisted on keeping the car for a week to work on repairs. No chance! I was so determined to keep our trip alive, I decided not to adhere to the experienced mechanic's advice. I knew he was a seasoned mechanic and gave me solid advice, but, again, I was determined to keep this trip alive. I was using knucklehead philosophy.

I left the house, heading to meet my partners in crime at North Park University. I was driving on interstate 90 with a mouth full of chew, grinning ear to ear, resembling the Joker, thinking how much bigger, faster, and stronger I would be, rolling into camp stylin' and profilin'. As I was sitting in my car waiting, I had no idea if my crew were even going to make it. Since we didn't have any cell phones, we were relying on conversations we had weeks ago. We penciled in a date and time, but things could have changed. What if they changed their minds and didn't want to go through with this anymore? When I got to North Park, I drove around campus looking for my teammates. The campus was dead silent. You could hear a pin drop because all the students went home for summer break. I was patrolling the campus, but there were no signs of life. Cowards! Just a bunch of lip service.

I drove for about ninety minutes searching for them and was ready to head home disappointed. As I was pulling out of the parking lot, I noticed a large, grizzly man from the corner of my eye approaching my car. As he got to my car I could tell it was only one of the members of our team. He knocked on the door and entered the vehicle. He was excited to see me and apologized for being so late. I asked him where the other team members were. He explained that one backed out at the last minute and couldn't make it and we had to drive another hour to pick another teammate up, delaying our journey further. We were already delayed and now we were going to travel another hour in the wrong direction. I was agitated now and just wanted to get the show on the road.

He also requested that we make a pit stop at his apartment. Pissed off, we drove to his place. Little did I know that we were stopping there to steal a jar full of coins from his roommate. This was intended to pay for the tolls. Let's add theft to the bonehead decisions made on this trip.

God was telling me not to take this journey across the US. At this point I was ready to head home, but my teammates' excitement kept my energy levels high. All of our spirits were high as we embarked on our journey. We had just completed finals and were on summer break traveling cross-country. Life couldn't be better. The summer had just started and it was already off to a great start. What's the worst that could happen? We go down to Mexico and can't find anything? At that point that was the worst thing I imagined. Boy, was I naïve.

We started to make our way down south, not a care in the world. Apart from gas and a few meals, we didn't stop to rest. We were renegades hitting local diners and splitting without paying the bill, leaving tire tracks in parking lots as we raced away. We drove in shifts, making great progress. As we were getting closer to Texas, I knew things were not looking that great with my car. The sounds my car was making did not bode well for us, but who cared! We were almost there. We were headed to the Texas and Mexico border to meet the fourth member of our team. He was connected with some of the local Mexican pharmacies and had the hook-up. He was patiently awaiting our arrival.

We made our way through Missouri and Kansas, finally reaching the Lone Star State. We were about thirty minutes outside of the Mexican border.

My car was getting worse, howling at me to stop. Once we got to the fourth member's house, my car could rest. Caked with insect guts on the front of the car. We all took a quick shower and jumped into a truck heading towards the border. Viva Mexico! The sun was dying, but the heat index was still over one hundred degrees. We weren't used to that type of heat living in Illinois. We were sweating profusely as the sunset was beaming down on us. Our eyes were on the prize and there was no turning back.

I figured when we got to Texas, we were going to hang out for a little bit and maybe grab a bite to eat. I was wrong because my accomplices were all business and wanted to head to Mexico immediately. This was a business trip, nothing more.

Our fourth member thought it was a good idea to hire a mule to take everything across for us, but the price was too steep and we declined. The Texas local mules didn't seem to have any qualms about going across the border and getting gear. They made this trek dozens of times.

As we arrived in Mexico, border patrol was rampant. The K-9 dogs were sniffing each car extensively. They were rummaging through people's trunks, coolers, everything! My adrenaline was already rushing and self-doubt was racing in my mind. This was our first of many checkpoints. There were people being searched and cars being taken apart, being searched for drugs right before my eyes. I didn't think it was going to be like this. I started questioning our decision. As we reached the border of Mexico, the hairs on the back of my neck were raised and my heart rate was elevated. We were heading into Mexico with nothing but the clothes on our backs, so we had nothing to worry about, but seeing all the local officials made me apprehensive. Our Texas local and driver told us not to worry, and driving into Mexico was a piece of cake. The border patrol agent looked at us and told us to proceed. We were now in Mexico.

We were all big dudes and drew a lot of attention. We finally parked and started trekking through the Mexican streets of Nuevo Laredo. Locals were drowning the streets and the nightlife was booming. A lot of the locals were gawking at us. Some were even pounding their fist against their chest proposing combat. There were already bullseyes on our backs. We brought on a lot of unneeded attention. We got across the border, fielded a few questions, and parked the truck. There was an uneasy feeling walking the streets of Mexico. Pharmacies were scattered everywhere. We had a sense of uncertainty, but we didn't drive 2,000 miles to turn back now. We were living out of the car for the past twenty plus hours, fatigued.

Our fourth member sensed something wrong and said, in Spanish, that border patrol was heavy today. *"Pesada patrulla fronteriza hoy."*

We decided to ignore his opinion, and instead decided to proceed so we could leave that same night. There were many signs telling us to rethink the idea, but we had no idea how strict border patrol was with drug trafficking. As soon as we crossed the border, we could see bright neon lights with the text, *Farmacia*. There were three in a very close radius. We initially started testing the waters, checking what they had to offer. We were greeted like royalty as each clerk knew we were gringos ready to empty our wallets.

Each pharmacy had a wide assortment of products. I realized how cheap some of this stuff was. I felt like a kid in a candy store. We were in awe seeing how much gear we had at our fingertips. There was so much variety, all four of us were frozen, examining the content.

All the pharmacies had clear glass windows connected to other stores. The other customers were rubbernecking, pointing and laughing. I felt like they knew something we didn't. We brought a lot of attention to ourselves and everyone knew why we were there. The spotlight was on us and why not? We all looked different from the masses of locals.

We loaded up and bounced from La Farmacia. I didn't realize how much we had until we walked back to the car. The fourth member looked panicky as he was eyeing our volume. We had grocery bags filled to the brim. He kept saying we had too much and we were going to get searched.

We were probably in Mexico for about an hour and a half. We decided to make a second trip and go back and buy even more. We started cramming gear in our socks, in our pockets, and wherever we could. I should have kiestered some of this stuff. We were walking with Clenbuterol in our socks and pockets as we approached our first checkpoint. This was the first checkpoint in Mexico that we needed to pass before reaching our vehicle. It was 1 a.m. now and we were all exhausted.

Day 12: The Key to my Cell

The fourth member was sweating profusely and kept saying, *"Vamos a quedar atrapados."* I did not fathom getting caught in Mexico and spending jail time in another country, especially one piled with prison gangs and brutality.

Mexican jails were ruled by prison gangs like Surenos, Nuestra Familia, and the infamous MS-13, notorious for playing soccer with their rival's heads. The bureau of prisons had little compassion for drug users. They put you away and threw away the keys. I realized quickly that we were playing with fire trying to smuggle this much gear, but we had traveled too far to turn back now like cowards.

As we approached the customs agent, he asked for IDs. At the time, I was on a traffic violation and did not have my driver's license to show the agents. The only type of identification I had was my North Park student ID. I did not even have a state ID. To think that I drove cross-country from Illinois to Texas with no driver's license gives you an idea of what my mindset was when I was in college. I was a troubled youth and had issues focusing on what mattered most, which was getting a quality education. Still to this day, I cannot comprehend why I acted the way that I did. We live from our mistakes, I guess. Knucklehead philosophy!

I remember walking across the border with a bunch of anabolics hidden on my body. I never, at any point, thought about the ramifications of getting caught. I was like a blind man skipping and whistling in a minefield without any sense of getting my head blown off. Everyone was staring at us with stupid grins on their faces, knowing we were going to get caught. We didn't recognize the warning signals. I was walking slowly to the border while the patrol officers were screening people and checking IDs. Our pockets and socks were bulging out, noticeable to everyone. I was in big trouble because my school ID wouldn't cut it. As I approached the patrol officer, he looked at me and asked for my ID. My hands were shaking uncontrollably like a cocaine addict jonesing. I gave him my North Park school ID and he pushed it back to me under the thick glass window, demanding more information. I apologized and explained I was on a US ticket and authorities had my license. He proceeded to ask me questions about the US. Where did I live? Why was I visiting? How long? He asked me basic questions that a customs agent would ask anyone. I started to regain my composure and was answering each question with confidence. He took one more long look at me and asked me if I worked out. I said yes, I am an American football player in university. The customs agent stared at me for about five seconds which felt like an eternity. At that point the interrogation was over. The officer let me go without even patting me down or checking my pockets. What a relief.

Row

As soon as I cleared border patrol, there was another stop we needed to clear to make it onto US soil. This was going to be by car. We emptied our pockets and socks, and combined all of it in a duffel bag. The duffel bag we brought from Illinois was filled to the max. We couldn't figure out a hiding place in the truck, so we decided to stash the loot in the glove compartment. We just increased the border patrol's chances of catching us to 100%. I don't know if we could have been any dumber.

As we were looking through our gear we were all shaking our heads in disbelief. We purchased way too much. Our fourth team member started coming down on us for making him do this. He thought we were in Mexico for a few bottles and didn't anticipate the quantity.

We had a few thousand dollars' worth of anabolics and in order to get through border patrol we had to drive. Our driver was against this responsibility and wanted to hire a drug mule. Hiring a drug mule to cross the border would cost a lot of money, and there was the uncertainty of reclaiming our gear. We didn't want to take that chance. I did not want to pay a mule a few hundred-dollars, especially since we were told mules are undercover patrol agents or thieves. The risk level was too high. I didn't want any part of this, and we were at a standstill. Both of my North Park teammates did not want any part of it either and took the easy way out, walking across the border empty-handed. I told the driver I would drive with him across the border. If we got caught we would both go down. As we got in the car, the driver looked at me and shook his head, asking me if I was ready to go to jail.

As we got to the border, everyone paid a toll. We were in jeopardy of paying a toll with our lives. As the driver reached his hand to pay the toll, the border patrol was inspecting the car with a flashlight. Dogs were roaming the perimeter ready to pounce on anyone dumb enough to smuggle drugs across the border. This was standard policy, so you could understand how difficult it was to smuggle a large quantity. The agent asked us to pull over for further inspection. We were now petrified. Sweat beads were racing from my forehead in the searing heat. The humidity that evening was unbearable and we could cut the tension with a knife. What if's were now circulating in my brain! How would I explain to my family that I was imprisoned in another country for drug smuggling? My heart was racing a mile per minute, as if I had just run a marathon.

Day 12: The Key to my Cell

The driver had done this hundreds of times, but I could see in his face that he was terrified. His early inclinations were right. Greed overcame our intellect. We flirted with disaster, especially after border patrol asked us to get out of the truck and stand to the side while they searched the vehicle. Four armed customs agents circled the vehicle.

My body was paralyzed with fright. I contemplated making a dash to US territory, abandoning the loot. At least then I would be tried as a US citizen. The patrol agent approached and was enraged, howling obscenities in Spanish. He was infuriated with something he saw in our truck. The driver yelled back. I felt like my heart was going to explode like a grenade. I couldn't control my anxiety. I was eighteen years old with my future balancing on foreign-speaking officers. How did I know they weren't in cahoots trying to blackmail three gringos? I was walking the tightrope, losing my grip as my life was hanging in the balance.

First, I almost got pinched hiding drugs in my socks by one patrol agent, and now border patrol had stopped us, searching our vehicle with a magnifying glass. I thought I was getting locked up without a doubt. Since the driver had a truck, the patrol agents spent a lot of time looking back there for secret compartments. They finally made their way to the front of the car. My body was trembling with fear. I knew we were looking at a serious bid in a Mexican penitentiary. How the hell would I survive jail in another country?

The border patrol put a flashlight under the passenger side and the driver's side seat and then put a flashlight on the glove compartment. The driver and I gazed at each other and looked down. We were defeated and it was time to start thinking of a story. The agents started to feel around the steering wheel and then one patrol member opened the glove compartment.

I bent over and started gasping for air fighting for every-last breath of freedom. We made a valiant effort, but it was time to succumb to our fate. It was time to throw our hands up and ask for leniency.

I was hyperventilating, but couldn't let the border patrol agent observe my anxiety. The glove compartment was wide open now and there lay the bag with our stash. As one of the patrol members opened the glove he noticed the duffel bag and started moving it around, looking for something else. Instead of looking in the bag, he overlooked it. He must have thought nobody was stupid enough to put drugs in the glove compartment. He never checked the duffel bag! I was in complete shock. My anxiety was lowered, but we weren't out of the woods yet, as the patrol agents were still rounding our vehicles. The duffel bag sitting on the passenger side wide open for any of the other border patrol agents.

Then, shockingly, the agent closed the glove compartment. He started walking towards us. He yelled something in Spanish to other agents. They all looked at me and walked away. The main patrol agent thanked us for our cooperation and told us to enjoy the rest of our trip. We walked back to the car, traumatized by the experience. We had officially smuggled drugs across the border.

As we sat in the car going to pick up the other accomplices, both the driver and I did not utter one word to each other. Dude was fuming, so I kept my big trap shut. I stepped up to go in the car with the driver, but I realized how stupid that was. You live and learn, but this was not the way I wanted to learn. Smuggling drugs 101: What not to do.

Little did I know that our adventure had just begun. We still had a long journey ahead traveling back to Chicago; in a rusted Ford Escort, which was in no condition to be crossing state lines.

We finally made it across the border back into native land. We were all jovial; our plan had come into fruition. I figured we would get much needed R&R from a very long day of driving. We would wake up early the next morning and head home. I knew this was a business trip, but driving nonstop was crazy talk. As we arrived back to our headquarters, my teammates were adamant about hitting the road immediately. I couldn't believe they wanted to drive back, as we were exhausted and needed quality rest. I did not agree with our approach, but at that point I also wanted to get home. I was ecstatic about getting on anabolics, especially after seeing the size of the players in college compared to high school.

We arrived at the driver's home, gave him a hug goodbye, and thanked him for everything. We had just driven twenty plus hours nonstop to purchase drugs, and, without hesitation, decided to hit the pavement back home. At this point I was worried about my ride, which had struggled to make it to Texas. Would it make it back to Chicago in one piece? We were young and dumb. Thinking irrationally came naturally.

It was around 2 a.m., and we started back on the road. The driver warned us that traveling at night was risky because of all the checkpoints. The stretch of highway that we were going to traverse was notorious for drug busts. It was the same stretch that popped Michael Irvin, Hall of Fame football player from the Dallas

Cowboys, for cocaine possession. I thought that once we crossed the border we were free. Nobody said anything about additional checkpoints.

The first stop we hit was frightening because both of my teammates were counting sheep when the patrol officer pulled us over. He checked my North Park ID, my ticket, and went around the car several times with a flashlight and dogs sniffing for drugs. After a few minutes, he handed me my ticket and waved us off. My teammates didn't even wake up through this ordeal. It was a piece of cake, and now I was confident that the rest of our journey was going to be smooth. My car seemed to get its second wind as well and stopped making that unusual noise it was making before.

We were carefree and left the gear in the back seat of the car, in the duffel bag. You would think we would find a safe location in the Ford, maybe somewhere stuck in the seats or somewhere less distinguishable. That didn't even cross our minds.

It was 4 a.m. now and all three of us were zombies. I contemplated pulling over and sleeping on the side of the road, but all the serial killers slay their victims in these scenarios so I pressed on. I was ready to pull over and take a nap, but we were still a long way from getting out of Texas and stopping on the side of the road with a few thousand stacks' worth of gear was not the smartest thing in the world.

I started thinking about how great our summer was going to be. All I wanted was to be an All-American football player. It consumed my soul. I would have taken smack if I knew it would make me invincible.

When my teammates asked me to go to Mexico with them, I felt honored. I said to myself, these guys chose me. Out of everyone on the team, they chose me to go to Mexico with them. I never thought this whole excursion was a drug stop, wait, who was I kidding? I would have gone either way.

We were making a lot of headway as morning approached. We were now rejuvenated and driving in shifts, taking power naps in between. At the pace we were going, we were going to be home within twenty hours. I was exhausted from driving and the overall trip, but we were full steam ahead.

We were still in Texas cruising behind a truck, when suddenly I heard squad car sirens behind us. 5.0 was screaming at us to pull over. Both of my teammates jolted up from the sound like jackrabbits. My heart went from zero to sixty within seconds. I figured it was just a routine stop, but we hadn't done anything wrong and weren't speeding. As we saw the cop car, the blood drained from our faces and we were silent. It looked like we saw a ghost because nobody uttered a word. My heart leapt out of my chest like I was having a heart attack. I couldn't catch my breath and the car started to swerve. This was the Mexican border all over again.

Why did we get stopped? We did nothing wrong!

What I had failed to realize at the time was that traveling with out-of-state license plates made us more prone to getting pulled over.

I pulled over and came to a complete stop on the right side of the expressway. The state trooper got out of his car and approached my Escort. Hat tilted, shield shining, with a neatly pressed uniform, and a leather duty belt equipped with a pistol, pepper spray, and a baton. This guy meant business. As the officer came to the window, he asked for license and registration. I proceeded and gave him my ticket with my insurance card. His next question was what we were doing in Texas. "What you all doin' in my state?" I told him that we were visiting a school friend. He told us that the reason why he stopped us was because we were tailgating a semi-truck for too long and were getting too close. Wait what! He then proceeded to ask us if he could search the vehicle. I swallowed very hard and hesitated, but didn't have a choice. It was either say no and wait for a search warrant, or comply and maybe the police officer would ignore the trunk. Not a chance!

I gave the police officer the green light. He instructed me and one of my teammates to step away from the vehicle and sit Indian style on the curb. He was clearly intimidated by all three of our sizes and was ready to call backup.

He ended up searching the front of the car first. I had a feeling he was going to search the trunk next and spend the most time there. I was having a panic attack as he inched his way to the trunk. He ordered my other teammate to come with him. He finally made it to the trunk and opened it. He started to rummage through the empty protein shake bottles and half eaten protein bars. My car was an absolute mess. He proceeded to find the duffel bag. Jack pot! Our hearts sank into the ground and we thought that our lives in the free world had ended. All day sentence was awaiting us. The judge was going to throw the book at us and make examples out of us so nobody would ever try to smuggle drugs again. Those thoughts were racing through my mind at a million miles per hour. I couldn't bear to watch my life being flushed down the toilet. We were going to feel the wrath of no holds barred Texas law and order.

Day 12: The Key to my Cell

The officer opened the duffel bag, and there were the drugs. He took out each bottle, rediject, and each vial, examining everything. Copper's expression didn't change as he checked everything we owned down to our dirty rags. I was positioned in the front of the car squatting on the curb, but I could see out of the corner of my eye. As soon as the officer picked up the duffel bag, the third member of our team looked up at us and gave us a pale, blank stare. His face resembled a dead corpse in a mortuary.

With the drugs in his mitts, the officer got on the radio calling for backup. He asked a few questions and moved to the front of the car, where I was motionless. He asked us to turn around, put our hands behind our backs, and read us our Miranda rights. Soon we were cuffed and sitting in the squad car. It all happened within ten minutes. The cold steel was pressed around my wrist. The pain from the handcuffs was cascading through my body. I was angry and wanted to punch a hole through this cop's face. He didn't have the right to search our vehicle. We were driving too close to a truck? What a load of crap!

All three of us were thrown in the squad car like longtime felons. I had no idea what was going to happen to us, but I knew that I was going to prison for a long stretch. All the hardcore prison flicks like *Lockup*, *Shawshank Redemption* and *Escape from Alcatraz* were racing in my mind. I was now going to be one of those cons.

Our drive was going to be a few hours to the Fabian Dale Dominguez State Prison in San Antonio. The whole process was an experience I would never forget. Chicago was no longer going to be home. I was going to enter prison at the ripe age of eighteen years old, bug-eyed and scared to death.

On our way to prison, my teammates and I were pleading with the officer to let us go. That wasn't going to happen. Texas police officers play it by the book. The car ride felt like hours before we finally arrived in San Antonio.

I will never forget when we arrived at the jail. The concrete fortress surrounded by watch towers with gun-wielding snipers salivating for inmates to pull a jackrabbit parole. The compound was bigger than a shopping mall and was filled with over two thousand inmates.

My heart was pounding and I knew right then that everything you hear about prisons was true. I was in shock, in handcuffs instead of home. A few days ago, I was sleeping on my cushy mattress counting sheep. Now I would be sleeping on a hard cot. I just shook my head as the officer led me out of the squad car. As we stepped out, all eyes were glued on us like prey in the savannah. All the new prisoners were congregated in a straight line. We were getting scoped out by all the inmates like fresh meat. I was told to look down and keep walking. The problem with jail was that hierarchy rules and if you're alone, you're in deep shit. I was fortunate to have two people who had my back, but that wasn't enough. Gangs ruled Fabian Dale prison just like every other prison. They controlled the daily structure of everyday prison life. If they wanted to start a riot, they would start a riot and there was nothing prison guards could do about it. I had thought that if I ever went to jail I would always be able to handle myself, but I knew this place wasn't for me.

As soon as we arrived, the prison guards smiled at us, thinking we were three punks with extensive rap sheets. We weren't criminals. We made a stupid mistake. Every time the prison guards asked us to do something, we complied and followed with a "Yes, sir" or "Yes, ma'am." We did not give any of the officers a hard time when we got booked. They were doing their job and we committed a crime. It was that simple.

The booking process can take hours with uncooperative inmates, but it took us thirty minutes to get booked. We weren't stupid and we knew that the more respectful we were, the better off we would be in the end. My biggest fear was that I would end up being split up from my teammates.

You hear that prison gangs own the prison system and if you're an outsider, you better comply with their rules and regulations. Well, guess what? I am a Pakistani inmate in a prison with a Pakistani population of zero. At least my friends were going to blend in just fine with the woods. I was not ready for this and had to man up really-quick. I figured that as soon as we got booked, we were going to our individual cells, but luckily, we got put in an arctic holding cell which was a little bigger than a regular cell and given a razor thin blanket. We were told to get comfortable as we were going to be there for a while. All three of us were together with another Hispanic detainee. He didn't speak a lick of English and was on some hard stuff because he was completely incoherent. As soon as we got in the cell, we all looked at each other, shook our heads, and didn't say a word. We lay down on the cold steel and tried to get some shut eye. There was about an hour of silence before we started jawing with each other.

Day 12: The Key to my Cell

This whole experience was new to us, so we couldn't plan our next steps. Being with each other gave us some comfort because we were together. Our cell consisted of a metal sink and metal toilet. We had to sleep on the concrete floor caked with past inmate bodily fluids. If we needed to go the bathroom, we had to go in front of each other. It was exactly how they portray it on television.

After a few hours of contemplating the situation, we lay down and fell asleep. We were stuck in a small holding cell with no light, no windows, and no communication with the outside world. I quickly realized that this situation we got ourselves into was real, and I could not rely on Mommy and Daddy. This was my major screw-up and I was going to face the consequences of getting tried in a different state. This was my first major offense so I thought to myself, maybe the judge would be a little lenient with me, but then again, I was thinking about Texas as the state that imposes the death penalty. I was being classified as an out-of-state drug smuggler. Put that on my résumé.

After a few more hours of thirst and hunger, all three of us were finally escorted to our individual cells. We were all called up at the same time, so I had no idea what to expect. I figured we would get cells right next to each other. That was not the case at all, and when we got separated into different cell blocks that was the last time I would see them together. I was escorted upstairs and my cell was right next to an inmate who allegedly strangled a man to death in prison. I always thought I was tough based on my upbringing, playing sports, and playing through all my injuries. It was in that moment that my confidence was shaken. I wasn't as tough as I thought I was.

Just a few days before my trip to Mexico I was chillin' at home having dinner with my family, and now I was rotting in prison with rapists and murderers, with robocops looking up my stink hole. My luck changed drastically. Just like the great Walter Payton said, "Tomorrow isn't a promise to anyone." I was going to have to succumb to prison life without the certainty of freedom. Not having my friends and family around me made me realize I was going to have to face the music alone. At this point I was starving, but my hunger was put on hold because being in a cell was a lot easier than being out in the population with hoodlums.

Row

I didn't want to step out into general population because that was the lion's den. Those guys were some of the scariest people I had ever seen. All tatted with no fear. One of the inmates housed in my cellblock was one hundred pounds soaking wet, serving an all day sentence on a murder rap. His cell was across from mine and he scared me to death. I could never make eye contact with him. He was well respected in jail by both the prison staff and the inmates. He kept to himself and didn't bother anyone, but he was a force to be reckoned with. Everyone knew to leave him alone and let him do his bid, which was life.

Many of the convicts in Fabian Dale were in prison for lower offenses and waiting to go to trial. I still had to be careful because these men were backed into a corner and ready to shank anyone. They would leave me for dead as quickly as they found me. I had one thing on my side and that was respect. I spoke to everyone whether it was the guards or the inmates with a level of respect. Believe it or not, having manners in jail will get you places. A lot of guys that walk through the halls of incarceration have disdain for their peers and superiors, so they end up having a tough bid. Most of the cons were never going to see the light of day and, if they did, they'd be in and out of prison, never leaving their footprint on society. They become a number in our penal system, constantly pushing the penal code of conduct. Violence and intimidation were what these inmates lived for. Confrontation was probably a game to most of them. They took pride in being the biggest adversary to prison rules.

I was the only Asian inmate in my cellblock. I might as well have had a bull's eye on my back. What gang would I join? Come on. Gangs are all about numbers and staying within their own race. Gangs like Aryan Brotherhood, Mexican Mafia, MS -13, Black Guerilla, Nazi Low Riders, etc. This place was the jungle and I was a jungle bunny. I couldn't show any fear. Cons detected fear and jumped all over it. They might ask to borrow some soap at first. Then ask for part of your lunch. Then ask you to do their laundry. Slowly they have made you their bitch without you even knowing it. They were like CEOs of their criminal enterprise, pinching every last ounce of pride from you. They were like sharks in water, miles away from a drop of blood. They could sense fear. I wasn't stupid, though, and had street smarts from my days growing up in Chicago. I knew how to talk to people with respect and detect shady activity.

I had to stay incognito since I didn't fit in with the inmate population. Prison was a melting pot of races, all vying for the most power. Even though we were all crammed in a tin like sardines, there was still a lot of segregation. The Whites hung out in one area, the Blacks in another, and the Hispanics in another.

I always had to keep my eyes down and not make any sudden movements. This place was like the Serengeti and from what I heard, was like cupcakes compared to some of the other prisons. Places like where I am now and Pelican Bay were like war zones with overpopulation, and different races clashing over power, money, and prestige. Thinking about it now, Fabian Dale was a cake walk.

I was already adapting to the lifestyle and, believe me, there was no rehabilitation. The cons were there to buy their time and get back out on the streets and hustle. Committing crimes was their hustle and prison was their academy. They came to prison to become better criminals.

I had to make sure I fit in or else I would become an outsider quick and becoming an outsider in prison was like being an African American at a KKK rally.

Luckily, I could make phone calls and talk to my family. It was extremely difficult talking to my parents. Here I was, going to college, getting a better education, and playing college ball. I was making them proud, but I let my parents down big time, especially after they forbade me to go to Mexico. I could tell in their voices that they were petrified. Not knowing the prison system, they could only imagine the harsh treatment I was going through.

I came to realize that bad decisions were a recurring theme. I had to start making better decisions in life or I was going to go down a path of destruction. I would lose my name and become a taxpayer's nightmare. I would become the problem in the US, rather than the solution. Instead of prospering and becoming a self-sufficient human being entering adulthood, I took a step back. My knuckle head philosophy was going to define my whole life. I was going to get sentenced for seven years in a state penitentiary. I would carry a felony on my record for the rest of my life. How would I ever get a job? My life was ruined, but all I could think about was my parents and how they would have to explain that their son was caught trying to traffic drugs into the US.

When I was booked, processed, and able to make my first phone call, I called home and my sister picked up the phone. I had to explain to her that I was in trouble and locked up. My sister had no clue I took a trip to Mexico. She thought it was a big joke, but she could tell from my voice that I was dead serious. I could sense the shock in her voice. It would have probably been easier to tell her that I had a terminal disease. Once I hung up the phone, I started imagining my family and how they would adjust to having someone locked away. Would I get visits all the way in Texas? How many years was I going to get? Hopefully the Texas Bureau of Prisons would grant me a transfer to Illinois.

I wasn't in denial like a lot of the other inmates. Some of the other inmates that had already put in years behind bars thought they were on a bum beef. I was guilty. I committed a crime and it was time to man up and put in my time behind bars. Whether it was going to be a couple of years or a few months, I was ready for the next chapter. I had to settle into my new life as a convict.

My impression of prison was confirmed when I was given my grungy orange jumpsuit and orange flip flops. The only thing unique about my wardrobe was the six-digit number pasted on the back. I would have never imagined putting this attire on in my whole life. Having the world at my fingertips to three-hots and a cot. That is all you get in the joint, three meals and a cot to sleep on.

My first meal was breakfast once I got released from lockup into general population. I didn't eat anything and was starving.

By that time everyone knew my business and knew what I was in for. I had no idea how they found out, but they did. I didn't want to disrespect anyone, but wanted to make sure that nobody punked me. I grabbed my tray and sat down. I didn't make eye contact with any of the brownies and made sure I wasn't sitting in gang territory. I was told that if I kept to myself and didn't get in anyone's business, I would be okay, and that was exactly what I did.

Out of the five judges in the area I was arrested in, I was told we were getting a cold-blooded woman who was notorious for handing out stiff penalties. Even though this was our first offense, inmates told us to get comfortable because it was going to be a long trial. She was known to make life miserable for out-of-towners, especially for drug-related offenses. She epitomized the tough Texan attitude. I was nervous at this point, but my main concern was getting bailed out and getting my freedom back. I wanted to put this out of my head. I knew this could take months, possibly even years. I knew the longer it would take, the larger my sentence. I was going away for at least a few years, barring some miracles.

My fellow inmates advised that we should get a lawyer within the same court system because the Texas judicial system was tough and bringing an out of state lawyer wouldn't be taken well by the court officials.

I didn't know when I was going to get bailed out. There was no certainty and the waiting process sucked. I knew the day would come, but when you expect something to happen, the minutes feel like hours, and the hours feel like days. The worst part about this was that I knew I would be making multiple trips back to Texas for my trial, my sentencing, and ultimately my fate. I'd better get comfortable with Texas. I was going to relive this nightmare over and over.

One day, as I was making my way back to the common area, I finally heard the words I was anticipating, "Mr. Ali, you're processed!" There was a sudden roar amongst the inmates. Multiple inmates bum rushed me and started congratulating me like I won the lottery or something. My family arrived and I was relieved to go home. The whole booking process was painful. My family had to wait hours while I was getting released. While I was getting processed, I thought they would see me with cuffs and my orange jumpsuit. That would have been a lasting image my mother would never forget. Her son the criminal. The first people I saw were my mom and brother-in-law. I could tell my mom was scared, worried, and tired. She didn't sleep for days and, why should she? I had put her through hell. She had begged me not to go to Mexico and I knew exactly why. It was a mother's intuition and I should have listened. Knucklehead philosophy, I guess!

After we left, I told my mom I needed to drive home. The three of us promised each other that we would finish this journey together no matter what. My family insisted I ditch my car with the other two guys and head home on the plane. Once again, I ignored their advice. It was my car and I wanted to make sure it made it home in one piece. I should have listened because our nightmare had just begun. You would think we had been through enough, but getting home was the second battle. All three of us got released at the same time and headed back to Chicago. My family went back to the airport and headed home. I remember having this strange feeling that this dreadful experience wasn't over yet.

Row

Our last task was to visit our parole officer. He went through the drill of checking in weekly and made sure we understood the ramifications if we didn't comply. If we fled and didn't face our sentences, warrants would go out for our arrests and bounty hunters would stalk us down. After we left the parole office, I kissed my mother good-bye and left. My mother, as frightened as she was, showed no sign of distress. As usual, she was strong in the face of adversity.

We were traveling through Oklahoma and then through Missouri, making some good progress. The car was running smoothly. We were a defeated crew and just wanted to get home.

It was going to be creatine cocktails all summer, but that was the last thing on my mind. We just wanted to finish this journey in one piece because our families were waiting for us to get home. We didn't say much to each other. There wasn't much to say. We committed a crime and knew we weren't closing this chapter of our life. It had just begun, but we wanted to turn the page and get home. We didn't want to get into any more trouble because we were on the verge of taking out our anger on something, or someone. We were on edge and tempers were flaring. We were trying our best to keep our composure, but, boy, was that hard.

We were switching off driving every few hours. When it was my turn, the other two were sleeping and it was getting late. I was exhausted but stopping for a rest break was not in the itinerary.

My eyes were getting heavier and heavier. I started to daydream about this whole treacherous experience and how it could easily have been negated if I had listened to my parents.

Suddenly, I lost control of my vehicle. We were on the freeway heading north-bound and next thing I knew, we were on the shoulder of the road heading straight into a ditch. I quickly gathered myself and started to maneuver off the shoulder, but it was too late. My car was traveling seventy miles per hour and it darted into the abyss. I was struggling to regain composure, but luckily eluded the guardrail. My car skidded off the road into open pastures. I was still traveling fifty miles per hour off road into a long stretch of greenery. Once again, we were fortunate; my car landed in an open landscape. A few hundred feet ahead of us was a bridge with a 200-foot cliff. It was the first time I fell asleep at the wheel. It was an uneasy feeling, especially when you have other people in the car relying on you to get them home safely. We ended up driving in a farm field, but it could have easily been off the cliff. The car finally came to a halt between two trees.

It was a horrific experience thinking about how fortunate we were that I didn't drive us off a cliff. I couldn't imagine what my teammates were thinking. How could they trust me to drive again? We were still hours away from reaching Illinois and then another ten hours from the southern tip of Illinois to Chicago. Our journey was only half complete, with another day of driving ahead of us.

We agreed that I relinquish the wheel and catch some z's. In fact, we all agreed to stop at a hotel. We hadn't had a decent shower in over a week. Our clothes were dirty, wrinkled, and we smelled like death. We stumbled into a dingy hotel, seeking refuge. The front desk manager on duty took one look at us and turned us away immediately. I was wearing the prison wrist tag and he noticed. We pleaded that we'd had the week from hell and were just looking for a warm shower and soft bed. He told us to take a walk and that he would call the police if we came back. We took the walk of shame back to the car with our tails between our legs.

We decided that it was too late to continue driving around and getting off route looking for a hotel. At this point we were exhausted and decided to sleep in the car.

The sky was gloomy and a storm was brewing, so I imagined we rested at a good time. We were all shattered and we didn't say much to each other while we were in the car. We were collectively pissed off not at the fact that we were rejected at a Holiday Inn, but at all the bad luck we had been having. This was literally the trip from hell.

It was difficult getting sleep in the car, but we managed to get a few hours. We woke up the next morning around 5 a.m. and wanted to get back out on the road. We downed some protein shakes and headed back out. The sky was still dark and rain was on the horizon.

Today was the day I was going to lie in my own bed. Home at last and this nightmare was going to end for the time being. I couldn't wait to get home and see my family.

Before I knew it, there was a full-on downpour. The rain was coming down hard within a few minutes. We all understood the importance of this day and slowing down was not an option. The rain wasn't ceasing and there were only a

Row

few cars on the freeway now. The roads started to disappear in the fog. The darkness in the sky was yelling at us to seek shelter. We did not want to mess with Mother Nature, but we also needed to keep pursuing our goal of getting home. Unfortunately, we were taking a beating, but we were hoping we were going to land the knockout punch and the storm would cease.

That did not happen and the rain came down harder and harder. It was two hours into the storm and we had to stop. We couldn't see anymore and it was becoming extremely dangerous. The storm was roaring, causing us to stop and examine whether we wanted to continue.

We were lucky thus far to reach all the way to Cairo, Illinois, only six hours outside of Chicago. We were nearly home as the rain continued, but we didn't consider the condition of my vehicle.

The rain finally subsided after six hours. The roads were flooded and desolate. We parked at a nearby gas station in Cairo, but due to the weather conditions, the station was closed. We were zombies at that point, but we knew that the storm could come back any second.

It was finally time to go home. I went to start the car, and nothing, not even a flicker! The engine would not even turn over. The engine was completely flooded. The lights wouldn't even turn on. The car was dead. After traveling all these miles continuously, going off road, and driving through these hellish conditions, the car threw in the white towel.

We were stranded in Cairo, with very little money. Just like the car, we were getting close to throwing in the towel, too.

I was already two weeks behind on my summer program, a criminal, and now I was losing my car. Not to mention some disciplinary action by the NCAA. Now we had to figure out a way to scrap the car and get a ride back home.

Tempers were at an all-time high. Nobody wanted to look at each other, let alone speak to each other.

Panic and fear turned to anger, and all three of us started pointing fingers. No more polite, positive reinforcement about getting home and putting this behind us. Now it was, "Who put this atrocious plan together and why didn't we plan better?" We were all aggravated, agitated, and appalled. I felt I lost the most in this stupid, irrational endeavor.

We had to wait over three hours before the gas station finally opened. I called the local junkyard to take the car. I got a measly $100 for it. So, there I was, convicted of a felony, dirty, tired, without my car, unable to get a hotel room, and stranded hundreds of miles from home. After I sold the car and watched my summer transportation disappear, we had to find a ride home. We weren't exactly the popular kids amongst our parents, but luckily my teammate's father was willing to pick us up.

When he arrived, we didn't say much to each other. At this point, all I wanted was to see the back of these guys and crawl into my bed.

I realized the repercussions of my actions that summer and recognized the trouble I was in. If convicted, we were looking at years in a Texas state penitentiary.

I made several trips back to Texas that year. I had my arraignment and then would receive my judgment. I listened to the inmates and hired a local Texan who knew our judge very well. He told me that since it was my first offense and I was a college student and athlete; my sentencing could be reduced from distribution to consumption. After all, Texas loves football and their football players!

The day of reckoning arrived and when I stepped on the stand to receive my judgement I was trembling. My lawyer already briefed me on my sentence, but trust was not something I was willing to grant a slimy lawyer I barely knew. When the judge passed down my sentence she gave me a gold-plated key and warned me that If I ever had any inclination to commit another crime, I should look at the key because that was the key to my cell.

She dropped my felony to a misdemeanor; I was looking at one thousand hours of community service, a hefty fine, and 1-year probation. That was a slap on the wrist compared to my initial charges. We weren't criminals and the judge knew that. We were kids that made a mistake and didn't deserve to spend hard time in a penitentiary. Having a felony on our records would have ruined our lives and made it extremely difficult to establish careers after college. She gave us a second chance. Hallelujah!

After our trial, we all went home for the summer. We could finally put this nightmare behind us and learned a valuable lesson about how quickly a dumb decision could change the direction of our lives. If that judge had wanted to make an example out of the three of us, we could have been sent away for a very long time.

All in all, this whole nightmare took four months.

DAY 11 JAIL JOURNAL: HIGH TIMES

"I'll die young, but it's like kissing God."
— Lenny Bruce, on his addiction to opioids

I don't have much to rap about today. Frustrating! I want to grab one of these robocops by the throat. Wannabe tough guys selling wolf tickets. Talkin' outside the side of their necks like I am some punk. I would love to bury some of these maggots.

❖

The above quote is the epitome of how I lived my life in my twenties. "Life in the fast lane, sure to make you blow your mind," like the song goes, sung by the Eagles.

To live life on razor's edge, you must exercise rebellion. I was a self-appointed crash test dummy, not knowing when to throw in the towel. I liked living life on the edge, walking towards the cliff not knowing how to swim in the water below. I like to say that I lived my life to the fullest, but I made a lot of dumb mistakes along the way.

In the 2000s, there was an opioid drug epidemic ravaging the US. Drug overdoses were the leading cause of death, with 52,404 deaths in 2015. Prescription opioid drugs were the most common cause of death, over HIV and homicide. Physicians were prescribing narcotics to patients like candy, padding their own pockets in the process. Some were going to jail for malpractice for prescribing unsolicited amounts of drugs to patients. It wasn't street drugs that were devouring the nation anymore, but the introduction of prescription opioids. The big pharma corporations were pushing doctors to prescribe drugs like Oxycontin, Vicodin, morphine, Percocet, Dilaudid, and a host of others. There were medical advances in pain management and these were the medications that were dispensed. For many of the patients dealing with pain, opiates were the holy grail. It wasn't the Pablo

147

Row

Escobars and Griselda Blancos slinging mass quantities of narcotics into the states. It was our very own corrupt white coats that have long been hailed as heroes.

Manufacturers, pharmacies, and doctors were all profiting like a billion-dollar crime syndicate. There were commercials on the tube advocating these drugs as a non-addicting form of chronic pain relief. Patients with chronic pain were being cured of their ailments and starting to live normal lives, while the medical industry was profiting by the billions. Opioids not only helped relieve pain, but also produced pleasurable effects in the brain. It was a win-win for everyone right?

That was all fine and dandy, but patients were not clued in about the lasting effect, and addiction was soon to follow. When the pain subsided, the addiction kicked in and that was far worse than any surgery. In 2012, 259 million prescriptions were written for opioids, which is enough to give every adult their own bottle of pills.

We spent billions of dollars on sending our troops to Afghanistan, trying to kill the ultimate villain, Osama Bin Laden, who supposedly led the 9/11 attacks killing thousands. This mass murderer was not only behind the terrorist attacks of 9/11, but also behind ambush killing of other human beings. The attacks to our beloved country killed thousands of innocent civilians, while leaving our economy in a mist of chaos.

We were so hell-bent on revenge that we failed to realize that the number one killer to Americans is not terrorist activity. Terrorists can blow up hundreds of buildings and it won't even come close to the annihilation caused by drugs.

Americans overdose by the thousands every year. It's happening right on our front door and nobody does a damn thing about it. Why? Because drug distribution is highly profitable and the margins are substantial. Granted, there are the Drug Enforcement Agency, Federal Bureau of Investigation, and police officers patrolling the streets trying to rid America of this epidemic, but it is too little too late. Law enforcement could only put a band-aid on this bullet wound. Too much blood has already been spilled. The damage has been done and the almighty dollar is too powerful to rid the world of these kingpins.

❖

DAY 11: HIGH TIMES

The truth of the matter is that we all love drugs. This is going to shock a lot of people who know me and read this, but I am a huge fan.

In my twenties I was always chasing the high, chasing the dream of having a flawless physique and being high while doing it. I wanted to live like a rock star, be feared like a serial killer, be respected like a mob boss, and be loved like a newborn baby. I always told myself I was doing nothing wrong, but I was slamming needles in my arm every day. Sometimes I would be in the bathroom slamming the needle into my arm, desperate to find a vein so I could get that euphoria I craved. I didn't think I was doing anything wrong, but when I looked at my arms it was easy to see that I was a junkie. I wasn't a hardcore junkie. Well, that was what I believed.

Reminiscing about my past always put me in a state of denial. I always told myself junkies were homeless, sleeping in abandoned buildings, feening for their fix. Nope, they were everyday people. You could be sitting next to one on the bus and not even know it.

Looking back, I didn't realize the damage I was doing to my body. I was training like a madman twice a day to become the best and then banging needles in my arm sometimes four to five times a day. I was a thrill seeker, enjoying the chase, and I didn't care what the consequences were. Who cares about a little drug abuse when I am working, paying my bills, and taking care of business? We all have our skeletons, right?

I never let anyone know about my addiction. I never let anyone know about my deep secrets. I lived a solitary existence, secluded from the outside world. I never let anyone get too close. I was a rebel without a cause. I traveled the road less travelled, which turned out to be my own path of destruction. Even though nobody truly knew me, I knew me, and I knew what I was doing was wrong. But I didn't care. Not a lot of people understood Evel Knievel and his ridiculous acts of courage. Not a lot of people understood how a Frenchman, Philippe Petit, wanted to walk on a wire between the New York Twin Towers. It was to do whatever they wanted, whenever they wanted, regardless of what people thought about any of their endeavors. They were journeymen chasing the ultimate thrill. I was much the same on a much smaller scale. When I was pumping iron and winning state titles nobody questioned me. I guess nobody knew.

My addiction was my business and I didn't want to open the doors to anyone. I always kept that piece of my life private because I knew it was going to bring a lot of criticism. I got enough of that in bodybuilding. You try to train as hard as I did, endure the breaks, pulls, and tears, and sometimes you want to relieve that pain instantly by self-medicating by any means necessary. By ANY means necessary!

My drug years were a span of eight years on and off, maybe longer. Like most, it was a time when I wanted to experiment like a hippie did in the 60s. It was also a time when I thought that I was indestructible.

Nothing could hurt me and nobody could tell me what to do. I was ignorant to say the least. During those times, I didn't care if I lived or died and I wasn't scared of anything. In retrospect, I was a young punk that didn't know the true meaning of life. I devalued life, making decisions that would put me in compromising situations. I didn't learn from the trip to Mexico. The gold-plated key the judge gave me was just a toy that hung from my neck.

I wanted to think I was tough, but I didn't know the true meaning of having responsibility and taking care of something or someone. That was the definition of tough, I realize now.

I will try my best to explain some of the drugs that I experimented with and how they made me feel, but it has been a long time since I have taken anything. I've tried to eliminate these thoughts from my mind, but I think it is important to explain to my friends and family during my last few days. When I was taking my drug of choice I never thought of myself as a junkie, but I was. I was a prisoner to whatever I was on.

Sitting in my first Narcotics Anonymous meeting, I realized my infatuation with drugs was not different from others. Their vices were just like mine. Their daily struggles maintaining a sober lifestyle were like mine. I knew without a doubt that if I continued this path of self-destruction, I would be dead. I envisioned each moment cherishing the outdoors, traveling great lengths, and accomplishing my life goals, sober. I didn't have to push one hundred-pound dumbbells anymore. I was never a belligerent abuser and people around me during that chapter in my life could not have imagined that I was using.

I am fortunate to have been imprisoned sober. There are a lot of inmates that get pinched while addicted to a drug. Their first few weeks in prison are sheer torture, going through withdrawals while confined to their cell. There is no assistance as they are living in misery, shaking, vomiting, and withering away in agony.

Once you start taking drugs for the wrong reason you won't stop. I even went to the extent of mainlining vodka. Yes, the alcoholic beverage, vodka. I saw a documentary on Motley Crue being so strung out on heroin they would inject vodka just so they could get satisfaction from injecting into their veins and drawing blood. They hit rock bottom, trying to crawl out of the basement, and struggling from relapsing. I never understood why anyone would inject something into their vein if they weren't going to obtain that euphoric release.

I realized quickly how good it felt injecting and pulling back the needle, watching the blood rush into the insulin needle. Minutes before I would train, I would pull back the shaft and plunge one hundred units of vodka into my bloodstream and the burning sensation would set in immediately. It was excruciating pain, but exhilarating at the same time. As you're injecting, the burning sensation pulsates like a hot iron penetrating the skin. It hurts like a mother beep!

When you get strung out on drugs, you can never get enough. The more you use, the more you want, and that is when the addiction sets in, like fungus settling on fruit. The drug consumes you, and every day is a struggle trying to get your fix.

If you have never mainlined drugs before you have no idea. I started my addiction as normal addicts would. You take your first hit of something light, and then you start hitting harder drugs. It's the circle of life for an addict. I started taking painkillers and never realized how addictive opiates were. I was addicted within weeks of regularly taking Vicodin. I got Vicodin from pain doctors and low-level street pushers who had a few lying around and wanted to make a quick buck.

I remember the days that I got off Vicodin, how horrific I felt. Vicodin is classified as a mild narcotic. When I stopped taking Vicodin cold turkey, I had no clue what withdrawals were. I remember calling a friend and questioning him about why the hell I felt so terrible. I was depressed and couldn't get out of bed. My muscles in my whole body were aching. He told me that I was going through withdrawals. I started looking up the term "withdrawals" and thought I was going to die. Cold sweats, nose running, diarrhea, throwing up, and muscle cramps were just some of the symptoms I was experiencing. The scariest part of this whole ordeal was that I did not know how long I was going to feel this way.

Next up on the hit list was a drug called Nubain. Nubain is a narcotic to treat moderate to severe pain after surgery or childbirth. I wanted something that would take away the pain during those strenuous training sessions and function every day. During my bodybuilding days, I was introduced to Nubain. This was another pain medicine that a gym acquaintance introduced me to. He would be able to get boxes and boxes from the pharmacy so he was always stocked. He advised it was a lot stronger than Vicodin and I could form an addiction quickly. At the time, I couldn't care less because I was feeling terrible. Plus, winning is all I cared about. So, there I was, taking a new drug that was more potent. I knew nothing about Nubain, nor did I care. I just wanted to stop being in pain. Lifting thousands of pounds continuously day in and day out paralyzed my body. I needed something to take the edge off and continue training hard.

My acquaintance at the gym could get Nubain whenever he wanted. He was reliable, and he was the only one I knew selling Nubain. I couldn't resist. He was also in the bodybuilding scene, so, as I did well in competitions and built my brand, he would slip me a freebie here and there. We formed somewhat of a friendship. We even trained a few times together. If I needed him to meet me somewhere, he was there. When I was a little light, he spotted me a kit on the house. He was a huge advocate of my bodybuilding career and wanted me to succeed. Now, whether he cared if he was feeding my addiction, I don't know, but he was making $100-$200 every time I paid him a visit.

Nubain was the only drug that I could get my hands on at the time, but if smack had been an option, I would have probably experimented with that stuff. That would have been the worst mistake I could have made because once you are on smack, the percentage of people that get off is slim. The only ways you get off smack are by being behind bars or in a casket.

Nubain comes from the opiate family and can be mainlined or taken in the muscle. I started taking it by pinching my stomach and injecting it in the fatty tissue, but then I wanted a bigger high and started mainlining it. I would purchase two to three kits at a time for $300. Each kit came in ten crack-off ampules containing twenty mg in each ampule. I didn't only enjoy the high from Nubain. It was also an unparalleled pain med. I am sorry, but glutamine and amino acids didn't do the trick.

The first time I bought Nubain, it came in a 10cc bottle, and I took about one cc in my stomach. Within minutes, I felt a rush of euphoria. It was climactic and I couldn't get enough. The euphoria was inexplicable. I had never felt like that before, not even on Vicodin. Vicodin has a slow release, but Nubain hits you like a Mack truck. Nubain was the answer to all my problems; it masked all my pain, nobody knew I was on it, and I was always on cloud nine. My injuries from years of working out, performing labor-intensive jobs, and playing all manner of sports imaginable were no longer an issue. I won the lottery with this stuff!

I didn't want to tell anyone my secret. Nobody needed to know what I was taking. The only reason people in the gym scene were talking to me anyway was because of my accomplishments on stage. When I got incarcerated, I never got a phone call, letter, or visit. Nothing! I quickly realized that I didn't have any true friends in the bodybuilding world. All the people I met were consumed by their own self-interest. All those man hugs and congratulatory exchanges were superficial. Everybody was around for the ride. If I had a dollar for every time someone came up to me and sparked a conversation leading to a conversation about bodybuilding, I would be a millionaire, straight up.

The drug was expensive, but I could afford it. Plus, when your so-called friend is a local drug dealer, Nubain was always on tap. I had no worries — except that if my source went dry, I would have bigger problems than before. Trust me, Nubain withdrawals are no joke. The stuff you see in movies about addicts trying to get clean, running out of money, losing their connection, and stopping cold turkey are all true. Addicts throwing up, shitting on themselves, and foaming at the mouth? Those side effects are all true. I can go on and on. It is sheer torture. Forget about it.

Ever seen the movie *Basketball Diaries* with Leonardo DiCaprio? Leonardo DiCaprio hit the nail on the head with his portrayal of a heroin addict going through withdrawal. His depiction of agony and torment while locked away in Reggie's dingy one-bedroom abode, pleading for one more hit depicted the real mental anguish an opioid addict faces.

Row

He was foaming at the mouth, crawling out of his skin, fighting an endless battle, and craving just a taste to curb his withdrawal symptoms. After weeks, his symptoms finally subsided.

What fascinates me is when people say things like, "Oh, I would never get addicted to drugs," or "If I did get addicted, I would just get off." I have seen some of the hardest dudes crying because they were going through withdrawals. One of my oldest friends asked his friend to lock him in his basement and not let him out until he was clean. That lasted for about a day and the poor bastard broke down the door. I was there trying to force him back in the basement, but to no avail.

I thought Nubain was the best painkiller out there, but it's filthy. It's filthy in a sense that you can get addicted very easily and your tolerance becomes high extremely quickly. I began shooting eighty IUs a day and before long, I was up to 100 IUs twice a day. My tolerance got as high as 300 IUs twice a day. That is more than half a bottle, coming out to sixty bucks a day worth of Nubain.

Nubain was strong. It was probably as strong as morphine or methadone. They give women in labor Nubain, so that should tell you this stuff was legit and did the trick. After about six months of use, I started taking Nubain every day, three to four times per day. I wasn't taking it for bodybuilding anymore. I was taking it for the high like a piranha chasing a gold fish. The high of playing college ball, competing on the bodybuilding stage, lifting more than anyone in the gym, working every day, sponsorships, businesses, or the high of sticking a needle in my arm; it was just part of my pathetic life. I had an addictive personality and had all the drugs I wanted right at my disposal. It was hard to say no when it was right in my face. I knew all the bad side effects. I knew I was entering a dark room, flirting with disaster, but at that time in my life, chasing the dream and winning at all costs outweighed anything else. I was selfish, what can I say?

After a while, I stopped thinking about anything except for getting high. I was calling my dealer every two weeks. Most dealers were difficult to get a hold of and addicts had to play by their rules. If they wanted to meet in another state, then guess what? I drove to another state. My guy was my friend and easy to get a hold of. I would be able to call him and meet him that same day.

The source of the problem was my juice. I was always making a bankroll. Sitting in my cell now, I contemplate how much money I would have if I never touched any recreational drugs. I was living the high life, plummeting off the deep end in shark-infested waters. I couldn't be contained. Even though I was working and living on my own, it was hard to maintain my tolerance.

❖

When I said Nubain was filthy I wasn't playin'. Combining Nubain with another drug was entering the devil's playground. Damn right, stupid. Believe me, I went through it plunging into a blazing inferno. The term for this was "precipitated withdrawal," which means "pure misery." Precipitated withdrawal is when an opioid-dependent user takes an opioid antagonist like buprenorphine. Basically combining two powerful drugs.

I made the mistake of combining Nubain and methadone, which put me in precipitated withdrawal. This was insane and foolish. I walked through the gates of hell and looked the devil right in the face. I learned a valuable lesson that day, and that was how dangerous these chemicals were to my body.

I was clueless about what was going on, thinking I was dying. I was in my car ready to kamikaze into a birch wood so I could be seen by a doctor. It was crazy!

It all began around 8 p.m. I entered my sanctuary after a hard day of work and training legs. My gas tank was on empty. All I could think about was cracking off the top of the vial of Nubain and positioning the syringe in the liquid. The clouds were grey outside, amidst a downpour. I envisioned chasing the ultimate high all day, combining whatever chemicals I could get my hands on, trying to get some jubilation. For some reason Nubain wasn't good enough. I needed to stack it with something. Always pushing the envelope.

Excitement was rushing all through my body in anticipation. I anticipated the ultimate high, which for an addict was supreme. It was supposed to be the most electrifying, euphoric feeling that I ever had.

Without doing any research, I took ten mg of methadone, chased by mainlining a full ampule of Nubain. I stabbed the needle in my vein, pulled back and watched the blood rush into the syringe. Then I slowly plunged the liquid into my vein. Pure ecstasy!

Uh oh! Something was terribly wrong. The euphoric feeling quickly disappeared and I was consumed by a sudden hot spell. It felt like my body temperature went up twenty degrees in seconds and I felt my whole body getting tight, followed by severe cramps that left me handicapped on the ground. I was trapped in my home, alone and in sheer agony. I was puking, having diarrhea, intermittently getting hot and cold sweats and experiencing cramps. My bathroom floor was covered in puke as I was unleashing in the toilet. I thought that my life was over. I thought that I had received some bad gear and I was overdosing.

I was naïve thinking that combining the two would be a mind blowing, orgasmic high. Within seconds of taking the Nubain, it felt like someone was lighting me on fire. My bathroom was a disaster zone. I was having a panic attack, shaking uncontrollably, and it felt like I was staring death in the face.

After minutes, which seemed like an eternity, I scraped myself up from the floor. I felt like I'd been hit by a 250-pound fullback. Vomit was dripping from my lips and sweat beads from my forehead. Veins from my forearms and neck were bulging. I gathered my clothes and stumbled outside to my car, leaving my bathroom in disarray. My withdrawals were so intense at that point that my vision was blurry as the rain started to pound the pavement. Seconds later, I was stuck in a downpour. I started to make my way to the hospital, my car swerving in and out of lanes. I had visions of destroying my car just so I could get some medical attention. I couldn't stomach going to the ER and admitting myself as a drug user, but I had no choice. This was my only option. I only made it about a mile down the road when my car slammed into the curb. My forehead smashed against the steering wheel violently. I felt a cold liquid sensation dripping from my forehead and realized I had a laceration on my forehead.

Bloodied, bruised, and covered in my own vomit, I ended up rethinking the plan and headed back to the crib. If I was overdosing I didn't have enough time to make it to a hospital. Once I pulled into the driveway, I called a friend, fumbling as I tried to dial the numbers. He heard my voice and came right over. Within minutes, he was banging on my door like a bounty hunter. I put my full trust in him because I didn't have another choice. He rushed over and witnessed me in a severe state. I was sweating profusely in the dead of winter and shaking hysterically. The symptoms were getting worse. My eyes were still glazed and my nose was running like a faucet. My friend laid me down, gave me ice-cold water, and wrapped me up in blankets. He knew the anguish I was going through. He turned the television on and sat right next to me while I drifted away in deep sleep. I woke up about twenty minutes later and he was still sitting next to me. The withdrawals were still prevalent, but nowhere near as severe. He was an addict and knew how dangerous precipitated withdrawal could be. He rode that roller coaster many times.

A few hours later, the withdrawal symptoms subsided and my body temperature stabilized. I don't know what I would have done without him. Later, I found out about precipitated withdrawal and why it was so stupid for me to combine two powerful opiates. It has been said that people have died going through precipitated withdrawal. Instead of obtaining the high of my life, I spiraled into my worst nightmare. The chemical reaction I experienced could have been fatal. I will never forget that experience; it scared the hell out of me, but, unfortunately, not enough to stop.

There was nothing like indulging in morphine for the first time. I no longer had virgin veins. It was easy to cover them up with vascularity and bulging muscles. Most experience morphine at a hospital, dealing with some sort of pain ailment. Not me. I was a morphine junkie getting my fix at gyms from power lifters, bodybuilders, and straight up gangsters. I even knew someone who was on a large cocktail of medications and suffering from chronic pain. What helped me build up my street credit was my physique, which did a lot of the talking. I didn't fit the mold of a junkie, but, believe me, before the pills, I was injecting up to three to four times a day. Morphine, on the one hand, was the opiate of opiates, but, on the other hand, it was also extremely expensive and difficult to find on the street. Low-level street hustlers weren't slinging that type of medication. Only top-level suppliers were dispensing morphine.

My morphine addiction was short lived, but what a ride. It was like taking the plunge off a cliff in Negril, Jamaica, or jumping out of a plane in the vast lands of the United Arab Emirates. The sheer ecstasy of morphine was a thrill ride. Cliff diving had its merits. Skydiving, like the Road Warrior Hawk would say, "Ohhhhh what a rush." Morphine was superior to those feats and, believe me when I say this, if I was outside these concrete walls and you put a bottle of morphine in front of me, I would spoil my ten-year sobriety in a heartbeat. Forget about it. You don't walk away from orgasmic highs like that. Why? Because you don't get them too many times in life.

Row

Mainlining morphine was a high indescribable. Granted, the high only lasts a few minutes, but those few minutes were like liquid elation. I traveled far and wide to experience that jubilation. As soon as the liquid struck my blood stream, I went into a dream state, experiencing complete euphoria. My pain vanished and I started reflecting on greener pastures. I would score the pills from my dealer and hurry home. I knew how great the feeling was so it was hard to contain myself, but those few minutes felt like an eternity. I crushed the pills into a powder and mixed it with a teaspoon of bacteriostatic water into a spoon. I warmed up the bottom of the spoon and watched the white liquid bubble, ready to export into the syringe. I took a cotton swab, soaking up all the liquid, allowing the syringe to fill up with liquid bliss. This was my favorite part of the process, watching the cloudy liquid explode into the syringe. I know it like the back of my hand.

Once all the liquid was in the syringe, I was ready to ride the shock wave to paradise. The anticipation was unbearable. Exhilaration was already kicking in, as I'm waiting to inject liquid heaven into my arm. To an addict, the anticipation was like the foreplay leading to that bite of the forbidden fruit. I wouldn't take that feeling away for anything in the world, as I would be plummeting into pure excitement. Like I said before, once you're an addict, you will always be an addict.

I kicked my morphine fix pretty quickly but jumped on my next vice, which spiraled me back into the jungle.

Methadone was another opiate pain reliever that I dabbled with during my knucklehead years. Methadone was like making a deal with the prince of darkness. It will rob you of your soul and leave you jobless, moneyless, and family-less. Getting off methadone was one of the biggest challenges I ever faced in life. It was a constant battle with addiction and the everyday ups and downs were difficult.

Methadone handicaps addicts and leaves them never capable of getting off opiates. Addicts become lifelong methadone addicts, chained to outpatient clinics. Many addicts remain on methadone for years, trying to kick their habit. Methadone, unlike other opioids, stays in your bloodstream longer so when a prescribed patient's pain wears off, the drug hasn't. It can lead to overdose, respiratory failure, and even death. Methadone is said to stay in a user's blood stream for up to 59 hours.

Day 11: High Times

I was prescribed methadone with multiple refills when I pulled my hamstring a few weeks into training for my bodybuilding competition in 2005. I was performing leg curls and felt a strain. I decided to perform a few more repetitions and then felt a severe pull. It felt like knives were stabbing the back of my leg. My hamstring bruised instantly and I made the decision to continue to train, which made the injury worse. I have pulled my hamstring over a dozen times and it's hampered my training. I didn't have time to kill on a little pulled muscle.

I decided to see a physician and told him that I pulled a hamstring while training. He asked what my pain was on a scale of one to ten. I gave him a number and walked out with a prescription for methadone with a refill. Good ole U.S.A. Unbelievable! He told me good luck with my bodybuilding career, probably thinking I would be back to see him in a few weeks, begging for more.

When I asked, why methadone, he told me not to worry. If I took it properly under his guidance, I wouldn't gain a dependence. Well, that was false, because after sixty ten milligram pills, I was hooked. My hamstring healed, but now I had to deal with another vice, an addiction to methadone. I reached out to the prescribing physician, stating that I took the medication as prescribed and now I was going through withdrawals. I was advised to check into a methadone clinic and they would help me lower my dose and eventually get clean. Click! That same physician has probably prescribed methadone to thousands of patients, lining his pockets. Yet the DEA is going after Gulf Cartel, Zetas, and Knights Templar Cartel, when the real enemy is right at our doorstep. White coat told me that my symptoms were not uncommon and since I wasn't a heavy drug user, my withdrawal symptoms would subside after a few days. What a load of crap.

Fortunately, I had pills left and I slowly weaned myself off, which was a painstaking process taking over three months. I was left in the cold, trying to get off the prescribed medication on my own. There wasn't a lot of material on the Internet to help me get off the drug. I adhered to the prescribed medication and was left in a tailspin. I could only imagine how challenging it is for longtime heroin users to get off the drug.

Next on the hit list!

My longest battle with addiction was with Suboxone, a deadly narcotic used to assist patients with other opiate addictions and assist with mitigating chronic pain. Suboxone was introduced in the 80s, but didn't make it big until the opiate epidemic started in the early 90s. Back then there was no proper guide on how to take Suboxone. There still isn't a proper guide on how to take it. I see cons trying to dilute it and then slam into their arm, drink it, snort it, you name it.

Suboxone, like any other opiate, has awful side effects, especially when you start weaning yourself. Out of all the opiate cocktails I took, Suboxone was the only narcotic that kept me relapsing over and over. I couldn't get the monkey off my back.

Suboxone gets a hold of you and doesn't let you go, like an anaconda wrapping its coils around your body and squeezing the life out of you second by second.

A lot of drug users took Suboxone after getting off harsh drugs like heroin and Oxycontin. The reason why doctors had been prescribing this medication was that it has a longer half-life, which means that it stays in your body for a longer period than heroin. Therefore, you won't go into withdrawals as quickly while taking Suboxone because of the longer half-life, meaning less frequent dosages. Also, drugs like heroin can be injected, inhaled, snorted, or smoked. All these ways can kill you on the spot. Suboxone was taken sublingually under the tongue, which was much safer. Yeah right. It is also much easier to get Suboxone than other opiates like Percocet or morphine.

I was prescribed Suboxone for pain relief. I felt like an old dog ready to be put down. The process of getting Suboxone was much easier than driving 80 miles to obscure locations. I would go to the nurse at the outpatient every month, wait thirty minutes, and within an hour I would have my prescription in my hand and head to the pharmacy. It was simple.

I recall the first time I tried to wean myself off Suboxone. I started at 16 mg. and slowly worked my way down in two months. My last dose was a small film I placed under my tongue, much less than 1 mg. I had to take tweezers to insert it under my tongue. That was how small my dose was.

I still couldn't wean myself off and within twenty-four hours I was shaking uncontrollably with severe muscle aches. Suboxone withdrawal has been categorized as worse than heroin withdrawal. It was unbelievable that something so small can take over your life and that was what it did to me.

Day 11: High Times

I started taking Suboxone when I was in dire need of pain medication. My body was yelling at me that enough was enough.

When I initially went to a physician to discuss pain management, I told the doctor I didn't want any medication that was addictive, or anything that would get me high. He wrote me a prescription for Suboxone and told me I could take it for thirty days as a trial and see if it helped me with my pain. He wrote me a prescription for 16 mg daily for thirty days.

I eagerly took the medication and it worked wonders for my pain but left me in an opiate-induced stupor, constipated, constantly falling asleep, and unable to consume any food. I took eight mgs in the morning and eight mgs at night. I could fall asleep anywhere, anytime. Both work and my workouts suffered, as I was lethargic all day long. I was concerned, but the doctor was confident that this would alleviate my pain without getting addicted. I questioned the method as well as the sizeable dose. I explained I didn't have an appetite and the little I ate made me vomit. It was worth it, though, as I put all my trust in the doctor, and if this would cure my chronic pain, I was all for it. No pain, no gain, right? Knucklehead philosophy!

Lo and behold, thirty days in, I was addicted like a two-bit crack whore. I went back for my follow-up, and the doctor didn't blink at writing another thirty-day prescription. Jackpot! He had completely ignored what I said about taking addictive medication. He had completely ignored the fact that I wasn't eating, I was lethargic all day, and I was constipated. In fact, he tried to get me on another drug called Nuvigil, which was a stimulant that could assist with the fatigue. I stated that the reason why I was experiencing overwhelming daytime drowsiness was because of the Suboxone. That was the last time I saw that doctor. When I needed a refill, I would see a nurse practitioner who wrote my monthly prescription. I guess I asked too many questions. Silly me.

I had already gotten myself off methadone, Nubain, morphine, Vicodin, so I thought Suboxone wouldn't be difficult. Years later, I still had the monkey on my back battling the addiction. I was a prisoner, self-medicating myself.

Just like Nubain, Suboxone was very accessible. It was not accessible from street level drug pushers, but from the men and women we hold to a higher standard in the medical profession. My health insurance covered the prescription and the nurse had no problem writing me a script, sometimes with refills. Every time I walked into that office I was a prisoner succumbing to the prescriber. I couldn't walk out of there without my prescription. Anyone who knows anything about narcotics knows that doctors should never write refills, especially for addicts.

Years later I was finally able to kick the habit. It took a good four months after my last dose to finally live normally. Depression, anxiety, restless shoulders and legs, insomnia, and that was just the start of my withdrawal symptoms. Not to mention constantly sneezing, diarrhea, glassy eyes, and muscle cramps. Get the picture? My mind and body craved that euphoric feeling I was getting from years of substance abuse, but I knew every day clean was a new day.

The drug game was not something you want to mess with. The lifespan of a drug abuser and drug dealer are short lived. You either end up in prison, or six feet under.

DAY 10 JAIL JOURNAL: COLD TURKEY

Listen up. There are a ton of casualties in my extraction from the world. You think taking my life is going to make things easier for my family and friends involved? No chance in hell.

It sucks living in these walls, wasting away, knowing I could make a difference in the free world, especially when I know I'm not repenting, but waiting for my destiny. I will be taking the back-door parole as they call it here.

I am so fed up with everything in my life. I survive in a white chamber, surviving on nothing, and knowing that I am wasting away. There are so many aspects of life that irritate me while I am incarcerated. So many things that I would love to change, but can't. I will never get an opportunity to make a difference anymore. What I did in my past is probably a distant memory for many. What I will be remembered for is what I did to get myself locked up.

I sit here in my cell this morning as the prison is on lockdown. The 411 was an Aryan Brother got into an altercation with a Mexican mafia member at chow hall. It was probably over something as minute as cutting in line, but you can't break the prison code of conduct. Cell block B erupted with a full out gang war. No casualties, but, believe me, this feud just started and there will be cons leaving on meat wagons. Death and destruction always follow the Aryan Brotherhood.

Violence is a daily occurrence in San Quentin. I hear about a stabbing almost once a week, but when you're on death row you're locked away from the prison violence. I rely on the newjacks outside my cell and their big mouths.

I have seen some crazy shit in here. It's not just the violence, but all the other crap that happens in the big house.

Row

During my first week at San Quentin, I was in my cellblock and another inmate in the cell across from me was puking his guts out. In prison, I mind my own business. I don't ask about anyone or anyone's situation. I keep my mouth shut and live one day at a time, or else danger will scope me out quicker than a needle finds a junkie's veins.

When he scraped his face from the toilet, I could see his pale, lifeless expression. He was going through withdrawal. He was living the nightmare that millions of Americans live every year. The same nightmare I lived. The diarrhea, vomiting, glassy eyes, running nose, constant sneezing, insomnia, muscle cramps, restlessness, shakes, and overall distress. That same expression was on my face not too long ago. He was dope sick, broken in half by heroin. His skin turned oily, eyes distorted, no hair, teeth rotten and missing. Heroin abuse took a toll on this man and I witnessed it.

He was a substantial heroin user and now he was trapped in a cell without his fix. Cold turkey! Before he got locked up he was slamming 1000 mgs of black tar heroin a day. His symptoms were only going to get worse and his troubles had just begun. I could see him trying to rock himself to sleep each night and then rushing to the toilet, spewing everywhere. I wanted to go there and help him, but I didn't want to be pigeonholed as a punk.

Withdrawals were a major reason why addicts stay on drugs. Addicts can't go through the pain of withdrawals. A lot of us don't have the coping mechanism. If you think you know how it feels to go through withdrawals, believe me, you have no idea. It can make the strongest soul crumble into ashes.

It feels like cutting yourself with a small razor blade thousands of times and letting the blood drip off your body one drop at a time, draining your body and putting you in a state of agony as you stare, paralyzed. That's what withdrawals feel like. It was sheer suffering all day long without any recourse. There was nothing I could do and there was nowhere to hide. My muscles ached all day long and my brain was in sheer trauma, screaming for it all to be over. It was the feeling of getting hit by a truck without anyone knowing how miserable I was. I have known friends who have gone through withdrawal who had to check into a rehab center. It was rock bottom with so-called "trained professionals" trying to figure you out and investigate the reasoning behind your abuse.

The word "withdrawal" will make an addict shiver with pain and discomfort. Waking up with severe depression each day, anxiously waiting for the agony to subside. Not knowing when the pain would subside, relying on stories from past recovering addicts. It was the hardest thing in the world. It's not a pain that I could relate to from a torn muscle or a broken bone. People I have spoken to say it's all in an addict's head and if they were ever to get addicted to a drug they would be able to easily get off. I wanted to smack those people in the face because of how many lives drugs have demolished.

When I broke a bone, I was in a state of suffering as pain receptors dealt with the break. I knew that my body would be able to bear the pain as days passed and the discomfort would subside. Withdrawal was completely different and drained my life one inch at a time by breaking my will. There was no turning back once I was in a state of withdrawal. I was in a deep hole, stuck without anyone there to help. My only savior was a little white pill or needle filled with liquid ecstasy. I would sell my soul for just one hit. I bet that inmate who lived across from me in cell block B would kill an Aryan Brother if a hit of heroin was dangling in front of him.

I was never going to write about withdrawals, but it was something that I went through repeatedly. Writing about withdrawals is difficult; re-living the helpless feeling of drowning in a pit of sorrow. Revisiting this phase in my life has been tough because it's like reliving rock bottom. I experienced the opposite effect from taking drugs as I did withdrawing. Often the lines were blurred between physical addiction and mental illness. The walls were closing in as I was paralyzed, trapped in confinement.

I didn't see the light at the end of the tunnel. I tried to scrape myself from the pavement, trying to live a normal life without the consumption of drugs.

Row

Withdrawals were the hardest affairs I ever faced. It wasn't playing football with a broken arm or getting ready for a bodybuilding competition with a torn bicep. None of those compared to going through withdrawals. The feeling you go through is inexplicable, but if you speak to anyone who has gone through it, they will tell you the same thing, "It is hell."

It felt like being run over by a truck and living through the pain without any medication. The pain and anguish was indescribable, as my body was in a state of panic and craving medication. Everyone on drugs is hiding past hardships in their lives and trying to mask the internal pain, not knowing the true suffering of weaning off the drugs that still lies ahead.

Saying I have an addictive personality was true, but being an addict was not something I was born with. I loved taking drugs and loved the euphoria of taking drugs. Part of the problem was I couldn't let go of great feelings and certain drugs made me feel on top of the world.

Nobody truly knew about my addiction and what I went through. It could turn a kind person into a monster. I wouldn't wish that grief upon my worst enemy. For those of you that have gone through withdrawals and dealing with addiction, I say keep hope alive and keep fighting. This chapter puts me in an uneasy state, reminiscing about my past turmoil and how difficult that stage of my life was. The good thing about withdrawal was that sooner or later it would end and you would start to feel somewhat normal, but once an addict, always an addict.

For me there was no such thing as getting off drugs cold turkey. I could not kick my habits, even though I tried several times. It was impossible and people have tried, but, ultimately, everyone succumbs to their poison. The torment can kill you. That's why there are so many treatment facilities in North America for addicts. Funny thing was these facilities are there to help you, but they cost a fortune. They get you at your lowest point, preying on the weak like vultures. When you're all beaten up and have very little to live for, they come and try to scoop you off the ground, emptying your bank account in the process.

I recall when I tried to seek assistance coming off methadone. I called a rehabilitation center based in Orlando, Florida. I was rudely interrupted and told to pay a $500 deposit as a sign of commitment. They then wanted me to book a flight to Florida and attend their recovery seminar. They would deem if I truly needed recovery. The agony in my voice wasn't good enough. The process of getting into their program would take five grueling days, which was an eternity for an addict going through withdrawal.

Shit, I got off drugs myself. I got so pissed off at myself that I weaned myself off whatever I was on, methadone, Nubain, Vicodin, morphine, Suboxone, etc...

The perception with drug usage was once you start you cannot stop, and for the most part it's true. You just jump from one opiate to the next chasing the thrilling high. Part of the reason is that the initial high becomes part of your life, consuming you into its dark world. I lived for it. It was my oxygen.

When I was addicted, it was the first and last thing I thought about when I woke up and went to bed. If I did not have any drugs, I knew I was in for hell. It was not only about the actual pain of withdrawals, but it was also the actual pain and grief of not having drugs and having to deal with sobriety. The drug game didn't discriminate between race, religion, creed, occupation, etc. People who use drugs are not always at the bottom of social circles. Doctors, lawyers, and scientists are self-medicating. I have known friends who were in the medical field prescribing pain medication to patients, while strung out themselves.

I was at my low point a few times, but I never truly hit rock bottom until I hit the slammer. If you asked me if I could have one thing right now, what would that be? Vacation anywhere in the world? Any meal I wanted? Or have a hit of any drug? I would choose a hit of any drug, hands down. My day and life used to revolve around it.

My support circle refused to believe I was on drugs because the drugs did not make me fumble around or slur my speech. I took drugs and functioned, which could be difficult for users. The bathroom was my sanctuary. I would go to the bathroom, shoot up, and continue with my day. Once you're hooked, you're hooked, and there isn't a thing you can do about it. Hook, line, and sinker.

Pop pills and train hard. That was my motto. I trained harder than anyone, but my vice was my addiction and that I just couldn't shake. I always told myself I couldn't train as hard without my pills, but that was only an excuse. Pills were masking my inner demons of trying to be the best and doing whatever it took to achieve greatness. I ate, slept, and fantasized about football and bodybuilding. I didn't care about anything else. I was selfish, but I did what I needed to since I didn't have the genetic makeup to survive in alpha dominant sports. It's not like I was trying out for the badminton team.

Row

Life didn't seem that great when I was off drugs. Things that made me laugh before weren't funny anymore. I enjoyed watching movies, playing music, traveling, reading, and exercising, but those didn't make me happy anymore. I wasn't myself.

Unfortunately, nobody knows what you're going through, dealing with withdrawals, because everyone has a different story. Everyone was on a different dose of medication for a different period. The longer you stay on drugs, the harder it is to get off. If you think that you can dabble with drugs on the weekend and then work hard during the week, you're dead wrong. Slowly those weekend highs become weekday highs and then you're hooked on riding the high life.

It took a while, but I finally started to feel normal again. The monkey was finally off my back. Sick and tired of self medicating, hiding, isolating myself. I got clean so I could live a better life with my family and friends. A more meaningful life.

My life of debauchery was over. No more crawling into a black hole, isolated in my own transgressions. No more waiting at a doctor's office, or driving in a remote area fiending for my fix. No more!

I was finally clean and life was great.

Let me be your voice of reasoning. If there is one thing you get from reading this book: drugs are never the answer. I was fortunate to kick my habit, but it took years. Take it one day at a time. Each day not taking drugs was a win. Be your own motivation. You don't need anyone to get you clean apart from your iron will and dedication.

Day 9 Jail Journal: Dope Man

I must choose my last meal before they put a mask over my head and I go to the other side. Stairway to heaven, I hope. The last meal is a customary ritual for a condemned prisoner facing the big bitch. I guess the Bureau of Prisons wants to offer some level of dignity and compassion to the condemned. I didn't need any charity from any of these bugs. My only request was not to be shackled and handcuffed before I take the walk to my execution. I wanted to walk to the chamber with dignity and stare my fate in the face without the metal restraints. I don't need my last words and I sure as hell don't need a last meal. I told the guards I was going to have whatever meal they would shovel in my cell that day. Give me a goddamn ladmo bag filled with moldy bologna for all I cared. I have heard of notorious criminals getting lavish last meals such as lobster and filet mignon with creme brulee and champagne. Brutal murderers like Tim McVeigh requested two pints of mint chocolate ice cream; John Wayne Gacy had shrimp, KFC chicken, fries, and a pound of strawberries. I didn't care for any of that, as I threw the empty piece of paper under the jail cell. I looked at the guard after he picked up the paper and that was my middle finger to him and the Bureau of Prisons.

The Bureau of Prisons attempts to mask the inevitable by trying to ease my mind, giving me one meal of my choice after years and years of the ghastliest sustenance. I couldn't care less what they fed me the day before. My stomach is turning everyday like a revolving door. I can't hold anything down. I am waking up with cold sweats. Feed me properly while I am dwelling behind these metal bars, while wasting away taxpayers' money.

Lights out!

Row

I hate those words. I will remember those words for the rest of my time on God's green earth. Well for me, this cage. I don't get to see God's green earth, being sheltered, caged, tortured, no name, just a number. Lights out means exactly what it says: LIGHTS OUT! It's time for all of us condemned in cages to rest our eyes. Then all hell breaks loose, but nobody sleeps in a place like this. We just rest our eyes momentarily until we hear prison commotion. I go through multiple iterations of cell counts, chow, and other prison protocol daily. Sleeping is a luxury, having to constantly give heed to prison officials and their demands. I wish I could take a one-way ticket to paradise, getting away from these awful people. Things I have heard behind these walls are unrepeatable. Life slowly passes, I've overheard the gargling sound of a man choking on his own blood and a man screaming while getting raped by ten Nazi Low Riders. Those voices don't disappear from my head.

Correctional officers vanish when it's lights out. They circle the perimeter, securing the fortress so none of the inmate's escape, but within the confines, controls are not set in place to track prisoners during the twilight. The predators lurk, preying on the weak. These prisons aren't monitored 24/7. They are monitored from 5 a.m. to 11 p.m. The six hours in the dusk are when the lions come out to feast, showcasing their blood-stained prison blues, seeking another prisoner who has broken the sacred prison code of conduct. Like in the Serengeti, the lions in San Quentin are on top of the food chain, displaying their tats and gang affiliations.

There are two types of lawbreakers in SQ, the shot callers who hold the key and who conduct themselves with honor and dignity for their gang and then you have the sucker duckers: guys that were living the thug life on the outside, but are frail and timid inside the joint. Renowned serial attackers like the Boston Strangler and Jeffrey Dahmer were all victims of prison violence. The apex killers that preyed on helpless civilians become helpless themselves. If you enter here as a gazelle, you better figure out a way to become a lion real fast.

I came into prison as a sheep and became a lion in an instant based on my criminal offense. It made me a force to be reckoned with because convict law in prisons governs the system. Death row inmates are treated differently. We are the celebrities notorious for a criminal endeavor, while staring mortality in the face.

Often, while I was in the cell block, I would get convicts asking me how I did it. They wanted to know every last detail, often asking me how much blood was spilled. These criminals weren't men. They were weak human beings. I had to give the impression that I was sadistic, glorifying each detail. I am someone the other inmates don't fear, but respect and, in jail, respect comes ahead of fear.

Don't get me wrong, I was scared as hell walking into prison, with inmates and COs eyeing me up and down, trying to punk or take advantage of me. The weight pile gave all the inmates a reason not to mess with me. I walked in lifting more than any other convict in the joint and that got me respect. Then they found out that I was an ex-bodybuilder and football player and had competed in multiple hand-to-hand combat sports. Attention is not something you crave in prison unless you are a shot caller, but I did my thing and lifted weights hard. I didn't yell while I was training, or make myself known. I buried my head in the sand and acted like a soldier on the outside, but on the inside, my body was trembling with fear, hoping somebody wouldn't try and punk me.

I let my actions speak louder than my words and I let my force do the walking. That is how I handled myself on the streets. There are too many chatterboxes out there forcing their idealistic views on others on social media. If someone wanted my bench, I gave it to them. I just grabbed another machine, stacked it up with weights, and lifted it without sweating.

Inmates were impressed and COs liked me because I didn't cause any beef. I didn't make eye contact with anyone. Making eye contact was construed as a sign of disrespect and making eye contact with a gang lieutenant was rock stupid. I am just doing my bid. No matter how quiet I am in prison, everyone found out my story. So, if you are a Chomo, you might as well do the dutch because you are at the bottom of the food chain. You are small krill that whale sharks devour by the millions a day.

I never talked to any of the other inmates about my addiction or any of my other short-comings. I couldn't. I never wanted to show a kink in my armor. If they saw a weak spot, those animals would jump on it like a pack of hyenas on a gazelle. Remember, I was not only dealing with the inmates in here, but also the robocops every single day and that can be far worse than dealing with any con. Robocops are COs that take no prisoners. They were firm in their assigned duties and displayed force at any given moment. I never pissed these guys off because they could make my life miserable. Then you got the cowboys; the wet-behind-the-ear CO's who thought they could really make a difference and reform some of these guys. They learned pretty quick that San Quentin was not a place for reform. Some COs abide by the law and come in to work, put in their grind and go home to their loved ones. Some COs are no better than us inmates. They are crooked.

When I was on the cell block out on the yard lifting, I would have COs coming up to me all the time, asking me where they could score roids. They wanted to know who the hook-up was. I had to be careful about how I spoke to the COs. I knew I had to have a good relationship with them or else my time, no matter how short, would be a living hell.

❖

When I was on the outside I enjoyed being high on life. I was always flirting with some drug. Even inside the block it was easy to get whatever I wanted. heroin, marijuana, crack, cocaine, Oxys, Vikes, etc.....Whatever my heart desired, but I knew I better be able to pay for it upfront. Don't ever think someone in the joint was doing you a solid passing you a couple of pills on the house. In prison, being nice will get you dropped like a bad habit.

I made that mistake my first thirty days in the can. I needed something to take the edge off. I didn't know how long I had to live and dealing with my new home was brutal. Every day, I was a ticking time bomb ready to explode.

DAY 9: DOPE MAN

My anxiety was too much to handle and I was hanging from a cliff. I met an inmate who I thought was looking out for me and truly cared about helping me cope with life behind bars. Wow. Thinking about it now, I laugh at myself for thinking anyone in here would be here to help me. Naive!

I was given a few pills of methadone and told it was on the house. Well, the house came three weeks later, asking for two packs of bats, which I didn't have. I don't smoke, so my commissary always consisted of food. One thing you must realize, in the clink every inmate was desperate. Bats are a hot commodity and the only way to obtain them was by trading or gambling. The problem was I didn't have anything to trade.

I was lucky this inmate was not well liked and classified as a cell warrior. At that stage in my incarceration, I didn't know the difference between a shot caller and a regular inmate. If he was a shot caller, I would have been dealt with. I learned very quickly how to act and who to avoid. My addiction was survival each day. I was a deer in the African plains watching over my shoulder for a pack of wolves to attack. Every day could be my last and I needed to make sure I had eyes in the back of my head. My best friends were my fists and my education. I was educated enough to speak to inmates and officers with respect and not look weak. That was very difficult, believe me, because inmates prey on weakness, and correctional officers do not care too much about inmates on death row. They knew my time was limited.

❖

Another issue that fed into my addiction was that I could afford my drugs. Yes, they were expensive, but I could fund my drug habit, which made my drug appetite even hungrier. The more I took, the more I wanted. I craved it like a dump truck wanting a doughnut. I needed that feeling of euphoria. I was becoming my drug dealer's preferred client. I didn't know how many customers he had, but I knew his profit margin was over seventy-five percent. This guy was making stacks hand over fist. He was driving a pimped-out Escalade and always carried a phat stack of cash. Here we are, hardworking Americans trying to do the right thing, paying forty percent taxes to Uncle Sam and then you have someone breaking the law, feeding the opiate epidemic, and making thousands of tax-free dollars on the-daily. Let me get some of that action!

Of course, what he was doing was a crime, and the drug game was a very short-lived existence. You either get pinched or killed. I just can't understand how the world works, but if you can't beat 'em, join 'em.

For years, I contemplated becoming an entrepreneur and starting a business dealing, but after the trip to Mexico I was always apprehensive. I was young and dumb and didn't accept sound advice from people I should have. I always remembered what that judge in Texas told me, but it didn't always affect my actions.

Taking drugs was one thing and counted as a misdemeanor pending the substance and the quantity, but when you start slinging, then you are playing a whole new game where your sentence can multiply by over ten years. It is not something I wanted to take a chance with BUT...

Deception, deceit, and lying were all things that I did when I was dealing. I was a small-time hoodlum, but that was how Pablo Escobar and William Hung started out.

I didn't want a reputation that preceded me, especially since I didn't know what I was doing. I was controlled by greed and the almighty dollar. In a strange way, I thought I was helping people. Idiot! People relied on me for a product and it wasn't like I was slinging crack rock. I was a low-level hustler. What's the big deal, right?

The kingpin controlling our operation was supposedly a close friend. Little did I know my supplier was a wolf in sheep's clothing. I wish I could have taken flight on that punk. That weasel ended up stealing over six stacks from me and disappeared, leaving me to answer to some pretty-intimidating goons. I wouldn't mind seeing that scumbag before I perish. I would put a shiv right in his kidney.

I would get the supply from the distributor at one price and dispense it to my clientele for another. My profitability was through the roof and I was making double, almost triple. I was staking my claim in a saturated industry. Demand was high and the supply was always at my fingertips. I was selling performance-enhancing supplements to gym rats. As a bodybuilder, I had the hook up in the industry and being in the gym training at all hours, looking the way that I did, I ended up meeting people and striking up conversations, which eventually turned into conversations about getting jacked. People were always approaching me, seeking mentorship and asking me questions about exercise and nutrition. Eventually, they always wanted the secret ingredient they thought was in a bottle, and were willing to pay any price.

I was selling everything from Deca, Winstrol, D-Bol, Anadrol, test cypionate, propionate, growth hormone, and the list goes on and on. Everything was at my fingertips. I wanted to make a little extra money. Why not? It was the law of supply and demand. If it wasn't me, it would have been another hustler taking advantage. I was young and dumb and obviously didn't learn from the monumental mistake I made in Mexico. I thought I was untouchable. There was risk, but at the time, my eye was on the prize of making quick stacks of cash. I didn't worry about getting pinched and my business was growing exponentially. I had knucklehead philosophy all day!

I just started my bodybuilding career with no sponsorship, nutritional business, personal training studio. I was starting from scratch. Being a competitive bodybuilder required a bankroll. I had to purchase quality foods and spend on supplements like protein powder and other bodybuilding formulas. Bodybuilding was a very expensive sport and before I was sponsored, I had to purchase everything on my own. I bought my supplements and food, and paid for guidance so I could compete on stage successfully. It was a very expensive endeavor and those who think all you do is train are dead wrong. I didn't want to participate. I wanted to take over.

Looking back, the return was not even close to the risk. I was one wrong deal away from getting locked up and becoming a lifelong felon, again! That gold-plated key to my jail cell was no longer draped around my neck; instead it was in my drawer, caked in dust. It was now just a knick-knack.

I dealt for as long as I could. The heaven was raining down on me because I lost my connection. Probably the best thing that ever happened to me. Like I said, the punk that stole from me took my money, disappeared into the twilight and was never found. He probably ended up in a ditch somewhere in Vegas. Good riddance!

Drug dealing was a short-term engagement with a two-way street to either jail or the grave. I was making a lot of mistakes in life. My early years in adulthood were

Row

diluted by troubled thoughts, which led to a lot of misdeeds. I am glad I survived and didn't end up a statistic like most who dabbled in the drug game.

The fun didn't end there, though!

DAY 8 JAIL JOURNAL: PIPE DREAMS

My rationale in my twenties was flawed, so San Quentin was never far from the truth. San Quentin was in my windshield and it was just a matter of time before I hailed the concrete barriers, fine dining, and residing at San Quentin, CA, 94964.

My views on the prison system change every day in isolation. Being locked away for so many hours, my mind goes in circles.

While on trial I educated myself on the prison system. I learned the ins and outs. I wanted to acquire as much knowledge as possible before becoming a statistic. I analyzed prison data in order to be ready for whatever came next.

In 2005, US prisons held 81,622 in segregated isolation. Out of those inmates, 7,400 come from California state prisons. Does California have the worst criminals? Why the hell are so many of us caged for twenty-three hours a day with barely any sunlight? Left to survive with just the bare essentials. I could scream as I lose my lucidity. Solitary confinement was supposed to be reserved for the worst of the worst felons. Inmates like Barry Mills and Tyler Bingham, the notorious lieutenants of the Aryan Brotherhood, who have been responsible for hits across state lines. Career criminals who constantly commit crimes end up in solitary confinement. Not people like me!

Now, solitary confinement has become a control strategy as the first resort for criminals. Today, the Bureau of Prisons hands out solitary confinement like candy. The Bureau of Prisons grabbed me from my cell, where I was an obedient inmate. I was prospering as a model inmate with my cellie and suddenly I was sanctioned to live out the rest of my sentence in isolation.

❖

Row

When there is darkness, there's imminent danger. Gambling was the Grim Reaper with millions of degenerates betting and ultimately succumbing to the high stakes world. The gambling industry was rich and filled with billion-dollar whales or malnourished individuals who were playing one vice to feed another.

Don't get it twisted, the dangerous world of gambling spans over the entire universe, caging its victims. It has no prejudices. Gambling is the ultimate high with winners and losers. There are millions and millions of dollars exchanging hands all over the world in sports betting, lottery, dice, raffling, pitching quarters, bingo, slots, casino gaming, and the list goes on and on.

Right now, there are high stakes Texas hold'em games proceeding in thousands of underground taverns around the globe. The stench of cigar smoke, bad breath, and degenerate stink fills the air as the gambling world consumes millions. The casinos fill with degenerates ready to cash in their paychecks and second mortgages for the chance to sit at the winner's circle at the World Series of Poker with Doyle Brunson. Those pipe dreams are the visions of so many captivated by the world of gambling.

Boiler Room, Casino, Scarface, and Wall Street. I loved all these movies that embellished how easy it was to make a quick dollar. These movies were very popular when I was going to school. I watched these movies and wondered, why am I even going to school? Was I a sucker, paying an institution over $100,000 when I could get away with making millions? It was risky, but if I performed a few crimes I could be set for life. Why not steal from some of these fat cats making millions off the backs of their employees, taking enormous bonuses to fill their shallow lives? The same guys sipping on Chateau Margaux, snorting thousands of dollars of coke, and sleeping with their secretaries.

When you're young, dumb, and broke, the power of money is overwhelming. It can overpower your morality. Remember the beginning of Casino when Joe Pesci was talking about Robert De Niro's character, Sam "Ace" Rothstein, and how he could win any bet he placed? He knew exactly what angle to analyze for gaining a competitive advantage and would eventually win millions before going on to manage his own casino. The movie was brilliant and precisely what I wanted to do. I wanted to be the kingpin that would win every week. I wanted the bookies to tell me they didn't have any more action because I was unbeatable. I wanted to tell people my car, clothes, shoes, and house were all paid for by my wisdom of gaming. The quest was my high. I wanted to make gaming classy, just like Sam

DAY 8: PIPE DREAMS

Rothstein. Why couldn't I be the next big wig in the world of sports betting? Gamblers lived by one motto, go big or go home.

Professional gamblers made gambling a science and spent countless hours studying each game. You can't become a card shark if you don't put in the grind, and I was willing to put in the work.

The main attraction for me in sports gaming was making money without having to work for it. I was the CEO of my own company, making decisions on which pawns I thought would beat the other pawns. I liked the mystery and the uncertainty of gambling, as well as being a businessman, understanding the odds and making bets based on my analysis. Each game I gambled, I weighed the outcome. Was the team playing at home? What was the weather? What were the odds? What was the over under? Who was injured? What was the outcome of their opponents they had already played? I wasn't trying to make a profession out of sports gambling, but it was intriguing and easy money.

NCAA athletics, work, and school didn't seem to keep me from starting bookkeeping and carrying multiple accounts in gaming. My gambling career spanned over a year, but just like any addiction, it could haunt me at any time. I must have been joking thinking that I could have made money sports betting. At one point, I was thinking of quitting my job and gambling full time. Knuckle-head philosophy! I started betting $25 games to $3,000, all while going to school and paying tuition. I quickly made waves as I started betting on high limit games. My bookie knew who I was. In the gambling world, that is not a good thing.

I ended up hitting it full speed ahead. I was fortunate because I could have gotten caught up with some very dangerous people. I was gambling with money I didn't have. I was a student, working part-time, making enough to get by, but I was living on the edge gambling. I was entertaining a lifestyle of greed and regret.

When I was going to school, I met a fellow student across from my dorm room who knew a few bookies operating out of Chicago. He wanted to see if I wanted an account to place some bets. Just a few bets here and there, nothing major. Just something fun to do on my free time.

Row

Many of the NFL teams were in mid-season form. This also meant Las Vegas was bringing in a million dollars a day from gaming. It was the busiest time for gamblers and bookies because of college football and NFL. There weren't enough bookies for the action. My roommates and I were avid sports viewers and were always glued to the television on Sundays. We were a bookie's wet dream, young and prime for picking. We were ignorant, playing on games with coin we did not have.

When I initially started gambling, I told myself, "What the hell? Let's live life on the edge." I was only allowed to play upwards to $50 bets and my limit was $250 in the hole. It was child's play. I didn't think there was anything to lose besides a little bit of money. Gambling on a few games a week for my enjoyment was the whole purpose. It was football season anyways so I would play well-educated plays and enjoy watching the games. I was treating this as a hobby, but it turned into a lot more than that. I never thought that I would start betting with money I didn't have, but sometimes you get ahead of yourself and that was exactly what happened. I was controlled by greed.

I went from placing $25 bets to placing $3,000 bets. Now that was not a ton of money, but for a college student $3,000 is unattainable without some illegal activity. I became addicted while trying to maintain my academics, work, sports, and everything else in my life. At that point, I was researching more on sports betting than I was on my classes. It was an odd time in my life, as I was trying to adjust to a new school and adapting to my roommates, as well as thinking about life after football.

When I originally gambled on my first game, I won, which led me to win $150 my first week. I thought I had the gift like Sam Rothstein from Casino. I was delusional to think that a few games would make me into a gaming shark, but for a short time I was living the dream.

By the end of the month I was up $1,000. I jumped in my car, headed to Best Buy with a bankroll of dirty cash, determined to furnish my room with the newest gadgets. I purchased a 32-inch television, DVD player, surround sound system, and PlayStation with games. I was balling. I thought I was a gangster laundering dirty money. I even kept my money like a wise guy in a tight bank roll with a hundred on the top.

Sports betting was deceptive because I was never winning a lot of money when I was playing conservatively and trying to build a bankroll, but when I started losing money I would bet the house to regain control. That was when bad habits formed. I told myself the highest bet I would make would be $25. Who was I fooling? Within a few short months, I was making $500 to $1,000 bets on a regular basis.

Gambling was effortless. All I needed to do was call in a number, provide my account details, and take whatever game I wanted. It was just that simple and made watching sports exciting. That whole thing about playing with a $50 limit was false. Those gangsters didn't care how much money we bet if they were paid.

I quickly realized how serious gambling was with my college roommate's addiction. We all kept our games in separate binders, tracking all our accounts and making sure our numbers were the same as the books. The last thing I wanted to do was call in a game referencing the wrong account number. We were now full-time gamblers and part-time students. That was all we were talking about. School, work, and even football were taking a backseat. Gambling was consuming my life.

My roommate was a heavier player than I was, with a larger bankroll, too. What he possessed in wealth, he lacked in sports acumen. He thought gaming was going to be his way of paying for school, betting on multiple games each night. He didn't do any research on any of the bets he made and thought gambling was about luck. He was putting money on college basketball, hockey, football, baseball, and the NBA. He was addicted to the fact that he could make money by watching TV. His priorities were gambling first, everything else second. His grades dipped, his girlfriend broke up with him, and he was fired from his part-time job. His life was spiraling out of control.

I wish gambling was as easy as he made it out to be. He instantly found that his good fortune could turn at any point. During March Madness, he was taking a lot of action because every time he would place a bet, he stepped out of the room. I would hear him announce a laundry list of games to the bookie. Gambling on over ten games a night like a degenerate. He kept a little black book resembling the Old Testament with all his games. He kept it lying around for everyone's viewing pleasure. I was always respectful of his things, but one night he left his book wide open, displaying his week's action right next to my International Business hard-cover book. All I could see were negative balances and by Friday night he was in the hole over $10,000. For a small time gambler $10G's was a fortune.

Row

Gambling was one of those addictions that could get out of hand. If gambling addicts weren't dropping dimes on games, then there wouldn't be any casinos. Gambling was one of the worst types of addictions because it was difficult for people to identify who was an addictive gambler. I am an addictive gambler, but stopped as I was getting carried away. I recognized my threshold before it was too late. And believe me it was almost too late. I was one game away from getting my head put in a vice.

I loved betting on everything. I have bet on poker, Texas hold'em, blackjack, 5 card draw, basketball, football, hockey, and baseball. Shoot, I have even bet on board games like Monopoly.

When my roommates at Benedictine and I started gambling, we had no idea the tornado we were walking into. It was the first time I was betting through someone. I told myself I was only going to play small games for $25 at the most, but that soon changed as I started taking games for higher amounts. Dollar games started becoming nickel and dime bets. Luckily, I was winning and not having to worry about losing money. The money that I was winning was a few hundred here and there. I was on top of the world, creating a bankroll and acting like a small-time hustler. Knucklehead philosophy at its best.

The tides turned when I started losing. Like a heroin addict, I was crashing hard into a deep black hole. Gamblers are degenerates that tend to raise the stakes when their chips are down. Placing bets is like calculus and I made sure that every game I played was carefully researched. I reviewed tendencies, stats, record, weather, odds, over, under, parlays, prop bets, and whatever I thought would be advantageous. If I was going to bet my hard-earned money, then I will damn well make sure I did my investigation. I tried to learn as much about matchups as possible, but time management was not on my side as I was juggling commitments and trying to adhere to my responsibilities.

I had no idea how I would have paid my gambling debt off if I lost Super Bowl XXXVI. I would have gone to my bookies and asked for leniency, paying my debt in blood. That was my only option.

The Super Bowl was right around the corner. Super Bowl was a bookie's wet dream. It could make or break a bookie because of the different prop bets. Gamblers ended up spending their whole salary on one game. You could bet on how many passing yards the quarter back would have and how many points each team would score each quarter, half, or the game. You could even bet on which team would win the coin toss. The opportunities to make a quick buck were endless. The Super Bowl was a gambler's fantasy. It was the biggest sports betting day in the entire year, estimating $3-$5 billion in bets, though most of it is illegal wagering in an underground, unregulated forum.

The week of Super Bowl XXXVI, I was down two large. I couldn't catch a break leading up to the game. Every game I played was on the losing end. I never lost so many consecutive games. I was playing into the bookies' hands, as every degenerate was doubling down and trying to regain control. I was sleep deprived and all prior commitments were delayed. The more I focused on gambling that week, the more I lost. The Super Bowl was going to be my redemption. I hope.

Super Bowl XXXVI would live in history for me. I watched the game isolated from the outside world, watching each play like it was my lifeline. Every play momentarily stopped my heart. I felt as if I was playing Russian roulette with the last bullet in the chamber, ready to blow my head clean off. It was the first time in my life that I didn't have an answer for my stupidity. I was in a deep hole and left without any options. I couldn't stop making bad decisions, as if it was in my DNA. I always seemed to hit a bump in the road and overcame each one, but I may have bitten off more than I could chew this time. I had a knack for beating the odds, but I couldn't control gambling. I was playing for my life because if I lost, there would be no way I would have come up with five large. The gaming world didn't take any prisoners. The voices at the end of my phone call when I played a game were scary men who demanded payment by any broken bones necessary. They didn't hand out loans or payment extensions. They handed out beatings. I heard the men tied to my accounts were part of the Chicago mob syndicate.

The New England Patriots, with a wet-behind-the-ears backup quarterback, against "the greatest show on turf" in the St. Louis Rams. The Rams were a seventeen-point favorite, which was the highest spread in Super Bowl history. Both defenses were meager and this contest was primed to be a shootout. My mantra that week was to fulfill my prediction that both teams combined would score over fifty-three points. It was a sure bet if I ever saw one.

I was deep in the hole and didn't have a bankroll to fund that shortfall. My school jobs were barely enough to pay for a happy meal let alone my hospital bills if I didn't pay. It was not something I was proud of, but I had a week to come up with this money and if I didn't, I would have had to sell my kidneys to the black market to pay off the mafia. Excuse me, the bookies. I had to make a move and the move was taking the Rams and Patriots offense in a high scoring affair. I knew Kurt Warner, the Rams' quarterback, was going to light up the scoreboard like he did all year. The other quarterback at the time was a second-year QB named Tom Brady. I was hoping the Patriots malignant offense could muster twenty to twenty-five points and the highly potent Ram's offense would cover the rest.

2001 was the year the St. Louis Rams were unbeatable and arguably the biggest offensive juggernaut of all time. They could not be beat, assembling an aggressive attack featuring four Hall of Fame players Kurt Warner, Isaac Bruce, Orlando Pace, Marshall Faulk, and future Hall of Famer Torry Holt. They annihilated teams by throwing in tight windows and capitalizing on the opposing defense's weak secondary. They were dominating and I knew they would beat up on a lucky Patriots team that was squeaking by in the playoffs. The Patriots didn't have the firepower and were playing a backup quarterback drafted in the sixth round of the NFL draft who only played a handful of games in the NFL. This was going to be a sure thing. Even though my back was against the wall and I was going to put $3,000 on that game, I felt confident that I was making the right decision. I would seize a golden opportunity.

I was an emotional mess. The whole week was a nightmare as I was going to class and thinking of one thing. How was I going to come up with this money if I lost? I still had a few days to place the bet, but didn't know how I would build up the courage.

Super Bowl Sunday arrived and in a few short hours I was going to make the most important phone call of my life. The man who was on the other side of the phone was known as Mr. X. I was a young 21 year old punk and had no idea whom I was dealing with. Playing with fire back then made the business venture even more appealing to me. I asked our middleman, "What would these guys do if payment was not received?" He snapped back with glaring pupils, demanding me to pay what I owed. He was clear and decisive, and told me never to put them in that situation.

It was 3 p.m. and I had to make a move or else I would miss the deadline. I was franticly pacing back and forth in my 9' x 11' room like a caged lion. I needed someone to push me off the cliff, or in this case, force me into making a phone call. I could cut the tension with a knife, as I couldn't hide from this predicament. With my heart racing, I dialed each digit on my cordless phone, knowing my play. I heard the ring of the phone, realizing that the other person was probably a ruthless gangster. If I didn't have money to pay him, I would be paying him in blood.

It felt like ages, but someone finally picked up. It was the same man that was taking every game. His thick, raspy voice resembled the Ice Man, Richard Kuklinski, who was a notorious mafia contract killer. He sounded like a guy that would come and find you with a chainsaw, imitating Leather face, if you owed any money. I envisioned him as a true rough neck with bad intentions. A real life knockaround guy.

I was hoping he would not let me place the bet and tell me something like, "Hope you learned your lesson," but we all know the world of underground gambling doesn't work that way. Bookies feast on people in my position. I would need to man up and either pay my debt or make a play. It was time for me to back my statements I made all week, and that was the Rams and Patriots in a high scoring affair. I hesitated a few seconds, gripping the phone as I murmured, "Give me the under for $3,000." WHAT?! I was possessed. Something came over me, preventing me from saying what I wanted. There was no turning back now as I placed the bet and hung up.

The whole damn week, I was milking the idea of the Rams and Patriots scoring a ton of points. When it was time for me to place the bet, I folded like a table and succumbed to the pressure. This wasn't going to be a low scoring contest, as all the expert analysis was proving a shootout. St. Louis Rams were one of the highest scoring teams in NFL history. They were the greatest show on turf and they were going to exploit the inexperienced New England team. What the hell was I thinking?

The game finally started and lo and behold, the Patriots shut down the Rams. The Rams were going nowhere and punted the ball back to the Patriots' inept offense. The Rams were getting stopped and their Hall of Fame quarterback was rattled, getting hit from all angles by the bone crushing Patriots defense. The fans were in complete shock as the Rams' prolific offense was prevented from moving forward.

I watched every play like the game was on the line. Like my life was on the line. I was sweating, terrified about the outcome, but after the first quarter I was sitting on my throne. I was like a young businessman that just made the biggest move on Wall Street. Okay, maybe not, but for a college student it was a big deal. I ended up ducking a beating as the Rams and Patriots only scored 37 points and I won that bet. Did I learn anything? Well...

My barrage of futile attempts to become rich quick were still in progress. I am glad I walked away from that ordeal unscathed, but as one terrible decision ended, another came along.

❖

As if gambling wasn't enough, I wanted to take it to the next level. I shake my head as I am writing this piece.

I came out ahead from gambling, but it got me thinking. Why should I have to go through this agony for a few bucks, when I could be the bookie, taking games? The demand was there and I didn't even need to be a supplier. All I needed was to take games over the phone and have a bankroll to manage. I needed to make sure the bets were not lopsided and I collected on the juice. Granted, sports booking in Illinois was illegal, but how is sports betting different from stocks? Instead of betting on companies, I was betting on sports teams. Tomayto, tomahto.

During the next fall, I was approached by another student managing the football season's gaming at our institution. There weren't enough bookies for the gambling action. Instead of saying "Hell, no," especially after my gambling ordeal, I decided to give it a try. He presented me with the idea of taking games from some locals in his neighborhood. I would be affiliated with the same group of men who petrified me. Without getting into the logistics of my job, I decided to jump in headfirst.

I would take NFL games with a maximum of $100. I was a small-timer, but then again, look what happened to my gambling addiction. I had an addictive personality and things could spiral out of hand very quickly. I was getting a taste of this lifestyle like a drug dealer giving an addict a smidge of ice. As soon as gambling hit my bloodstream like a shot of opium, I was hooked. The whole idea was pure entertainment, making the games even more stimulating, but it went to another echelon, as I had to become much more organized at operating from multiple accounts. I had a group of ten gamblers working with a $1,200 bankroll. I had a nice little racket going.

I was now managing ten accounts, MA40, MA41, MA42, and so on. Gamers would call with their account number and specific games. I was now that grizzly voice on the other line. I wonder if the gamblers knew they were dealing with a college student. Did they think I was some sort of mafia hit man?

I was only booking for a few months before I decided to stop. I walked away with two large. I could have continued and created a small empire, but it was time to walk away. Last thing I needed was another judge handing a correctional officer a gold key, this time locking me away for a long time.

The gambling industry was worth billions and I could have had a small piece of that pie. It wasn't worth it. I had too much to lose. I was becoming a cowboy in life, constantly making the wrong choices. I didn't learn from any of my bad decisions, and sooner or later, I was going to commit a major crime.

DAY 7 JAIL JOURNAL:
LET'S GETS READY TO RUMBLE

I am shaking my head at so many things wrong with the world. I'm fed up with the lack of change. I'm fed up about not having an ear to voice my concerns. I'm losing time as each second ticks away, praying for a government sanction to rescue me. Not going to happen. I got nothin comin' except for the stainless-steel ride.

I am so fed up with the government and their false claims about making the US a better country. Donald Trump is now our president and trying to make changes that will better our society. Please! Hey, President! How about getting jobs and shelter for our war veterans who were overseas fighting for our freedom? It breaks my heart to think that some of our veterans return home to find their homes foreclosed. How about helping clear up some of our national debt? The US owes trillions to other countries. I am so fed up with paying taxes for everything. When I was on the streets, I couldn't buy a pack of gum without paying taxes. I used to work hard for my money and Uncle Sam took damn near half of it every time. For what? Better highways, municipal buildings, military aid, and social security that my daughter will never get. There are inmates that make less than ten cents per hour and the government has the nerve to take some of that. Where is our hard-earned tax money going? I am fed up with illegal immigrants that cross our borders every day and steal the jobs of hard-working Americans. Start doing your job, Border Patrol, and protect our borders from foreign trespassers. I am fed up with US banks. Hey, idiots, stop giving people loans they can't afford to pay back. You are ruining people's lives and killing our economy. I am fed up with bullies and people who take advantage of other people. I hate criminals who prey on other people. I see it far too much in the joint. I am fed up with criminal lawyers that lie and cheat everyone to fatten their pockets. These leeches are the scum of the earth. I am fed up with today's youth. Hey, morons, put the video game controllers down and quit rotting your brains playing Grand Theft Auto, and do something productive. I am fed up with professional athletes. They have been given every tool in life to succeed and yet some of them find it hard to maintain a decent life without committing crimes. I am fed up with these rappers getting paid more than heart surgeons by yelling out profanities about killing and raping. I am fed up with reality TV stars. C'mon, who are you kidding? You guys are not real actors. I am fed up with people that can't stop complaining about everything. There are people fighting for their life with a terminal disease and you have people complaining about getting a parking ticket. Most of all, I am sick of myself. There is nothing in life worse than wasted talent. I had all the talent in the world, but ended up in prison decomposing. What a pathetic loser.

❖

I let my emotions out too frequently in my twenties and never realized the ramifications. Didn't care. I was quick to the draw, often letting my emotions get the better of me. I realize now my instincts were animalistic. When I was in grammar school, combating with students was a normal occurrence. My ferocious approach to life didn't cease even through my college days at North Park University. My razor's edge attitude was sharpened from encountering some of the big dogs on my team, with our egos often colliding. Playing a sport with over a hundred alpha males, I was certain to get into a bunch of altercations on and off the field.

My freshman football dormitory basement was home to a simulated Ultimate Fighting Championship. Combatants of all sizes and statures would duke it out like two pit bulls. It was our own fight club. The fights would cease when someone would get knocked out or quit. It was the art of dumb-ass aggression and testosterone that fueled us. I also got in a bunch of brawls on the street for nonsensical reasons.

On one occasion, I was walking the streets of Chicago after a party about a half mile from my dorm and about 100 yards ahead of my teammates when I was attacked by a handful of street thugs. The conversation was light that evening and fists were flying as my aggression took over immediately. My mind went blank and I went into survival mode. I ended up holding my own until the cavalry arrived. My adversaries went home counting their lucky stars that their carcasses weren't being scraped off the floor.

A lot of arguments were resolved in the dorm room with fisticuffs. When I had an issue with another teammate, we simply solved it by going into a dorm room duking it out while the audience waited outside for the outcome. Normally, the first person who walked out was the victor. Same thing in the joint. You got beef with someone, you find an empty shower stall and let the fists fly.

I took the beating of my life during my freshman year when one of my teammates, our starting tight end, took it upon himself to throw food at my head in the cafeteria. I guess this must have been a freshman hazing or something. I wasn't in the mood.

After I rendered multiple warnings, the food onslaught continued until I couldn't take it anymore and rolled up on him. The issue needed to be resolved and was taken to the dorm room. He was 6'2" and 260 pounds of muscle molded from granite and I didn't stand a chance. Dude was massive! We went toe to toe for seconds, which felt like an eternity exchanging blow after blow. His size outmatched me and the fight came to a sudden abrupt stop. I was a punk that day. I walked away from the fight battered and bruised, but the respect I earned amongst the upperclassmen was worth it. Remember, I was only a hundred and some change pounds. This dude was enormous. He ended up becoming a pro boxer. Go figure!

All my altercations should have knocked some sense into me. I used some of that aggression on the gridiron and applied it in a negative way outside the lines. I continued using the same poor judgment. I was using knucklehead philosophy until I had a life-altering clash, which changed my temperament for the rest of my life.

When I was at Benedictine University, I got a part-time position as a sales associate at General Nutritional Center, more widely known as GNC. I was about six months in at GNC and working towards a store management position at one of the stores. I was rotating from multiple stores, working with different colleagues. It was a job while I was trying to obtain my undergraduate degree. It started to become much more than a job. I was a shot caller in training and started working on my own, opening and closing on a regular basis.

One spring morning at the Woodfield Mall in Schaumburg, Illinois, I received a phone call from the district manager notifying me that ephedra was now officially banned and needed to be taken off the shelves immediately. Ephedra was a 5,000-year-old Chinese herb used as treatment for asthma, allergies, and fever, but also taken as a stimulant to increase metabolic rate, spurring the body to burn calories faster. Due to the ephedra-related medical incidents, the Food and Drug Administration decided to ban the supplement from the retail shelves. This was a huge moneymaker for the supplement industry, but it negatively impacted a lot of people. According to the New England Journal of Medicine, there were 54 deaths and 1,000 reports of complications linked to ephedra. The controversy was raised to epic proportions when multiple NFL players, like Rashidi Wheeler, Korey Stringer, Devaughn Darling, and Curt Jones all collapsed and died.

I was told to take all the ephedra off the shelves, so I started taking the Xenadrine, Hydroxycut, Speed Stack, Stacker, and so many other supplements containing ephedra. It took me the whole 8-hour shift to remove everything. When I was done, I looked around the store and I could see a lot of gaps on the shelves. Thousands of dollars' worth of goods removed. In the back room, there were bags and bags of ephedrine-laced products getting recalled. The amount of stuff I chucked away that day could buy me commissary for years.

Let's fast-forward to six months later. It was a brisk, ordinary October morning. Winter was approaching and there was a nip in the air. I was working my morning shift when a man entered the store. He was a tall, lanky man covered in ink, wearing a white sleeveless t-shirt, a sideways FUBU hat, and fashioning multiple gold chains, resembling a skinny Mr. T. I could tell right away he was going to be trouble. He was approaching me while I was tending the cash register. He was carrying a white bottle resembling one of the thermogenics, Xenadrine, which was extremely popular at the time. He approached the counter and tossed me the bottle, demanding a refund. He claimed the bottle was his girlfriend's and didn't work. I looked inside the bottle and there wasn't one pill remaining and noticed that the supplement had ephedra, which was banned six months ago. This dude was trying to con me. I proceeded to ask him when his girlfriend took the product and he said two weeks ago. I asked him for a receipt and he couldn't provide a receipt. I denied his request straightaway, which infuriated him. After multiple profanities, he commanded that I grant him a refund. He was irate as I tried to diffuse the situation by calling corporate. I knew this man was lying through his teeth, as Xenadrine did not manufacture any more products with ephedrine and I personally had removed that product from the shelves months ago.

I got off the phone with corporate and told him he's got nothin comin'! I was very careful delivering this news to him, as I could sense his aggressive nature. He grabbed the bottle from my hand and ended up whipping the bottle, hitting me square in the nose while yelling obscenities at me.

I remember that moment vividly. My head swung back, feeling like I got hit by a sledgehammer. My eyes started to water like a faucet as I tried to regain composure. Being hit flush in the nose and being called a bitch to add insult to injury was crossing the line. I needed to teach this punk a lesson.

A switch turned on in my head and I blacked out. I became an enraged bear, storming the man with reckless abandonment. I speared him like Bill Goldberg during one of his wrestling matches and dropped Vanila Ice like a fly. He didn't stand a chance. I loomed over him and started dropping punch after punch. My haymakers were connecting one by one as the man stood motionless. As I dropped my last punch I felt his cheekbone shatter. It looked like his face caved in, and luckily the mall security guard, whom I knew very well, came and pounced on me, preventing additional ground and pound. The man was pulled up to his feet and again started runnin' his mouth while being taken away, a bloody mess. I was handcuffed and taken to a holding room, awaiting the police. Dude was selling wolf tickets and had a monkey mouth. He needed to be dealt with.

As I sat in the holding cell inside the mall, I was looking at my hands which were covered with this man's blood. He didn't deserve this abuse. I was mortified by my actions. I was now entering a whole new realm of anger. I let my anger cloud my judgment in a major way.

I knew this was going to be my last day working at GNC, which was perfectly fine because I was going to be in a lot more trouble than just losing my job. I was taken to the police station and placed in a holding cell. I was bailed out by a friend a few hours later. I won't go into too much detail, but the man that started the fight had a warrant for his arrest and didn't show up to court. My charges ranged from mall disturbance to assault. I was acquitted of the charges and the case was dropped. Even though I was antagonized and assaulted, I should have kept my wits. I resorted to the behavior of a vigilante with no refrain. My parents didn't raise me to attack people, no matter how vile they were. I was let go from GNC. This changed my life forever. All the previous verbal altercations and all the physical confrontations didn't change me, but this altercation at GNC changed my life. I never knew I was capable of destruction until that autumn day. I could have killed that man! Anytime my temperament started to elevate, I used this incident as an example of taking the wrong action and letting my temper get the better of me. There are far worse things happening in the world than having a plastic bottle thrown at you. To this day, I regret my actions. To this day, I never obtained the man's name to apologize. I only wish I didn't leave a lasting emotional scar. He has played an important role in my life, whether he knew it or not. I wish I could meet him and apologize for my actions.

I was a changed man forever after that date. Worse events have happened to me since that cold autumn day, but I never let it get the best of me. It's true, things happen for a reason.

PART IV
Turn the Page

Day 6 Jail Journal:
Living the American Dream

San Quentin sucks! I hear other cons say that they're lucky that they aren't in an international prison. Glad they are serving time on US soil rather than in some rat hole. What?! San Quentin is a rat hole.

I live in a shoebox and get fed dog food. I only get a little bit of time looking at the blue sky gleaming with sunlight, but I guess I did that to myself. I had every chance to become a productive member of society while I was on the outside, and I took it for granted.

I am starting to wrap my brain around my execution, constantly re-examining my case, jury selection, my defense team, judge, and the whole judicial process. Was I tried precisely? Was there any prejudice against me when I was arraigned? When you are trapped in a cell with nothing but the prison blues on your back, it's difficult not to think within your environment.

Once you become institutionalized for as long as I have, you don't think of the outside world anymore. I don't think about being on the outside with my own family, wife, kids, house, car, clothes, etc...It's all a hallowed memory. It's hard to say, but I can't worry about politics, crime on the outside, or world order. I live in my environment, which is a small enclosure surrounded by J-cats, Chomos, bangers, shot callers, and whatever type of miscreant. It would be too depressing with the little time I have left to get accustomed to my surroundings, I have disassociated myself from getting my conviction overturned. It wasn't going to happen, because I was guilty and I didn't have OJ's dream team backing me. I wasn't going to be disillusioned like some of these other inmates, thinking one day a lawyer was going to rain down from the heavens and save them from the big bitch. Some of these inmates talk like they are going to be granted a stay of execution. I only have a short time on this earth and thinking about my doom wasn't going to be my serenity. I feel bad for the inmates that believe they would get another trial and would be freed. Guilty or innocent, the odds of that happening are slim to none because a murder trial can cost millions of dollars. A convict would have better odds of winning the lottery or getting struck by lightning.

❖

Success finally happened when I stopped my knucklehead ways. I traded in my roughneck attitude — always looking for trouble — for stability. I needed to step back and evaluate whether I was going to be a criminal or a success. I was finally able to turn the page and instead of being a debt to society, I became a better person. I wanted to be a better person not always bound by my tenacity to become something. Something, I probably couldn't even define during my knucklehead days.

I wanted to be a role model by my acts of humanity, not by what I did in the gym or the gridiron.

I wanted to have a career my parents were proud of and lend my hand to people in need. It was time! It was time for a change!

How do you win in life? Is it by the number of zeros at the end of your paycheck? Is it your status within your organization? Was that what winning meant? When we went to school we decided our occupation based on earning potential. People ended up being trapped under the spell of corporate America trying to climb the ladder to get to the top. Every generation X wanted to be the next bigwig CEO. I wouldn't envy any CEO's life because it's fake. Fagazi handshakes, fagazi hellos, it's all fake. Why the hell would anyone want that for themselves? During my early adulthood, I was grounded to the wolves of Wall Street. I was hustling countless hours for the corporate fat cats and then trying to maintain my business after hours. Where did it get me?

Good ole US of A, the land of the free and the land of opportunities. The opportunities were endless, and I am an example of that theory. I started my hustle at the ripe age of sixteen years old, working as a sales associate for Champs Sports. It was my first taste of corporate America. Getting a mere five dollars and fifteen cents an hour and then getting gouged by Uncle Sam thirty percent. After getting a taste for the almighty buck, I never stopped working. I worked my fingers to the bone. I had to hustle because I wasn't the sharpest tool in the shed. I barely got through high school.

I worked a lot of odd end jobs on the outside: security guard at multiple night clubs, sales advisor for a college, decal company, fitness center, academic advisor, retail sales associate at nutritional stores, data entry specialist for an engineering firm and my university, janitor, mover, construction worker, factory worker, aerator, weight room attendant, associate football recruiter, grounds crew for my university, cash collections, telemarketing, financial analyst, personal trainer, project manager, business owner, property manager. You name it, I tried my hand at it.

My corporate career started cracking when I started my tenure at a software company. This company was rated by Forbes as one of the 100 best companies to work for. I would normally get requests to work there on a monthly-basis. Everyone wanted to work there. I was blessed to work for a company this prestigious, especially after all my knucklehead choices, and this was the company where I would stay and establish my career. I finally hit the jackpot. Salary, bonus, benefits, stock options. Forget about it! I stayed with this company for over twelve years and continued my term until my trial. I didn't realize I was trading my neatly pressed button down to a tattered orange bonaru. I could have easily seen myself working at this company for the rest of my life. Shoot, I would have never retired. I was able to do some pretty cool stuff there. When I started, I applied for a temporary finance position in the Aerospace and Defense sector. At the time, I didn't realize how dynamic this company was. I thought a normal 9-5, no big deal. You either retired from this company or in my case, you get put in the slammer.

With over 345,000 customers and an army of employees operating globally in 130 countries, I knew this company was going to be sustainable and I would do well if I kept myself out of trouble. I also wanted to work for a company where I wouldn't be pigeonholed into one assignment and would be able to transition into different roles. Working for this company I traveled to places all over the world, meeting some pretty interesting people, and leading multiple projects. From top to bottom, it was one of the greatest things that ever happened to me. I was honored to work for this organization, my managers, and colleagues.

I was happy and making fat stacks of cash and doing it the right way. But … I still wasn't fulfilling a lifelong dream of owning my own business.

❖

Row

The land of free and the home of the brave. The US was also the land where survival of the fittest takes a stronghold on society. The US can be a nasty place and then you add money, power, greed and corruption to that and it can become ruthless. I always recognized that hard work was the recipe for success for me. Just like in football and bodybuilding I had to outwork people. I was going to set my own hustle, channeling my energy on venturing out and diversifying, just like my father.

My father had a work ethic that resembled that of some of the greatest business tycoons. Rest was for the weak, and he modeled himself after Fortune 500 CEOs. "Coffee's for closers," stated by Alec Baldwin in Glengarry Glen Ross. I also strived to have a similar mindset not only in business, but also in life. I always wanted to try my hand at different opportunities, never relying on just one hustle. No rest for the wicked.

If you have the mindset, then the possibilities are endless. If I could choose one characteristic from my father, that would be it. Work ethic! He hustled when others were off and always tried to do things above and beyond his call of duty. First one in and last one to leave. I tried to emulate that trait throughout my whole life. I always wanted to grind harder than all my peers at my craft. One example of that was during my senior year at Benedictine, when I was taking twenty-one credit hours and scrubbing toilets at Life Time Fitness, working the graveyard shift from 11 p.m. to 7 a.m. on the weekends, then I would drive back to my dorm, and work a full day from 7:30 a.m. to 5 p.m., busting my hump aerating customers' lawns in Naperville, Illinois. I was pushing for every dime. I was dedicated to continuing working as a student athlete, training the weight pile for hours, and working two jobs. I maintained that back-breaking schedule for months through the fall and spring seasons. Whatever didn't break me made me stronger, and that was my father's mentality.

I wanted to start a business not only for self-fulfillment and making money based on my vision, but I also wanted to create a business from scratch and help as many people as I could. I earned my commission when my clients came up to me and told me that I helped change their life.

I wanted to emulate my father's business acumen. I started two businesses in the health industry and even a small business with a couple of friends from an old employer in the lawn care industry. That tanked.

Day 6: Living the American Dream

I started a nutritional business in 2005 after years and years of self-experimentation, research, and winning my first bodybuilding competition. I received a great following after the Midwest Iron Man competition in Chicago, Illinois. Throughout the diet and preparation, I tapped into the dietetic aspect of bodybuilding, eating quality, nutritious foods and putting together a formula that would help me. I never thought my body experimentation would help me start a business, but it did.

After the competition, I was asked by many gym rats for the secret sauce. Again, it's just a little good ole fashion elbow grease. Within a few short months I dropped my bodyweight and body fat percentages and had championship results.

My bodybuilding mentor was operating a successful nutritional consultation business, assisting clients and making money hand over fist. He was successful in assisting some of the best talent in the bodybuilding industry and charging thousands for nutritional advice. Why couldn't I do the same thing?

Even before the Iron Man competition I wanted to start a business, but I didn't have the business vision. My father's vision of no holds barred mentality inspired me to start my own business as a nutritional consultant operating under the name "Fayaz's Nutrition." Pretty vain, I guess. My mission was to help clients incorporate a healthy diet and workout regimen tailored to each person's specified criteria and schedule. The business was designed to support everyone with his or her dietary needs and design a workout. I operated for over ten years and reached over 100 clients, successfully helping them manage a healthy lifestyle.

Fayaz's Nutrition was never supposed to be a big corporation. It was started with the intention of helping people, period. I wanted to start something small and gain leverage. There were a lot of facets to business that aren't written in a textbook and I didn't learn them in business school. I learned them from the hard knocks of working hours on end. The experiences I have had in business have been both good and bad.

My thinking was I needed multiple revenue streams to survive. My generation won't see social security, and pension plans are now becoming obsolete in the US corporate world. We won't be able to survive with our 401K to fund retirements. I don't even know where my retirement is now.

I funded myself by any means necessary. I didn't believe in borrowing money from anyone. I believed in living the American dream and fighting for everything.

Row

My businesses were never these huge enterprises, but they were mine, and my nutritional business was still operating until I got put away.

My ultimate goal was to open a personal training studio with my nutritional consultation business. I knew that wasn't in my immediate timeline back in 2005. I was going to continue to work full-time for my employer. I just received my graduate degree in Executive Business Management, earning the highest distinction on the Dean's List, which don't mean a damn thing, and wanted to work for a few years, leveraging my earned degree before I dived into owning a storefront and raising the stakes. I already had years of corporate America work experience under my belt and wanted to expand into an entrepreneur. What was the point of getting my graduate degree if I was going to work for someone else?

It was important to take the things I learned training and dieting and incorporating my own methodologies to help other people, using more of a hands-on approach by personal training. I was given the knowledge and gift to be a bodybuilder and I wanted to give that wisdom to whoever wanted to acquire it.

The fitness community was very robust. Anyone that walked into a gym around peak times slammed with yoga hot pants and muscle tees. Being a gym advocate was not an easy undertaking as it was very time-consuming. People have kids, jobs, spouses, and other life commitments that competed with going to the gym every day and investing an hour or two in their physical health. On top of that, they didn't have the insight on how to properly exercise or take in the right nutrients. That was where my expertise came in from years and years of self-experimentations and slamming weights.

There was an overwhelming population that wanted to exercise on a regular basis, but didn't have a proper regimen in place and didn't know how to exercise. The gym could be a very intimidating place, crowded with gym nerds waiting for the machine you're using as you try figure out how to use it. It would drive people away. I was a big advocate of training for a purpose. There were too many gym rats that love to exercise their muscles but also like to exercise their mouths. I trained hard, pushed myself, and then bounced. No chit chatting or lolly gagging. I didn't spend time making small talk. Hoodie, ear phones, wraps, chalk, and heavy weights, that's all I needed. Lift heavy or go home!

Exercising was the biggest investment I made in my life during my twenties. People purchase investment properties and stocks, always putting money away in a savings account in hopes of having a sumptuous retirement, sipping on champagne while getting a full body massage. Well, that retirement would be cut short if you weren't taking care of your body. I tried to initiate that life investment in every one of my clients.

My first few years, I was building a client base. My business was built the same way I built my physique, and that was through hard work and grind. I didn't ask for a handout from anyone. I didn't run to mommy and daddy and ask for help.

There were thousands of personal trainers, nutritional consultants, and dieticians, but only a handful that could assist in all aspects of health and fitness. I was a one-stop shop. The beauty of my service was that I wasn't reading books and then regurgitating what I read. I was designing programs for my clients based on my experiences, what I went through over years and years of exercising and dieting. I trained and was trained by Olympic athletes, professional athletes and world-renowned nutritionists. I gathered their expertise and developed my own practice. I took a lot of pride in designing programs based on my experiences. No sugar coating. My clients realized that my telling them to only eat certain foods and manipulating their intake all came from a place of personal experience and sacrifice. My bodybuilding days gave me a lot of credibility.

I met hundreds of people who wanted to lose weight, gain muscle, or just wanted to become healthy. Only a few people changed their lifestyle and made that sacrifice. It was a difficult prophecy, because people don't realize that it's a 24/7 commitment. Too bad I got locked up, or else I would have kept doing it.

I was finally able to open a personal training studio, fulfilling a lifelong dream. My training studio was a one-on-one training studio designed for clients to experience a workout in a very sequestered environment. I was training clients in a fully functioning studio, equipped with cardio and exercise machines. It wasn't the biggest facility, but it was mine. Right in the comfort of my own renovated garage.

I was training people under my terms. I didn't have the thousand-dollar machines, with Britney Spears playing in the background. My gym was hardcore, with rusted steel, blaring Metallica, "Harvester of Sorrow," in the background. No ventilation or central cooling. I trained anyone who wanted to work hard. I trained bodybuilders, athletes, blue and white-collar professionals. My gym only

Row

discriminated the strong from the weak. You had to come to train with your game face, or else I would break you down. It was my homegrown training methodology that I tested and proved on myself.

The years and years of training, eating right, and experimenting with my diet helped me to start two businesses, and the hard work was paying off. All the principles I instilled as part of my vision and mission were in all aspects of my life.

My business was doing OK, and I was helping hundreds of people, but I hit a speed bump. Life in the free world stopped.

Day 5 Jail Journal: Bleeding Heart

Instead of giving me a last meal, how about giving me a book to read? At least, while I was in general population I occupied my time reading, playing music, talking to my cellie. Something. How many pushups and jumping jacks can one man do. I used to love getting my hands on crime novels. Some of the best books I read were The Hot House, Tattoos on the Heart, No Angel, You Got Nothing Coming, Gang Leader for a Day, The Black Hand, and Lessons from San Quentin. All these books have one moral code. If you do the crime, you will do the time.

At least they have given me pencil and paper. Believe me, sitting in my jail cell, scripting my life, and detailing all my shortcomings is not easy, but it's my therapy.

The night of my incarceration is a distant memory, but the things that led to my imprisonment are imprinted in my mind clear as day. I examined every detail of my trial, trying to piece the allegations that were presented by the state. I can now live by what the state has named me, a menace to society, and told by the judge to lock the door and throw away the key.

Every day is a struggle between my inner demons and reality, which is death. Going through my trial, I saw people's true colors. Like the great Muhammed Ali said. When I got locked down, people I called friends dispersed. I was left to fight my own battle. I was classified as a corpse, forgotten about, and thrown into the trash. My accomplishments on the gridiron are now old news. My MBA is just a piece of paper locked away in my mom's cellar. All my humanitarian and corporate awards are probably sitting in a trash compound now. My nutritional business and personal training studio gone. Bodybuilding state titles, who cares. All my worldly possessions vanished. Everything about

207

my past existence has been repossessed, just like my family's beautiful ranch home. I might as well be executed, because I have been forgotten. Just point me to the chamber and I will go there myself.

❖

I did a lot of irresponsible crap throughout my life leading up to my incarceration, but one aspect of my life that I can hang my hat on was volunteering. I am not trying to be self-righteous here, but I don't believe that volunteering should be voluntary. Volunteering your time was not a requirement and has become a form of penance in the penal system. Many communities relied on punishment after a crime, requesting the individual to produce volunteer hours as part of their parole.

When I got pinched in Texas I was assigned community service, which I vowed to do. I never fulfilled my debt to society. I took the easy way out during my knucklehead days. Another cowardly act in my twenties. I owed a debt to society. One way or another I had to give back.

We are all responsible for lending a helping hand to the less fortunate. Some of us are dealt a terrible hand, filled with adverse consequences. We should all be helping humanity as much as we can. If it was up to me, I would do every illegal activity to extort money from criminals and give it to people who need it. Criminals like Bernie Madoff, Al Capone, etc.... The men that strong-armed innocent people and stripped them of their own wealth. The billion dollar corporations like the Lehman Brothers and Enron's of the world don't deserve to live. They devoured people's fortunes, ripping apart their pensions and retirement funds, leaving their families out in the cold. They are the scum of the earth. Drop those weasels in the SQ req yard for a few days.

With all my shortcomings in life, I also had a lot I was proud of. Being a servant to the less fortunate was one of them. I have always taken pride in helping people in need. I think we all get a helping hand along the way; giving back was always a necessity to me. Like I said, I owed it. I took the cowardly act and walked away from my obligations when I got apprehended in Texas. I was young and dumb, but when I got older I turned the page and realized what needed to be done.

Who knows where I would have been if I didn't get help. The more I gave back to my community, the more I enjoyed doing it. The wonderful aspect about volunteering was a lot of places needed the support. We live in a world of millions with a minute fraction of those lending their time.

There are tons of immoral people in the world, but there are also a lot of extraordinary people. You read about the people flying into Houston, Texas when the city was ravaged by floods. What about all the people volunteering their time during Hurricane Katrina trying to restore New Orleans. I always tried to be an example and volunteer with different organizations. My mother was the one who taught me to always give back no matter what. She gave her whole life to the good of society.

I volunteered for great organizations like Habitat for Humanity, building a home for a homeless family. It was a great experience watching a family whose home was ripped away from them getting a new home. Watching their faces as they walked into their new home was priceless.

KaBoom constructing a playground for an elementary school. Urban Outreach picking up trash in the Chicagoland area, Little City Foundation housing assistance for the mentally handicapped, Prisoner Visitation and Support motivational speaking to inmates, Care 4 Calais providing medical assistance to the refugees, Cancer Research Foundation running 5k, Disaster Relief Foundation performing a bake off and donating the contributions, Somerville Homeless Coalition serving food to families in need, to name a few.

Also, giving monetary contributions to organizations all over the world like Community Health, Housing, and Social Education (CHHASE), Sai Educational Rural and Urban Development Society (SERUDS). Sounds braggy right? But what the hell this is the part of my life I am really proud of.

My mother was always a very loving and giving person. She worked at Little City Foundation. I was always captivated by how she would be able to work with the mentally handicapped, giving back to her society. She served the community for years as a volunteer and house manager. She would call the residents of Little City her children. After seven years as a house manager, she left Little City Foundation, leaving a legacy behind which can never be emulated by another employee. I visited her on multiple occasions, discovering how revered she was at Little City. Everyone loved her.

Row

During the holiday season of 2009 and 2010, I volunteered at Little City. My initial experience was fulfilling the residents' Christmas present wish lists, gathering and donating as many presents as possible. It's the least I could do, as I was blessed to get presents from my parents every year, even when times were tight. My stockings were always stuffed.

My family and friends donated over 3G's worth of toys, fulfilling over 100 Christmas stockings. I remember taking bags and bags of toys. It felt damn good. It wasn't enough though. I should have given more.

In 2016 refugees from Iran, Somalia, Syria, and other various parts of the eastern hemisphere flooded Calais, France in hopes of a better life. Many of these refugees trekked long legs through various precarious situations, landing in Calais. The environment was extremely hostile, and poverty was rampant, as many families were residing in tents, trying to bear the harsh winter conditions. Families endured less than humane conditions with very little heat, water, and electricity, trying to better their lives away from a tyrannical government.

Calais was housing nearly 8,000 migrants in an area called "the Jungle." Reminded me of this joint with all the chaos. Migrants set up outhouses and living tents. They left their countries in hopes of a better life, ultimately trying to seek refuge in Great Britain. The tenants of the Jungle were all under the watchful eye of the French government, which wanted to enforce the strict French deportation laws. 5.0 was everywhere, strapped with rifles.

My wife, brother in-law, and I made a pilgrimage to Calais to volunteer in their medical tents, offering much-needed care to the residents of the Jungle. Lines would be out the door with people in need. My wife was the true hero, helping as many people as she could. We stayed near the Jungle, often hearing about the French police bulldozing the tents in the evening, trying to kick as many refugees back to their native land.

I walked away with an appreciation for life. The living conditions in the Jungle were awful; it was extremely over-populated, like chickens in a cage ready to be slaughtered. It opened my eyes to the harsh conditions that were going on in the world. I wish I could have done more to help the residents. Shortly after we left, the Jungle was torched down by the French government. Again, I should have done more.

When my wife and I were living in the City of Brotherly Love, I volunteered my time at Sunday Breakfast, which was a male homeless shelter. Sunday Breakfast was developed not only to house Philadelphia residents, but to also provide residents a warm meal for breakfast, lunch, and dinner for thirty days as well as the proper tools to get back on their feet. The program was designed to support, rehabilitate, and educate the residents to leave Sunday Breakfast and live a long, fruitful life. It was a great program, but I realized immediately there were more people in hardship and not enough people to support the residents in need.

I was overwhelmed at how many Philadelphia residents needed housing and a warm meal. I also recognized drug misuse was widespread, and addiction was affecting so many Philadelphians, driving them from their homes.

I saw some crazy stuff in there. An adolescent man waiting for a meal, dozing off on his chair, drooling, going into convulsions, being dope sick. Saw some of the same stuff in gen pop. Or watching grown men argue about not getting called up to eat sooner.

My responsibilities were serving the men a meal during dinner, cleaning pots and pans, and helping residents with their resume writing. I wish I could have done more; unfortunately, I was in Philly for a short stint.

My wife and I lived in Beantown for a couple of years. I always wanted to be part of an organization that looked out for the community. When the families of my community put their heads down on their pillows at night, I wanted to make sure I did everything in my power to help maintain their safety. I wanted to be part of an organization that kept the streets clean. I decided to apply to become a police officer. I finally turned the page after years of knucklehead choices. I was on the other side of the law now and putting on the blue and white meant the world to me. I was inspired to lend a helping hand to the United States judicial system. Crime all over the nation was growing.

Row

I was helping support the full-time police officers in patrolling the streets. Putting on my shield, uniform, duty belt, and spit shined boots, gave me honor and dignity.

Roaming the streets in my squad car I saw some crazy shit: fights, people having sex in precarious places, drug abuse, gang activity, violence. It opened my eyes to the disparaging world we live in. Brought back old memories.

It sucks being locked up. I knew that even before I landed in the joint. People make mistakes and get locked up for it, but that doesn't mean we are bad people. On the outside, I wanted to visit inmates who had been abandoned. By family, friends, everyone. Just like me now! I wanted to give back to those people. To try and give back to people who took a misstep in life and landed in prison.

I joined the Prisoner Visitor Support (PVS) program. PVS was devised to provide prisoners with regular, face-to-face, contact from the outside world to help them cope with prison life and prepare for successful re-entry into society. I started with PVS to offer a support channel for inmates to tell their story and have an ear to listen to them. I was there to provide motivation and teach them coping skills when they got released. I wanted to lend my time so inmates could speak freely and enjoy the company from someone on the outside of prison.

I wish I could speak to a PVS visitor now. I believe we are all criminals to some extent. We all live under different circumstances. I was very close to ending up in prison multiple times in my early adulthood. If the judge hadn't shown me some mercy, shoot, I would have been a felon much earlier.

When I finally cleared all the bureaucratic red tape to enter prisons, I was directed to volunteer at a medical facility, which housed over 1,000 inmates, known for notorious mob wise guys such as John Franzese, John Riggi, and Frank Locascio, as well as other notable lawbreakers like Peter Madoff, Roger Stockham, and the one half of the Boston Marathon bombers, Dzhokhar Tsarnaev.

The inmates were experienced criminals in their field. They were all guilty of their crimes and deserved to be in prison. I didn't pity their situations, but I realized these hardened criminals weren't going to get released and become model citizens without proper rehabilitation.

Day 5: Bleeding Heart

I gained an understanding of their mindset as they engaged in criminal activities, and how they felt during incarceration. I was working with a wide array of criminals with convictions that ranged from drug trafficking and armed robbery to sex offenses. One knucklehead was in prison indefinitely for threatening the President of the United States. Smart move! Another inmate I spoke to on a regular basis was part of El Chapo drug syndicate and worked as a drug mule for over twenty-five years. He would run four deliveries across state lines per month, delivering millions of dollars in blow. He was pulling in $75G's a month, living a luxurious life before being pinched. I would have signed up for that. To this day, he didn't dry snitch on any of his colleagues. He was very descriptive in recounting some of his deliveries and how he was ultimately captured. Pretty interesting stuff.

Every visit we would grab a table, sit, and break bread. What I would do now for one of those vending machine cheeseburgers!

I was most proud to volunteer for this place called ROCA. It was an outreach program that worked with youth gang members that got the short end of the stick their whole life and had to rely on their gang for money, food, love, everything. The vision of ROCA was to keep these guys out of prison. My responsibility was tailored towards mentoring the youth in a wide range of areas like resume writing, polishing their interviewing skills, and reaching out to youth on the streets.

I enjoyed talking to the youth. They too had a knucklehead philosophy, but still had the opportunity to change their ways. Their life growing up on the streets, coming from poverty and broken homes was a lot more challenging than mine growing up. I was ecstatic to see some of these young guys working so hard to change their lives and was honored to work with them.

The youth workers at ROCA were true heroes in my eyes. I was only volunteering for a short stint, but these guys were beating the streets everyday trying to change lives.

The most challenging work I did was for Crisis Text Line as a crisis counselor. This non-profit organization provides free crisis intervention for anyone who is dealing with suicidal thoughts. I found out quickly there are a lot of people dealing with chronic depression and anxiety. My purpose as a counselor was to offer an ear for people to voice their concerns and then help them mitigate the risk of killing themselves.

It was difficult working with people dealing with so much anxiety and depression; dealing with addiction, bullying, abuse, and a host of other problems. Depression is no joke!

Life is not easy. We deal with so much adversity, and the Crisis Text Line was another great way to give back. I was able to explore all my past experiences and share my insight to help other people that are dealing with similar issues.

All my volunteer experiences were humbling. I was granted opportunities and second chances in life. I always thought it was necessary to help as many people as I could in any capacity, whether it was donating money to organizations, mentoring people, or giving a few dollars to the homeless even if I knew they would end up spending that money on drugs. Who was I to judge? I was coached and mentored immeasurably in my life journey and I still made a ton of bad decisions.

I was granted a ton of extraordinary volunteer opportunities and thankful to the men and women who do this type of work every day. Despite all the great experiences, I still sit in my cell, pondering.

DAY 4 Jail Journal: Fantastic Voyage

Couple more days. Couple more days and they will be taking me away in a body bag, toe tagged!. It's like being in a zoo in the row compound, and I am the main attraction, viewed by everyone. I catch myself pacing back and forth, trapped within my thoughts. I probably complete 20,000 steps every day, constantly pondering what would have been. I am imprisoned in my own nightmare.

Living in a box is tough without any outlets to express myself apart from my writing. I must keep my mind free as I am serving my last few days. When you're serving back door parole like I am, you live your life reliving past experiences. My memories are all that I have. Mind over matter is easier said than done, but once you get to that stage you can conquer anything. This is my legacy. All my life's work is compiled in a few hundred pages.

We are prisoners of our space and our minds, trapped in a correctional facility for our entire lives. Where is the rehabilitation in that? Humans are not supposed to be confined to a small space and be expected to live in a peaceful manner. That is why you hear about so much violence in prisons. It's a common theme among some of the worst prisons, and San Quentin is the worst of the worst. You cram thousands of career criminals into a box. What do you think will happen? San Quentin is a time bomb, ticking away until an explosion, like the prison riots in 1971, 1982, 2006, and 2013. I have seen shanks made from toothbrushes, broom handles, pens, pencils … I have seen a con kiester a kesue in his permanent pocket. Whatever sharp object an inmate can grab is enough to put another inmate three knee deep. You puncture the right part of the body, and it could leave a man drowning in his own blood.

Luckily, I have only had one altercation and it was with an inmate who was outside of gang influence. He was considered a monkey mouth who constantly

Row

gossiped about nothing. This confrontation was when I was housed in general population. Luckily, I didn't have to deal with a mob, getting into an altercation with this inmate. I was at dinner, in the chow hall, when an inmate approached me, asking for my meal. He was a jail veteran, locked away on a thirty-year bid for armed robbery. He was a stocky meat head tatted with prison ink. He probably thought I was a lame duck and couldn't defend myself. He was dangerous and wanted to test me. He put his revolting muddy brogans on my stool, positioning his stained hands on the table, and was about to sink his stubby fingers in my food. Now, jailhouse cuisine is awful, but if I allowed him to take my ladmo bag, I would never eat again.

Prison food is worse than school cafeteria food, but it was mine, and I didn't want to give the impression that I was a punk. Giving one tray away would lead to ongoing harassment, not only by this thug, but by anyone, including correctional officers. Booty bandits would feast on my hide.

I told him that he couldn't have my dinner, and he proceeded to grab my shirt, trying to lift me from the ground. He wasn't very strong because I threw him off, giving him a chin check and dropping him instantly, like Tyson dropping Spinks in the first round. I could have pounced on him like a cheetah on a rabbit, but I restrained him until the prison guards came and broke it up. The warden ended up giving me one day in the hole, which was probably one of the worst days of my life, but from then on, I established the reputation that I knew how to use my hands.

Going in the hole was awful. We were already in a place where we are treated like children and told what to do every second of the day. Our adulthood was taken away because of the stupid choices we made on the streets. So why start something with another inmate and have our limited privileges taken away? knuckl

The inmate who attacked me ended up getting five days in the hole. No big deal. After the altercation, he was transferred to another pod. I don't know what gave him the impression that he could get my tray. I guess that's prison.

❖

Day 4: Fantastic Voyage

I would have loved to live a nomadic lifestyle, living off the land, and constantly moving. I loved traveling and exploring. I never wanted to be stuck in one spot. How ironic! I only wish I would have started traveling earlier in my life instead of making so many knucklehead decisions. The world is such a unique place filled with diversity. I was privileged to be able to travel for work and pleasure. I wouldn't let a month go by without taking a road trip or a flight somewhere. I was fortunate to have traveled to some amazing places and to have had some great adventures. Now the only traveling I do is in my head.

I loved traveling all over, but there was nothing like traveling overseas. I realized how different their cultures are compared to the ones I lived in. It was fascinating. Western civilization was so much more rigid compared to other places. I felt like we always focused on the American dream, which was outlined in a strategic format. Go to college, get a job, get married, buy a house, have kids, retire, and go six feet deep. Well, I don't think that was my path. Along the way, we developed a schedule around each milestone. We didn't truly live our own life. We became trained robots searching for answers, which we thought could be found in our daily 9-5. A lot of us lived to work. I couldn't live like that.

I loved traveling on my own and with my wife. We were tag team partners and loved to see the world and everything it had to offer. When we got married, we wanted to travel as much as we could before starting a family. We loved kids and wanted to have a big family, but wanted to enjoy each other and travel first.

During the first five years of marriage, we went everywhere; over 60 trips all over the world. We went to Maldives, Puerto Vallarta, Germany, Colorado, Houston, San Francisco, Toronto, New York, Washington D.C., Paris, Karachi, Orlando, Dubai, London, Oman, Montreal, Atlanta, Mexico, Jamaica, San Diego, Las Vegas, China, Los Angeles, Brussels, Budapest, Amsterdam, etc... These were just a few destinations we explored together.

We also moved quite a bit from Chicago to Philadelphia, then Boston, and then to Cincinnati. It's all about life's journey. We explored and wanted to see everything we could, eat everything we could, and engaged ourselves into as many cultures as we could. We loved it. Materials will come and go it's the memories that last.

Probably the best vacation I ever took was my honeymoon in Maldives, the tropical island near Sri Lanka, south of India. The natives called it Island Paradise.

Row

The place was ridiculous. Crystal clear ocean water, beautiful people, great food, amazing weather; what more could you ask for. During one of the evenings we had sharks swimming between our legs as we walked on the shores of the Indian ocean. We spent five days in pure bliss. I started to reflect on my life in the States, where I was consumed with living the American dream. I relieved stress by pressing 100 pounds of metal over and over again, while the natives enjoyed life on a beautiful island far away from people. I started thinking about leaving a life of stress behind and living on the island sipping on pina coladas and mai tai's. What a wonderful life.

I had some other great adventures before I got locked up; catching sharks deep sea fishing in the Atlantic, kayaking in La Jolla beach next to a whale, visiting Buckingham palace for brunch with the Queen, jumping from a plane high amongst the clouds, snorkeling with sting rays and dolphins, white water rafting class five rapids, hang gliding over the Florida Keys, cliff diving over the reefs in Jamaica, spelunking in caves, catching a moray eel in the Indian Ocean, hiking up the Atlas mountain in Morocco, zip lining through the Canopy mountains in Puerto Vallarta, racing up the sand castles in an ATV in Dubai, hiking up 1000 steps of the Great Wall of China, and kayaking up the Florida Keys among salt water crocodiles, just to name a few. I lived to travel, inspired by the journey to explore.

I truly believe life was about experiencing the good and bad. I didn't grow as a person until I went through the good and the bad. If I didn't expose myself to trying new things and adventures, I wouldn't live life to the fullest. It's not easy to try new things because you must be taught and that requires the ability to listen and learn. That was much easier said than done when we are children, but when we become adults we don't want another adult teaching us anything. We become stubborn in our ways. We know everything already, right? You must check your ego at the door and seek new quests and grow from those opportunities.

Put yourself in God's hands, cherish him, and realize he is both your maker and your destroyer. When it's your time to go. He will decide your fate. Even with my fate in a few days, the judicial system did not decide my fate, it was God.

PART V
<u>Lifeline</u>

<u>Day 3</u> Jail Journal: Leader of the Pack

I couldn't care less about life anymore. These people want to take it away from me, then so be it. Let them have it because I am going to a better place. I believe death is much better than spending life in solitude, left with only my meditations and prayers, being consumed with my sorrow and regret. My depression consumes me every second and life in prison creates an emptiness inside that devours every inch of my soul. Let's end the misery now. The anxiety of knowing there isn't much time left is unbearable. It's like having a timer on me ticking every second away. I wish I could drift away on my moped cruising the streets like the old days. Every day, I think about all the sorrow I have caused my loved ones and dying would relieve my family from thinking about me any further.

Even though I do wish to leave in peace, I know the day that I experience the surge of chemicals percolating through every vein of my body like heroin passing through the blood stream is going to be excruciating. Even though the pain will last a few seconds, the agony makes me think about all the other inmates that were once strapped.

All the pulls, breaks, tears, and trauma I faced on the outside won't compare to taking the stainless steel ride.

In San Quentin, I am declared a non-career criminal. A non-career criminal on Death Row is a rarity. I am like a black guy in a mosh pit at a Pantera concert. Non-career criminals are classified as prisoners who have a clean rap sheet, apart from a couple of crimes. They end up taking the wrong turn and end up in the slammer. I have paid my taxes, was a productive member of society, have participated in dozens of charities giving back to the less fortunate, worked hard my whole life, am properly educated, and so on, but my life didn't end up as I imagined. The last chapter of my life story is going to end soon. Hanging on by a lifeline.

My appearance is now only a shell of what it used to be. I am not talking about when I was a competitive bodybuilder jacked with muscle, but when I first arrived at San Quentin. I am only a shell of a man now, due to the lack of nutrition, exercise, sunlight, and substance in my life. I am emotionally battered and wouldn't be able to last another year. Broken dreams and broken promises.

I don't know how so many of my prison mates live this life. You will be surprised at how quickly your mind, body, and soul go to mush when you don't have anything to amuse yourself with. I spend time reliving my sentencing and past life. Often, my thoughts run into severe depression when I'm staring into the white cement, surrounded by cold steel. It's my metal casket.

I try to look through the walls, past the barricade onto a boat in the middle of a desolate ravine. My boom box blaring 80s classic rock, while I am fishing in the Indian ocean catching a 3-foot moray eel, watching dolphins soaring from the water. I was an avid fisherman growing up and would give anything to have one more day on the water with a rod in one hand and a two pound salmon in the other.

I overhear the prison bugs saying, "Mr. Ali is a smart man, but deep down he has an irrational, murderous rage lurking inside him. We should lock the door and throw away the key." When I hear nonsense like this, I think about my past mentors who helped me in school or in sports. They taught me how to be a successful person in life, not someone whom they portray me as — that heartless killer. Sometimes life can take a wicked turn for the worst.

❖

Carpenter, electrician, plumber, property owner, business owner, butcher, baker, deliveryman... The list goes on and on. Those were just some of the occupations my father acquired by working his fingers to the bone, providing for his family. He was a tireless, unselfish man, providing unconditional love to his children.

DAY 3: LEADER OF THE PACK

My father grew up dirt poor in a large family in Karachi, Pakistan. Even as a young boy he was destined for greatness. He wanted more in life than a three-flat bungalow. He aspired to have a large family and live a fruitful life in the good ole US of A. He always thought America was the place to be. When he was thirty-something he left my mom in Pakistan, moving to America by himself, with just a week's worth of coins. Within that week, he had to establish a life for his family or else he would be homeless. He packed a small suitcase and bounced from his native homeland, but he was driven by intestinal fortitude. He was the trailblazer in the family and was heavily relied upon by his loved ones back home. Not knowing anyone in the United States, he gave my mom a kiss and assured her he would set up everything in the US before calling her over. Forty years later, he owned multiple businesses and properties, lived in a beautiful five-bedroom house, made great friends, and raised three kids. Not only did he make a name for himself and his family, he helped dozens of people migrate from the subcontinent to the land of liberty along the way.

When my father first came to the States, he decided that Chicago was the place to be. It was a densely populated metropolitan city, bustling with an enriched economic presence in the late 70s and early 80s. My father ignored the harsh weather conditions he had never endured and ignored the crime rate, which was high because of gangs polluting the streets and drugs infiltrating many residences. He decided Chicago was the place his family would make a name for themselves. His intuition told him that his family wouldn't thrive under the harsh conditions. He made a courageous move, ignoring the warning signals staring him in the face. He understood the struggle he was going to face, being in another country with limited understanding of the English language and very little money. Most would cave under that pressure. Actually, most wouldn't have left, but my father was always a man that would face adversity head on and conquer any obstacles. He had that moxie.

His first job he was earning a whopping $1.60 per hour. Coming from a foreign land and not speaking the native language, there weren't a lot of job openings. He took whatever hustle he could or else he would have lived on the streets. Going back home with his tail between his legs was never in the itinerary. I think that is where my iron will came from. It was imbedded in me by my father. He tried so many different things in his life, never giving up on his dream of settling his family in the US.

Row

Under the harsh weather conditions in the Windy City, he worked for months on end, surviving on a few measly dollars a day living in a one-bedroom hut, saving every penny he could. He wanted to make sure his bride came with optimism. He delivered on his promise a few months later when my mom arrived in the US.

Living in Chicago during the frozen tundra months wasn't luxurious to say the least, especially with a minute cash flow. Heating was often run by a small heater that could barely heat up a bedroom. Hot water was a luxury. All the amenities that I took for granted on the outside were scarce for my parents during their early stages in Chicago. My mother and father survived on very little, surviving in a one-bedroom apartment smaller than a dorm room. The harsh reality of living in the land of opportunity was smacking them in the face.

Perseverance was the word that described my father. Not only was he a tireless worker, he was tough as nails. I remember my father working in the garage, cutting wood on his table saw. He was installing a waterbed in one of our bedrooms in our Hoffman Estates ranch home. I heard a loud thud, like wood hitting the concrete. Suddenly he entered the foyer of our house holding a dripping, bloodstained towel. My father cut his fingers to the bone on the table saw, leaving his fingers severed. He was losing blood rapidly and needed to be escorted to the intensive care unit immediately. We got in the car and he drove to the hospital; three kids in tow in utter shock. Never did my father panic and he kept his composure so his three kids would not panic. He ended up being admitted to the ICU for days. That's what type of man my father was and I tried to emulate that trait as much as I could. My father left a legacy behind and I wanted to try and preserve that legacy through my actions.

My father was a great man with an extraordinary talent for making people feel special. He had charisma and was the life of the party. He had that social capability, attracting friends. John Gotti was a beloved boss of the Gambino crime family known for his willingness to charm everyone he came across. He was loved by his family, friends, and much of the US. My father shared similar traits leaving a lasting impression with everyone he met. He had a talent for making whoever he was speaking to feel as if they were the most important person in the entire world. That was his gift.

When my father retired, he purchased four townhouses and became a property manager. Managing four properties was a retirement for my father, who used to work from sunup till sundown, six days a week.

Day 3: Leader of the Pack

My father was a family man, businessman, dedicated father, devoted husband, loving grandfather, and great friend. His legacy lives on in the hearts of the people who loved him, and he is sorely missed every day.

Rest in peace, Father.

DAY 2 JAIL JOURNAL: MOTHER

"What can I do to help? Can I get you some mud, water?" I am just lying in my bed with a stone-cold stare. This cowboy is obviously new and hasn't been tainted by the prison bureaucratic red tape. He should know better to ask me anything. He can stick that water and mud where the sun don't shine.

A CO stands watch twenty-four hours a day outside my cell. His job is to monitor me while I await my fate. He looks like he is in his twenties and completely wet behind the ears. Barely any facial hair on his gaunt little body. Punk was probably straight out of employment training getting thrown at the carnivores in SQ. This dude's a duck. Every noise he hears makes him giddy like a cheerleader getting asked to homecoming by the star quarterback. They put this kid at my side, one step closer to my execution. Tick, tock. I am glad he's here because he gives me something to do to kill the monotony.

Less than forty-eight hours. I don't feel like writing anymore. Sick of all the bs, but it was a promise to myself to get this journal completed. I constantly complain about solitary confinement, but it's much better than staring at the chamber. I wish I could get a little more time.

I am stripped away of my belongings. A different CO shows up at my cell asking me for my shirt size, pant size, and shoe size. Does he really think I care about what I want to die in. Talk about a pig at a slaughterhouse. I guess that is proper protocol. Another representative from the warden's office drops by to settle the final details, my last statement, and requests for final witnesses at my execution. Why would I want anyone to witness my horrific death? He hands me a death warrant with the golden seal from the state of California. This lengthy document resembles when I purchased my first piece of property a lifetime ago filled with legal jargon. He requests I read it over thoroughly and ask the warden if I have any questions. Coward!

Row

All day long, people continue asking me if they can help me. "Can we get you some water?" "Stamps for your letters?" More people have asked me if I needed anything in the last few days than in my entire life.

My mind remains scattered all over the place. I focus on my writing, but it's frickin hard. It is critical that I reach a place of self-forgiveness. I want to spend time writing a letter to family members. Writing these letters is going to be brutal. These letters alone are enough to make me beat my executioner to the punch. My killer is the lethal injection waiting for me down the corridor. A concoction which will be delivered intravenously traveling through my body, ripping my organs with sheer pain.

My fan club has been sending me mail nonstop, asking if they can visit before my execution. I have even received requests for boneyard conjugal visits, which are prohibited for death row inmates. Where were all these fans when I was rotting in gen pop?

The intrigue of death row prisoners before any execution turns into a bizarre fetish. These opportunists want to brag to their friends about how they spoke to a death row inmate before execution. Pretty sick. I don't get visitors or letters from any of my companions. The only mail I get is from what I call "jailhouse groupies." I feel like Richard Ramirez. When Richard Ramirez, the Night Stalker, who slaughtered women across LA, was on death row, he was getting piles and piles of mail from women. He became notorious in prison for having the largest groupie list. It was rumored that at one point, the prison mail system was two weeks behind because Ramirez was getting so much mail.

There is this sudden, eerie feeling in the prison spilling over into each cell, especially in the death row compound.

Each prisoner on death row realizes that one day their date of execution will come. The realization that one day each one of us living in this barred world is going six feet under is unsettling. My day of reckoning is coming like a bat out of hell.

DAY 2: MOTHER

Besides my family and a few of my friends, is anyone going to care when I am gone? Yes, it will hurt them for a while, but will it really impact anyone's life? It feels like I have been abandoned by everyone.

❖

When I expire, I want to make sure my mother knows this was in no way a reflection of how I was raised. Quite frankly, I came from a respectable home with a lot of love. My demise was not from a broken home or getting abused when I was a child. I made poor choices and became a menace to society because of my knucklehead choices. Sometimes the roads you travel render you on the right path and sometimes they don't. I was always swerving between the right and wrong paths. That is just how it was and I couldn't control some of the things I did.

My mother was the epitome of a kindhearted and loving soul, always wanting the best for everyone. She always put others' interests before her own. She was a nurturer, providing her children unconditional love. It can't be easy being a mother to a convicted felon, who is surviving in a maximum-security prison and getting ready for execution. She has been my lifejacket through this whole process we call life. It is true that a mother's willpower will always be by her children's side, through any adverse situations. A mother's love is constant and nobody will ever contest that.

Without her it would have been difficult to pull through my trial and then my incarceration. It's not easy for a mother to visit her son through glass, having to communicate through a phone. I can't say anything to her, except that I am sorry that I did what I did and for what I put her through. I can't imagine being in her shoes, watching her youngest son in shackles, labeled a menace to society, and receiving a death sentence. It would cause any mother to have a heart attack, but she is the type of person that always looks at the glass as half full and always takes the good out of any outcome. Even with my incarceration and knowing I was guilty, she knew God had plans for me in prison.

God would look out for me. My mother is a very spiritual woman, praying for her children every chance she gets, reading the Holy Quran over a thousand times, cover to cover. She was always praying for others' health and happiness. My mother's heart is bigger than anyone I know. If she could trade places with me, she would.

Row

My mother was a sacrificial lamb that always gave, gave, and gave. She never needed anything in her life, except for her family and friends. She never asked for anything except for her kids to be successful. She would do anything for her children and always gave me support in anything that I did. I feel like I let her down. I did let her down, and I spend a lot of sleepless nights re-examining my life, justifying my actions, and making sense out of all of this.

How did I go from being a loving and caring friend, son, brother, husband, and citizen to becoming institutionalized in San Quentin Correctional Facility?

If you took a survey asking how many people would sit in a room with Fayaz Ali, the convict from San Quentin, ninety percent of them would be petrified. I am now classified in the same breath as some of the world's most hardened prisoners.

One of the brightest spots in my life has been my mother. If I could communicate with my mom now, I would tell her not to worry and I am at peace. The fear of visiting God has prepared me to start making peace with my inner demons that haunted me for years. I was held captive for years sitting in a cage while the outside world was paying for my room and board. It's time that I meet my maker and atone for my sins.

My mother has been a positive influence in my life and has been my angel sitting on my shoulder. My parents provided an infinite amount of love and opportunity. They came from a third world country with very little and made me. They provided food, shelter, education, and whatever else I needed to thrive.

Growing up, my mother always tried to provide us with everything we wanted, even though we didn't have much money.

It kills me that I am so far away from my mom, thinking about her growing older without me. She was my inspiration growing up and has always been by my side. Through the ups and downs she has been a constant. People have come and gone into my life, but she has always been by my side through thick and thin. There are not a lot of people who stick with you like that.

When I was a kid, I remember to this day whining about wanting a lollipop in the wee evening hours. It was late at night and I could not stop whining about having a goddamn lollipop. My mother never wanted to let any of her children down and always wanted to fulfill all our requests. She ended up walking five blocks to the nearest convenience store. Our neighborhood was gang-infested and going out late at night was a terrible proposition. My mom walked all the way to the convenience store holding my hand with her head held high while thugs yelled profanities and threw things at her. It didn't bother her and she kept moving. Like a soldier. Her whole life she sacrificed and fought to put a stake in the ground for her family. My family and I could have been trampled in the mean streets of Chicago, but the perseverance of my mother and father gave us the iron will we needed to flourish.

❖

I learned so much during my early adolescence. The struggle that we endured has been burned on my mind.

My brother and I were always creating mischief growing up and had multiple altercations with some of the other children in the neighborhood. There was an occasion when we ended up getting into a fight with a neighborhood bully and roughed him up quite a bit. He ended up calling his mom, who was built like an NFL linebacker. My brother and I summoned our mom, not knowing the other woman's stature. My mom ran to our aid, not backing down one bit, submitting over six inches in height and probably fifty pounds in weight. Fisticuffs went flying and even though the other woman got the better of the exchanges, she walked away realizing never to mess with my mother again.

My mother's finest characteristic was her endless support. Whatever sport I played, my mother always backed me. She watched me go from playing soccer, swimming, baseball, wrestling, track and field, boxing, football, bodybuilding, mixed martial arts, etc...

Whatever sport I participated in, she always wanted to let me know that I wasn't alone. With the amount of sports and training I did, I always needed someone to take me to the hospital. There seemed to be a doctor's visit every month. She took me to every appointment, making sure I was safe. She never questioned any of the activities I partook in.

Row

When I broke my arm multiple times, I had a long cast, requiring a bag while I took a shower. She would always wake up to wrap that bag around my arm before I took a shower. Whatever I needed, she provided, and that is why I am the luckiest son in the world.

I will soon depart from this world leaving my mother to deal with loss. I love her with all my heart and thank her for her unconditional love, and for being my lifeline, always.

Mom, don't think I have forgotten. I haven't forgotten how you went hunting for my WWE wrestling ring when I couldn't stop whining. I haven't forgotten when you broke your ankle trying to carry me. I haven't forgotten when you drove hours lost trying to look for my soccer game. I haven't forgotten when I would wake up and the first thing I scream for you and you would come running. I haven't forgotten the million times you prepared a meal for the family after a long day's work. I haven't forgotten when I got in trouble in Mexico and you came to get me. I haven't forgotten all the doctor's visits you took me to. I haven't forgotten all games you attended. Rain, sleet, or shine you were in the stands. Mom I haven't forgotten all the sacrifices you made for the family and never complained. I will never forget how strong you were when dad passed away and what you went through. I will never forget. You're a true inspiration.

DAY 1 JAIL JOURNAL: INTO THE ABYSS

My hand's shaking. Pencil in hand trying to scribe my last passage before I travel into the abyss.

And so, it begins. I woke up today, disoriented. I barely got any sleep last night. Who can blame me? Today is my execution day.

Not a lot of people can say that, huh?

I thought I was ready for this moment, but I'm not. Nothing will keep me from being strapped on a gurney and rolled into the chamber.

I believe paradise awaits one way or another. Today I am going home to God. I am beaten down and destiny has dealt me a very bad deck of cards laced with the three of diamonds.

We are supposed to be living in the greatest place on earth and have confidence in our justice system. Who decides that a man should be executed? There are men in our current penal system who have raped, pillaged, and murdered walking freely in the prison yard, having access to all the prison amenities.

We get condemned by society for taking lives. We are displayed on the stand, exposing all our flaws, being plucked apart by the prosecution. We are given our future by a group of unqualified citizens who are forced to be in court. Those same scum bags are pressured to make a unanimous decision so they can be relieved of their duties. They don't want to be in court away from their families, even though it's their civic duty. I don't blame 'em.

Once the verdict is handed out, we are involuntarily shackled and restrained, taken away from liberty and transferred, now wards of the penal system. Marked as social misfits.

Row

It doesn't make sense. The only one who should decide another man's fate is God, even if a human being executed another human being. Capital punishment should not be accepted in modern society anymore. Who the hell do these people think they are to take my life?

The Bureau of Prisons has asked some state goon to log details about my last twenty-four hours before my execution. The log is designed to examine how the state carries out the death penalty. The record examines my sleep patterns, meals, activities, and even bowel movements. What the hell for? Does it really matter how much I am crapping before I get put to sleep?

It is sad for me to think there are people eagerly waiting for this day, waiting for the news to air, that on this day, I have been executed. I envision thousands of people waiting outside the doors of San Quentin for the warden's official announcement. I know I have hurt countless people with my heinous crime, but nobody deserves this fate.

The guards come to my cell door again asking for my height, weight, shirt size, and pant size. It's like living Groundhog Day. The tone in their voice the last few hours has been sympathetic and kindhearted. No more commands or barking orders. They know my day is here, as I opted out of petitioning for clemency. The prison board normally denies these appeals anyways so why bother.

My expressions and demeanor give the impression that I am ready for the seat at the chamber. I knew at some point the day would come where I would be facing my demise, but as hours come closer and closer, I can't stand the anxiety.

All becomes quiet, and the prison becomes like the middle of the ocean. I am left with my thoughts, and my thoughts these last few hours are inhumane. I contemplate the pain I am going to endure during the execution. The stench of the chamber of past deceased souls is haunting me. I get the feeling of chills running down my body, and then come the panic attacks. I am unaided in this blank concrete cell with my thoughts, a small notebook, and a dull pencil. These amenities were even a special request granted by the warden.

Day 1: Into the Abyss

I am thinking about my last day and trying to gain solace. Trying not to think about my impending doom and keeping my mind on my journal. The warden has been keeping a close eye on my temperament, spending hours in my cell, talking me through the process. He became a close ally and I could confide in him. He will be finishing up my journal and will pass it on to my loved ones as my only request.

There are a few positives about San Quentin and one of those is the warden. When I first came to San Quentin he greeted all the inmates and told each of us what he expected. He truly believes in reforming inmates before they are released. Unfortunately, my life will end today at San Quentin and I won't have an opportunity to atone.

The warden speaks to me and spends a few extra moments discussing life and the pursuit of happiness. We often talk about sports and my past. He tries to put me at ease as much as possible, knowing my fate. He asks the corrections officers to open the cell and leave him while we chat. He counsels me on my last few moments and prepares me for execution. The warden at San Quentin is a gentle soul, but no matter how amiable he is with me, he will eventually take my life.

Unfortunately, I won't be able to take this passage to the chamber with me, articulating my last breath, but I have asked the warden to assemble my last verses and use this chapter to an end.

I devour my last meal in the morning, which is the daily inmate intake of porridge, bread, scrambled eggs, and orange juice. The warden sits by my side, trying to lighten the mood. I am given a new pair of denim jeans and a brand new blue shirt. The anticipation and protocol is making me more apprehensive. I clear my mind and succumb to the process.

I transfer to a holding cell, which is called the Death House. I have nothing but my clothes on my back, notepad and dull pencil to complete my journal. I have the next few hours to transcribe my last thoughts.

Row

I try to summarize my last few moments of life. My hands are still shaking uncontrollably. I am starting to release myself into my own shallows into the depth of eternal damnation. Till this date, I have fully examined the details of the execution. I remove this inclination from my mind. I can't bear to think of the anguish I have caused my family and have requested this manuscript be sent to my immediate family as soon as my execution has taken place. I can't seem to make clarity of this. My mind is blurry, and my thoughts are scrambled.

I deny the prayers from the ordained minister and request to sit and ponder my last moments before I take the walk to the chamber. They keep shoveling people in my cell to talk with me. Just leave me alone!

I want to thank everyone who has supported me through my trial, my conviction, and ultimately everyone who remained a true advocate of my existence. I realize I have lost many past admirers, but I can't take away the past.

These are my last few moments I have before I enter the chamber. I would like to be remembered as someone who loved his family and friends and was able to venture out into the world and exercise his freedom. I lived my life the way I wanted to live. Mistakes were made along the way, but I own them. I am not perfect by any means, but I can rest my head knowing I accomplished what I set out to do. Just like my father, I was hardworking, establishing myself with sheer grit, bringing my lunchbox to work every day. I want to be characterized as being tough as nails, hard on the outside and soft on the inside with people who knew me.

The execution team leader enters my cell now. He shakes my hand and tells me his agenda. He is there to explain the execution process. The warden walks into the cell. He gazes into my eyes.

Now the warden is going to take over and begin his transcription of my last few moments. I am ordered to give up my possessions and my journal will end here. It's time!

I hand him my journal and pencil. "Take me to the chamber. It's time to die."

Day 1: Into the Abyss

❖

<u>Warden:</u> *He is ready. For his family and friends, I am going capture his last few moments to make sure his dying wishes are fulfilled. His one and only wish is to finish up this manuscript and release it to the custody of his immediate family. I will be doing so immediately after this execution. The time of execution will be 11:38 a.m. Eastern Standard Time.*

My inmate is administered three lethal drugs: barbiturate, paralytic, and potassium solution. The first drug will sedate him. Pancuronium bromide will then be administered causing muscle paralysis. The potassium chloride will kill the inmate and complete the execution.

He is now extracted from the cell, his hands and ankles in shackles. He is accompanied by myself and four correctional officers. We accompany him to the basement of the infirmary, where the chamber is located.

The inmate is silent as we walk through the hall of the basement about 100 feet from the chamber.

We arrive in the chamber adjacent to the spectator room which contains witnesses, state officials, lawyers, and people who have asked to watch the execution.

Inmate Ai has requested no family members be allowed in the spectator room. The minister, prison official, executioner, and physician are all present in the chamber to witness the execution.

The execution team prepares behind the curtain. The heart monitor is attached to the inmate's chest and positioned in front of the spectator room. The execution team injects two intravenous tubes; one in each arm which runs through an opening in the other room where the executioner awaits. I will give the executioner the signal when the solution will be administered.

My correctional officers strap the inmate in the airtight chamber. They will now leave the chamber and not return until the condemned is deceased.

At the eleventh hour and thirty-eighth minute, I will signal the executioner to release the lever, releasing the drugs into the bloodstream. I ask the inmate to make any last statements, and inmate Ali denies this request.

I instruct the inmate to breathe deeply, as this will speed up the process. I have now left the chamber, shut the door, and the inmate is alone. He is very composed and looking straight ahead. It is now 11:38 a.m. Eastern Standard Time and I have instructed the executioner to release the lever that administers the drugs.

11:41 a.m., inmate Ali is pronounced dead.

Author's Postscript

Truth and fiction are like the two sides of a coin: we can think of them as expressing complementary realities rather than as negations of each other. Often there is more truth in poetry or fiction than in a story in the news.

Fayaz was driven by competition his whole life. Through his hard work and determination he found success in a lot of different endeavors, when others might have failed.

This was the story about the sacrifices he made early on in his childhood through early adult life as well as a reflection on the bad decisions he made eventually landing him in prison and leading to his execution.

Bleak at times, uplifting at others, Fayaz takes you through his life and the things he was passionate about like football, bodybuilding, nutrition, travelling and humanitarian work while giving a history lesson on who and what inspired those passions.

Fayaz's roller-coaster life eventually ended prematurely, as a casualty of the United States penal system, but before getting executed, he accomplished his goal of completing his journal.

ABOUT THE AUTHOR

Shazad Carbaidwala is a husband, father, friend, humanitarian, and now author.

This is Shazad's first book, offering his readers an in-depth glimpse into parts of his life. His aim in this book is to capture his audience by positioning himself inside San Quentin Correctional facility awaiting the death chamber.

The book *Row* examines Shazad's life growing up as a youth in the mean streets of Chicago. *Row* takes you through his roller coaster ride highlighting his struggles and triumphs.

In order to write *Row*, he did countless hours of research, reading books on street gangs, jails, drug addictions, and death row inmates. He's also viewed numerous documentaries on capital punishment and inmates' lives in federal institutions, as well as the infrastructure at San Quentin prison. He did field research by speaking with inmates at Devens Medical Center located in Devens, Massachusetts, as well as with high risk youth for a non-profit organization in Chelsea, Massachusetts. He also served his community as an auxiliary police officer.

He, his beautiful wife, and his daughter currently reside in Chicago, Illinois.

www.ingramcontent.com/pod-product-compliance
Lightning Source LLC
Chambersburg PA
CBHW020442130626
46549CB00001B/257